CW00339679

SOLDIERS OF
MISFORTUNE

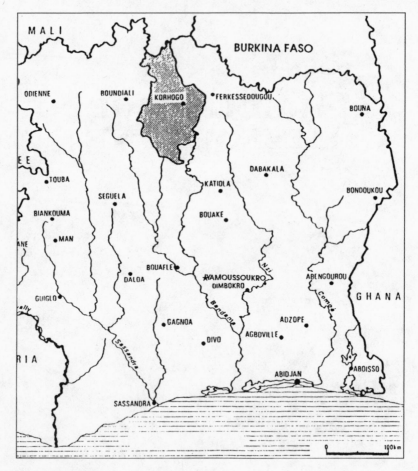

The Côte d'Ivoire

SOLDIERS OF MISFORTUNE

Ivoirien *Tirailleurs*
of World War II

Nancy Ellen Lawler

Ohio University Press Athens

97   96   95   94   93   92   5   4   3   2   1

Swallow Press/Ohio University Press books are printed on acid-free paper   ∞

LIBRARY OF CONGRESS CATALOGING-IN-PUBLICATION DATA

Lawler, Nancy Ellen.
   Soldiers of misfortune ; Ivoirien tirailleurs of World War Two /
by Nancy Ellen Lawler.
        p.   cm.
   Includes bibliographical references and index.
   ISBN 0-8214-1012-1
   1. France. Armée. Tirailleurs sénégalais—History—20th century.
2. France, Armée, Troupes coloniales—History—20th century.
3. World War, 1939–1945—Regimental histories—France.
4. World War, 1939–1945—Ivory Coast—Korhogo (Dept.)
5. Korhogo (Ivory Coast : Dept.)—History. I. Title.
D761.9.T57L38   1992
940.54'1244—dc20   91-24369
                                                    CIP

To my mother, Lillian Rubin,
and to the memory of my father, Albert Rubin;
et aux anciens combattants
de La Côte d'Ivoire

Contents

Maps and Tables

Illustrations

Unless indicated all photographs were taken by the author.

Acknowledgments

MANY PEOPLE HAVE PLAYED A PART in making this study possible. First and foremost, my thanks go to the many Ivoirien *anciens combattants* who were prepared to talk with me and to introduce me to their world. Their names will be found on pages 249–53. I am deeply grateful to each and every one of them, but very special thanks must go to Namongo Their names will be found on pages 247. I am deeply grateful to each and every one of them, but very special thanks must go to Namongo Ouattara, head of the Korhogo Veterans Association. He provided me with lists of veterans throughout the region and showed the greatest determination in making sure that I interviewed as many as possible. These *anciens combattants* welcomed the stranger from America with unfailing courtesy and warmth. They opened their homes and their hearts to me. They talked and I wrote, and as a result, their story is recorded for future generations. I thank them for everything and remain impressed that they never asked why a woman would be interested in war and soldiers. I also owe a debt of gratitude to Dr. Tenena Soro, then at Northwestern University, who labored so long to teach me Tyebari. Nonetheless, in this polyglot region I still needed the services of an interpreter. Sekongo Nahoua assumed this role and, in the course of our work together, came to be a dear friend. Wholeheartedly throwing himself into the project, he was an invaluable field assistant.

Other Ivoiriens also gave generously of their time and advice. In Abidjan, Professor Jean-Noël Loucou was always available for consultation. Professor Tiona Ouattara and his wife, Mme Fatou Ouattara, provided me with advice and introductions to their family and friends in Korhogo. M. Philippe Yacé found time in his busy schedule to assist me in many ways. Working in the National Archives was made most pleasant by the director, M. Dominique Tchiffro, and his staff. M. Guy Ahizzi-Eliam, president of the *Association Nationale des Anciens Combattants et Victimes de la Guerre*, was most courteous and helpful, and his letter of introduction smoothed my way in many parts of the country. My thanks also go to Nanou Guily for permission to quote his song.

Two good friends in Korhogo, Raymond and Madeleine Noble, took me into their family and introduced me to their many acquaintances in the town. Lanciné-Gon Coulibaly, *député* of the National Assembly of the Côte d'Ivoire as well as honorary citizen of Nebraska, was of immense help. *Père* Pierre Boutin, of the *Eglise S. Antoine*, not only opened his superb personal library to me but also shared with me his knowledge of the Senoufo people, drawn from his quarter century among them. My thanks also go to Korhogo's other *député*, Gon Coulibaly and to the prefect of Korhogo, Col. Emile Bombét.

As a graduate student at Northwestern University taking the first steps toward this project, I enjoyed the support and encouragement of Professors John Rowe and John Hunwick and the comradeship of my classmates, Jean Allman, Gregory Maddox, David Owusu-Ansah, and Timothy Welliver. For a decade I have had the benefit of the University's superb Africana Library. The staff have been unfailingly helpful, but my deepest thanks must go to Dan Britz, whose unparalleled knowledge of the collection made my task so much easier.

I must acknowledge my thanks to the Fulbright-Hays program for the fellowship which made it possible to work in the Côte d'Ivoire and to Oakton Community College for granting me the necessary leaves of absence. I am indebted to my best friend, Roberta Zimmerman, for her tremendous moral support and encouragement. And last, but only because he has a special place in this list, I am grateful to Ivor Wilks for his unfailing support for this project, from its genesis to its completion, and offer my apologies for occasional impatience with his rigorous standards.

Abbreviations

ACCCI	*Archives de la Chambre de Commerce de la Côte d'Ivoire,* Abidjan.
AEF	*Afrique Equatoriale Française* (French Equatorial Africa).
ANCI	*Archives Nationales de la Côte d'Ivoire,* Abidjan.
ANG	*Archives Nationales de Gabon,* Libreville
AOF	*Afrique Occidentale Française* (French West Africa)
BATS	*Bataillon Autonome des Tirailleurs Sénégalais* (Detached battalion of Senegalese Rifles)
BFL	*Bataillon Française Libre* (Free French battalion)
BM	*Bataillon de Marche* (A battalion formed for a specific purpose, consisting of men drawn from other units)
BMIC	*Bataillon de Marche d'Infanterie Coloniale*
BMTS	*Bataillon de Marche des Tirailleurs Sénégalais*
BTS	*Bataillon des Tirailleurs Sénégalais*
CFA franc	*Communauté Financière Africaine* (franc issued by the Central Bank of the French West African monetary zone)
CMIDOM	*Centre Militaire d'Information et de Documentation sur l'Outre-Mer,* Versailles. (Military Center of Information and Documentation on the overseas territories)
DFL	*Division Française Libre* (Free French Division)
DIA	*Division d'Infanterie Algérienne*
DIC	*Division d'Infanterie Coloniale*
DICL	*Division d'Infanterie Coloniale Légère* (Light Infantry Division)
FFL	*Forces de la France Libre*
NCO	Noncommissioned Officer
OACVC	*Office des anciens combattants et victimes de la guerre* (Veterans and War Victims Office)
PDCI	*Parti Démocratique de la Côte d'Ivoire*
PRO	Public Record Office, London
RAC	*Régiment d'Artillerie Coloniale*
RACLMS	*Régiment d'Artillerie Coloniale Légère Mixtes Sénégalais* (Light Artillery Regiment containing African and European units)
RDA	*Rassemblement Démocratique Africain* (African Democratic Assembly)
RIC	*Régiment d'Infanterie Coloniale*
RICM	*Régiment d'Infanterie Coloniale Mixte*
RICMS	*Régiment d'Infanterie Coloniale Mixtes Sénégalais*
RTS	*Régiment des Tirailleurs Sénégalais*
SAA	*Syndicat Agricole Africain* (African Agricultural Union)
SHAT	*Service Historique de l'Armée de la Terre,* Vincennes
WAFF	West African Frontier Force

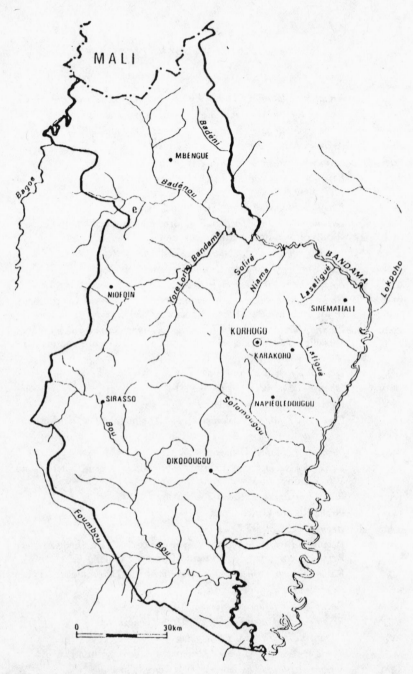

MALI

Bagoe

Badéni

MBENGUE

Badénou

e

NIOFOIN

Yoré Lorho Bandama

Soliré

Niama

Lasaliguè

BANDAMA

Lokpoho

SINEMATIALI

KORHOGO

KARAKORO

Latiguè

SIRASSO

Bou

Solomougou

NAPIEOLEDOUGOU

DIKODOUGOU

Foumbou

Bou

0   30km

The Korhogo Region

1
Preamble

The Problem

THIS IS A STUDY OF MEN FROM THE Côte d'Ivoire who fought and died in World War II. It has particular reference to those recruited from the Korhogo region of the north. They served alongside soldiers drawn from all the colonies of French West Africa in the *Tirailleurs Sénégalais,* the Senegalese Rifles. My interest in the topic had been stimulated by Amon d'Aby's work, *La Côte d'Ivoire dans la cité africaine.* "The declaration of war on 3 September 1939," he claimed,

> was not a surprise to anyone. The public had long awaited it, and now welcomed it with more enthusiasm than it had ever shown twenty-five years ago. This change demonstrated that the affection of the Blacks of the Côte d'Ivoire for the motherland had become more defined and deeply rooted since the last war. Through the medium of its elite, the indigenous population followed with interest, if not with passion, the preliminary phases of the war, the excessive demands and deceit of Chancellor Hitler, Munich, the invasion of Czechoslovakia, the dismemberment of Poland. . . . These aggressions aroused unanimous feelings of indignation. Public opinion, especially among *anciens combattants*, opposed any new concession to Germany and feverishly awaited the declaration of war.

Ivoiriens, d'Aby reported, flocked to recruiting centers, and after the collapse of the French army in 1940, thousands crossed into the British Colony of the Gold Coast to join *La France Combattante.* "They thought," he maintained, "that France, land of Liberty, should not be absent from the camp of Liberty."[1] Was it possible, I wondered, that Ivoiriens had so thoroughly identified themselves with France that they were able to choose, in the circumstances of 1940, between two Frances: between that of Pétain on the one hand and that of de Gaulle on the other?

It is well known, of course, that upwards of 160,000 West African soldiers, virtually all conscripts, fought in the trenches during World War I. Their contribution is excellently chronicled in Marc Michel's *L'Appel à l'Afrique*. [2] They fought, it is true, but there had been strong resistance when France attempted to introduce general conscription into her African colonies. Throughout the AOF, every means of evading the draft was used. In 1916 and 1917, there had been riots throughout the Côte d'Ivoire. Many Ivoiriens fled into the Gold Coast and Liberia. Such was the extent of the opposition to conscription in 1917 that in September the administration temporarily suspended it. [3] The next year, a renewed effort was made. Blaise Diagne of Senegal, the first African elected to a seat in the French Chamber of Deputies, was appointed a Commissioner of the Republic and charged with overseeing the new recruitment drive of 1918. [4] During his visit to the Côte d'Ivoire, he was able to calm the situation and convince both chiefs and people of their patriotic duty to aid France by accepting conscription. He was so successful that thousands of Ivoiriens joined the ranks of the *Tirailleurs Sénégalais* and were to fight and die in the bloodbaths of the final stages of the Great War. [5]

Those who survived to return home came to be regarded as men with *la force*, men of strength and power, men who had seen the land of the whites; who had fought side by side with some, and against other, white men; who had learned something of the language of the white men and had acquired many of their secrets. In the villages, they were held in awe as men apart. They commanded respect and they engendered fear. Yet, they did not gain much in a purely material sense. A few were selected as canton chiefs; others were employed as interpreters for canton and village chiefs. Most, from time to time, found themselves being mustered as official "greeters" for administrators on tour. They were expected to serve as examples to new conscripts at recruitment time, and on national holidays they were to appear as beribboned and uniformed symbols of France's imperial greatness. But that was it. They had no pensions and no hopes of advancement beyond these mainly menial roles. They were, by and large, reabsorbed into village society.

France was gratified by the part these men had played in the war and showed its appreciation of their fighting abilities by the passage of a peacetime conscription act in 1919. This act remained in force throughout the interwar period. Ivoiriens, like their counterparts throughout the AOF, had no choice but to accept a system of military recruitment by annual "class." Each class comprised those estimated to be 20 years of age. Every year, approximately 5,000 recruits were selected from the able-bodied young men of the AOF. They accepted it as yet another example of the black man's burden.

In the Côte d'Ivoire, military service was seen as but another form of forced labor, to be compared with building roads and bridges, thatching government residences, or being sent to work in the forests and plantations of the south. Service in the army, however, carried with it one advantage. Once completed—or so it was believed—the ex-soldier could neither be recalled to the colors nor required to carry out forced labor. The first of these beliefs was shattered in 1939, when veterans from classes as early as that of 1924 were called up after the declaration of war against Germany. But were they as enthusiastic about their return to the ranks as Amon d'Aby claimed? How did their attitudes compare with those of new recruits? How well did the *Tirailleurs Sénégalais* fight in the cause of France, or rather of the two Frances which would emerge after 1940? How did they view their role? How far did their experiences as *tirailleurs* affect them and their society after the fighting was over? These are the key themes of this study.

The existing body of scholarly work on the *tirailleurs* of the AOF in the 1939–45 period is remarkably sparse. Myron Echenberg's long-awaited book, *Colonial Conscripts*, appeared just as *Soldiers of Misfortune* was going to press and too late therefore to be taken into account. [6] Five of its ten chapters, however, existed in previously published form, and reference to them will be made. [7] Echenberg, in turn, was able to consult texts of this writer's interviews with Ivoirien veterans and drew heavily upon them. On the war itself, no one has yet produced a study of the specifically African contribution. Anthony Clayton's useful study of the French army in Africa contains much data on the *Tirailleurs Sénégalais*, [8] while Robert Paxton's equally useful history of the French army under Vichy has, in the nature of the case, little about them. [9]

The present study is not military history as such, although inevitably it has been necessary to provide a chronological and descriptive framework for the war and some account of the campaigns in which the *Tirailleurs Sénégalais* were involved. Insofar as this is a social history, it is of the kind often described, accurately although inelegantly, as "from the bottom up." Insofar as it is cultural history, it is that of a minority—of Ivoiriens abruptly moved from village and home and forced to take on new identities as soldiers of France.

The Interviews

The study draws extensively upon the testimony of ex-*tirailleurs*, veterans of World War II, interviewed between 1985 and 1987. It provides data which often usefully supplement official reports of battles and the like. This, however, was not the primary object of interviewing these *anciens combattants*. The essential purpose was rather to explore the ways Ivoirien soldiers interpreted the events in which they were involved and assimilated these events into their own understanding of their place in a rapidly changing world. I have let them, whenever possible, speak for themselves, albeit through my translations into English.

The veterans were, for the most part, eager to talk. They had a strong sense of being a lost generation. The tunes of glory, heard infrequently enough during the war, ceased to play for them as the cataclysm of 1939–45 receded in memory. By the late 1980s, they found their children, and certainly their grandchildren, little interested in the strange and wonderful stories they had to tell. They found they had little or no place in the new history with which the independent Côte d'Ivoire was rapidly equipping itself. In this new history, the focus was to be upon the nationalist struggle and upon the person of its leader, President Félix Houphouët-Boigny. To this new history, those who had fought (and died) in the defense and liberation of France became largely irrelevant. In a real sense, then, this study seeks to rescue the *ancien combattant* from oblivion.

In 1984, I found myself working on food production in the Côte d'Ivoire in the late colonial period. Much of this research centered on the Korhogo region of the northern savanna, then widely regarded as the rice and yam basket of the colony. Korhogo had another distinctive feature. After the Mossi areas of Upper Volta, it was regarded as the largest reservoir of forced labor during the colonial era. It was therefore natural enough to focus the present study of military service, which can certainly be seen as another form of forced labor, upon that region. There was another possibility. This was to carry out a series of interviews with veterans scattered over the country. This I rejected as unlikely to provide the depth of information I needed. I wished to work with a large sample of veterans who shared a relatively homogeneous background. As it turned out, I was able to interview an estimated one-fifth of the surviving *anciens combattants* of World War II in the Korhogo region.

The decision to use Korhogo as a case study inevitably raises a question about the extent to which the findings can be generalized for the whole of the Côte d'Ivoire — for the people not only of the savanna country but those of the forests and lagoons as well. I believe that a certain level of generalization is possible, not because I wish to argue that the people of Korhogo are in some sense or other typical or average Ivoiriens but precisely because those recruited, whether from Korhogo or any other part of the Côte d'Ivoire, were all brought together into a new and overarching military community and inculcated with a new set of values which eclipsed those of particular locality and ethnicity. The point was eloquently made, but with characteristic racism, by a writer in *Le Monde Colonial Illustré* in 1940.

> Bambara, strapping and stubborn, Mossi, proud but tenacious, Bobo, rough, but calm and hardworking, Senoufo, timid but faithful, Peuls, with the atavism of nomads who reject strong discipline, but are full of fire and likely to make excellent troop leaders, Malinké, more refined, good natured and quick to understand an order; all of them, with their diverse qualities, resulting from their *atavismes* and their temperaments fashioned from their adaptation to their natural habitats, all these representatives of the vigorous and prolific Sudanese race, all with their ingenuous souls and their devotion, make admirable soldiers, having the right to our recognition and to our solicitude. [10]

The combination of identical training and common combat experience in regiments of soldiers drawn not only from the entire colony but indeed from everywhere in the AOF, was to make the war a transcending reality for them all. Volunteer or conscript, villager or townsman, illiterate or *évolué*, and whether from north, south, east, or west of the colony, the army forced them all into the same mold. They emerged from their training, their service in Europe, their combat, and for some, their prisoner of war camps as soldiers of France, fiercely proud of what they had done and with a sense of apartness from civilians, who could never truly appreciate what they had seen and experienced. In the process they came to belong to a larger and newer "tribe," the great fraternity of men who had served in the army. In their conversations, they were always "we *Sénégalais*," never "we Senoufo," "we Yacouba," or "we Lobi."

This said, I did nevertheless carry out a shorter set of interviews with veterans mostly from the Man region in the mountains and forest of the western Côte d'Ivoire. Those in this control group were very different in background and current circumstances from the Korhogolese, yet proved indeed to share in that same new reality created by their years in the army. The men of Man and the men of Korhogo, so we shall see, demonstrated remarkably similar perceptions and interpretations of the events of 1939–45.

Those interviewed were asked primarily to recount their own life stories. No questionnaire was used, and the interviewee was given full rein to speak about whatever he thought relevant. Some were born raconteurs, and were able to take their own stories and view them against a wider setting of family, village, and army life. [11] Few of the interviews were held in private. There were generally in attendance, if not other *anciens combattants*, other men and women of the village, who never hesitated to offer their observations on the proceedings.

In Man, to have served in the army was a matter constantly referred to in public. Indeed, as one observer remarked of the Man region, it was virtually impossible in those days to get a wife unless you had done military service. Even after discharge, you wore your braid (*galon*) to show your status, "to show that you were a man."[12] In the Senoufo villages of Korhogo, by contrast, non-veterans were often hearing for the first time the stories recounted to me. There, the *ancien combattant* has tended to keep his wartime experiences, suffering, and sacrifices to himself. Lapon Silué of Topinakaha, near Korhogo, was among many veterans who told me why this was so.

> There were three in my family who did military service. We discussed things among ourselves. "I did this. I went there." We did not speak with others. Only among ourselves. Those who have not done it cannot be talked to. Only those in the same village who did it can talk about it. The army is like the *Poro*—if you leave for it—you know its secrets. We cannot divulge them.[13]

Thus bound by a self-imposed code of secrecy which looks on military service as similar to membership in a secret society, one whose rites cannot be revealed to the uninitiated, the Senoufo veteran lives out his life in his village, and finally, in words made famous by another *ancien combattant*, Douglas MacArthur, "just fades away."[14]

Why then were the veterans prepared to speak so freely to an American researcher, and a woman at that? To some extent, it was precisely my foreignness which enabled them to feel at ease and to have stories recorded which, as the veterans aged, they had been longing to tell. In the circumstances of the late 1980s, moreover, I was under no necessity of approaching them through chiefs or prefects.[15] They seemed gratified that I had arrived unannounced in their villages and displayed an interest in their lives. Their pleasure was compounded by the fact that I was more than willing to assist them in their perpetual battle with French and Ivoirien bureaucracies over their pension rights.

The interviews were for the most part taped, although in some cases this was either technically impossible or politically inadvisable.[16] In the villages near Korhogo, many veterans preferred to speak in Senoufo or occasionally in Dyula. However, when it came time to talk of purely military matters, the veteran often, despite a gap of almost half a century, reverted to barrack-room French, *parler tirailleur*. In Korhogo town and throughout Man, however, French was invariably used. The translations into English are mine. I have attempted to render the interviews as literally as possible and to preserve the staccatolike effect of the original conversations, including the use of repetition for emphasis.

The chronology given by the interviewees was often inaccurate. Their knowledge of geography was, to say the least, vague. Nonetheless, they had near total recall of their serial numbers, the names of their regiments, the ships on which they sailed, indeed even the dates of their passages to and from Europe and North Africa. Their descriptions of the campaigns in which they fought proved (after cross-checking in the military archives in Vincennes and Versailles) to be remarkably accurate in detail. If they did not always know exactly where they were and just what month it was, they certainly knew how the battles went. Their perspective was obviously different from that of the French officers who filed the official reports of these engagements, but there could be no doubt that all were referring to the same events.

We may note, in passing, that few of the veterans interviewed in the late 1980s had any advantage of hindsight. Most had virtually no access to films, television documentaries, books, articles, or radio broadcasts on the war period. They had a keen sense of their own part in, and importance to, the period extending from the battle for France in 1940 to the liberation of France in 1944–45 and of their fortunes—or rather, misfortunes—on repatriation to their homes. If the years have tended to make them remember their individual contributions to the war as possibly more heroic and dramatic than they were, it does not mean we are dealing with fiction. In the interviews we meet men not only conscious of their earlier existence as young, vigorous soldiers sent overseas to rescue France in her years of distress, but also at the same time aware of their survival as a virtual anachronism in their own land. For this study, their testimony on both scores is of importance.

The People

B. Holas's *Les Senoufo*, which appeared in 1957, usefully summarized the state of knowledge in the field at that time and also provides a useful bibliography of earlier writings. [17] It covers the Senoufo peoples of Mali and Burkina Faso as well as those of the Côte d'Ivoire. Much of the work, however, is devoted specifically to the *Cercle* of Korhogo, reflecting the heavy concentration of Senoufo in that region. In 1954, the *cercle*, 38,635 square kilometers in extent, had a population of 346,380 people. Of these, 262,241 were Senoufo, and 66,841 Dyula. It comprised the three subdivisions of Korhogo, Boundiali, and Ferkessedougou. Interviews in the present study were for the most part carried out in the first of these. The subdivision of Korhogo, 10,985 square kilometers in extent, had 193,940 people in 1954: 149,275 were identified as Senoufo, and 35,107 as Dyula. The census of 1963 indicated that the population of what had then become the prefecture of Korhogo had grown. About 240,000 Senoufo and 58,000 Dyula were counted.[18]

Korhogo town is at the center of the *cercle* and subdivision. Its traditional importance lies in the fact that it is the seat of a Tiembara Senoufo chiefdom founded (though this remains a matter of some controversy) in the mid-eighteenth century. Its history has been the subject of a broad study by Tiona Ouattara.[19] Nevertheless, Korhogo remained little more than a village when envoys from the Almamy Samory arrived there in the early 1890s and were informed by Korhogo's chief, Gbon Coulibaly, that the Senoufo were cultivators, not warriors.[20] The Tiembara Senoufo retained this stance when the French displaced Samory in 1898. They offered no resistance to the newcomers. Indeed, Gbon Coulibaly welcomed them with gifts of food and other supplies. The development of Korhogo from village to town, and then to city, resulted from the decision of the French, in 1903, to make it the administrative center for the northern Côte d'Ivoire.

The Senoufo were, and indeed are, first and foremost cultivators. They grow millet, sorghum, maize, rice, and yam primarily for household subsistence. A shift toward commodity production—mainly of cotton and rice—has gained momentum since independence. Nevertheless, the Senoufo peasant remains essentially concerned with household subsistence, though his children increasingly seek employment in towns to generate cash income. Descent is reckoned matrilineally, but household rather than matrilineage is the basis of production. The village, under its elders, possessed a high degree of autonomy. Small chiefdoms emerged in the eighteenth and nineteenth centuries, but those who held them had little direct political power. Their authority was based more upon their control, exercised through village and compound heads, of the initiation society (*Poro*), which managed the various *rites de passage* from birth to death and was custodian of the mores of the community. In 1978, Sinali Coulibaly's *Le Paysan Senoufo* appeared.[21] It is a comprehensive account of the social organization and traditional agricultural practices of the Senoufo specifically of the Korhogo region.

The French experiment in using Senegalese soldiers as their agents in the Senoufo villages was abandoned by the 1920s. They found it more expedient to rely upon local chiefs to sustain a flow of forced labor into both public works and the plantations and forests of the south. During the colonial period, then, chieftaincy in the Korhogo region was in a sense strengthened by being made an arm of colonial administration. It was only under the government of an independent Côte d'Ivoire, intent upon "modernizing" the new nation in part through the centralization of power, that the chiefs were not only deprived of the last vestiges of

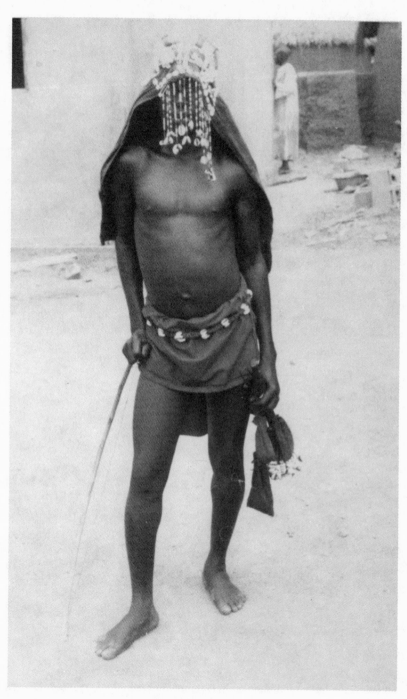

Member of Poro *Society, Korhogo*

Aerial view of Senoufo village

Granaries in Moroviné, near Korhogo

their traditional authority but often saw their people relocated as villages were consolidated into large and artificial units of production.

A broad overview of political change in the region is the subject of a study by W. C. Gunderson, spanning the hundred years from the 1870s to the 1970s.[22] The author argues that "local leaders had to operate within a variety of contexts as the needs and priorities of outsiders (Mande warriors, colonial officials and the leadership of the newly independent Ivoirien state) were translated into administrative systems and programs which disrupted local society to an ever increasing degree." Gunderson, however, ignores the role of World War II veterans in the process.

Gunderson's work is complemented by T. J. Bassett's study, completed in 1984, of change in the regional economy.[23] Bassett selected Katiali, some sixty kilometers to the northwest of the town of Korhogo, as a case study of the forces moving the Senoufo peasant from household subsistence to commodity production. He argues that "one of the major consequences of peasant involvement in crop and labor markets has been the transformation of the Senoufo lineage-based mode of production and 'culture of production' to a transitional mode." The transition in question has to do with the "functional dualism" between "the capitalist export-enclave plantation economy of the forest region and the peasant sector of the north which produced cheap food and labor for the capitalist sector."[24]

The Dyula are dispersed through the Korhogo region in villages of their own, in sections of Senoufo villages, and in quarters of the towns. Malian by origin, and speaking a dialect of Malinke, their migrations into the region have extended over a period of about half a millennium. They arrived to trade but identified themselves either as warriors, *tun tigi*, whose function was to defend their communities, or as scholars, *mori*, whose role was to maintain the Islamic values of Dyula society. The relationship between Dyula and Senoufo was essentially one of mutual benefit. That the Dyula did not seek to proselytize greatly diminished any potential for conflict between them and their hosts.[25]

The Dyula necessarily engaged also in farming for household subsistence. In the nineteenth century, however, they commenced production for export, using slaves to work newly created plantations. The old commercial links, maintained with other Dyula communities across the West African savannas, provided them with ready access to markets for their produce. The turbulence of that century, which witnessed the rise (and fall) of a succession of Muslim states across the Western Sudan, greatly stimulated those markets. The Dyula are credited with the introduction into the Korhogo region of a number of cash crops, notably cotton and tobacco, and with the development of manufacture, particularly weaving and dyeing. They have thus constituted an entrepreneurial factor within Senoufo society. In 1982, R. Launay's excellent book on the Dyula of Korhogo appeared.[26] He explores the nature of the symbiotic relationship which has long existed between Dyula and Senoufo and identifies the constraints upon the assimilation of the former to the latter.

The Dyula remain firmly attached to Islam, the Senoufo somewhat less firmly to their traditional gods. There are converts to Islam among the latter, and the process is a continuing one. Figures compiled on the basis of the 1954 census gave the Muslim population of the subdivision of Korhogo as 50,000, the Catholic as 2,100, and the *"animiste"* as 133,900.[27] The 1963 census yields no comparable breakdown, but the *Rapport Sociologique* suggests that Senoufo conversion was mainly an urban phenomenon. Almost 70 percent of the Senoufo in Korhogo town claimed to be Muslim.[28]

The interviews with veterans in the Man region, in the western Côte d'Ivoire, were conducted mainly with those who identified themselves as Yacouba (or Dan) and Wobe. These two peoples share a common life-style and culture, though the former speak a dialect of southern Mande and the latter of Kru. In the mountainous northern part of the region, rice cultivation has long been practiced. In the heavily forested southern part, yam is grown and hunting was formerly an important element in household subsistence. Traditionally, the Yacouba and Wobe lived in small settlements of, at most, a few families. Each family unit farmed for itself, however, there being little evidence of communal effort unless for ritual and defensive purposes. In the nineteenth century, and probably before, kola was extensively collected. It was sold to Dyula traders in exchange for salt, cloth, and other such commodities. Over the last seven decades or so, cocoa and coffee have been increasingly grown as cash crops, introduced with the "encouragement" of the colonial administration. Useful studies of the social organization and culture of the similar, and neighboring, Toura and Guéré peoples have been published by Holas and Schwartz.[29]

The early history of the Dan and Wobe has been outlined by J.-N. Loucou.[30] Unlike the Senoufo, the people of the Man area fiercely resisted the French occupation. "Pacification" of the area was only achieved after a series of campaigns lasting from 1905 to late 1908. Governor G. Angoulvant (1908–16), in charge of the operations, described the Dan as "unyielding savages," expressing surprise that "they wished to chase us [the French] from the country." Finally victorious, the French received the surrender of 670 rifles. Within the next seven years they were to seize and destroy almost 25,000 more rifles within the *cercle* of Man.[31] That the Man country was in time to prove a splendid source of volunteers for the *Tirailleurs Sénégalais* should scarcely be a surprise.

Like the Senoufo, the mass of the Dan and Wobe people remain strongly attached to the old gods. On the basis of the census of 1954, the sub-division of Man embraced 119,000 *"animistes,"* 15,000 Muslims, 4,000 Catholics, and 2,000 Protestants.[32]

When I first decided to study Ivoirien veterans and selected the Korhogo region, a knowledgeable anthropologist maintained that there were few such and suggested I "go west," that is, to Man. Perversely, perhaps, I ignored the advice. Nonetheless, it will now be apparent why he gave it. If not, perhaps the perspective of the Senoufo veteran Sekongo Yessongui will be convincing. Yessongui regretted not having stayed in the army once he had accepted the inevitability of being drafted.

> Military service was good for me. If I'd stayed in, I would be well off today. I would have a beautiful house today. But I didn't stay in. They asked me to reenlist as a volunteer, but I said no. After that came the war. They gathered us all together and they took me to war anyway. There I saw the same white who had asked me to volunteer. He said: "Hah! I told you to stay in. You said no. And here you are again." We didn't stay in because our parents made amulets so that we would stay here and work for them. That is why there was no spirit to stay in the army. Our elders had one single concern—farming. They only wanted us to farm for them. When we were children, they were only farmers—that's the only thing they knew—that's all they wanted. Now, if my son wants to leave here, I will give him my blessing. If you stay here, you don't do well.[33]

I found, indeed, that there were few Senoufo villages without their *anciens combattants.* On the face of it, this might seem strange in a society so devoted to agricultural pursuits, in which many had seldom left their villages even to travel to the towns of the region. The point was, however, that the Korhogolese had had little choice about serving in the army; class by class, age group by age group, they were recruited involuntarily whatever their personal predilections. So there turned out to be many Korhogo veterans but scarcely a volunteer or career man among them. But when I did "go west" to Man, I found that a significant proportion of the veterans were indeed volunteers, and men moreover who chose to serve their full fifteen years in the army. Those interviews proved, then, a truly useful control group. The administrator Gaston Joseph, who knew his Côte d'Ivoire well, had made the point in 1944. For him the Senoufo were "cultivators, extremely attached to the land, hard working, sweet, trustworthy, obedient to powerful chiefs." The Dan, by contrast, were "at the moment of the occupation, counted among the most backward people of the colony, being among the most savage, the most withdrawn and the most individualistic."[34]

The Winds of Change

It has become a commonplace that those Africans who participated in World War II became a driving force in the nationalist movement which brought their countries to independence in the late 1950s and early 1960s. The point was put in a different but telling way by Albert Tevoedjre. "When Africa becomes independent," he wrote, "we will have to raise a statue in memory of a cursed person in history, Hitler." [35]

There can, of course, be no question that World War II had immense consequences for Africa in general and for French West Africa in particular. Although Britain and France had experienced a radically different war, the six long years of conflict left both great colonial powers impoverished. Unlike Great Britain, however, in 1945 France was in the throes of a grave moral crisis resulting from the circumstances of its capitulation in 1940 and its collaboration with Germany between 1940 and 1943. Its savior in 1944, Charles de Gaulle, was the very man condemned to death as a traitor in 1940.

Winds of change had begun to waft gently into France's vast African empire following the signing of the Atlantic Charter in 1942. Not even the most radical thinker foresaw the abandonment of empire, but there were those who began to recognize that a transfer of power from the metropole to the colonies, the beginnings of a process of decolonization, would inevitably occur in the aftermath of the war. [36] Yet, if such thoughts were in the air during the later years of the war, it was to take the excesses of power practiced successively by the Pétainist and Gaullist regimes to create the stir of discontent in the colonies which was in time to swell into the nationalist movements and ultimately to bring independence. At issue is the role of the *anciens combattants* in this process, with particular reference to the Côte d'Ivoire.

The people of the Côte d'Ivoire, the African majority and the tiny European minority alike, experienced to the fullest extent the vagaries of France's vacillations between support of the Allied and Axis causes. No matter which side France was on, however, the Côte d'Ivoire still had to contribute its quotas of raw materials and forced labor. Over and above that, it had to provide tens of thousands of men for the armies of France. Ivoirien recruits joined the ranks of the 150,000 men who formed the West African regiments. [37] It is somewhat paradoxical that Free France, holding itself up as the champion of liberty and justice, in fact carried to new heights the economic abuse of the colonies. In the Côte d'Ivoire, the political goal of winning the hearts and minds of the white, pro-Pétainist *colons* was deemed so important that the

Free French administration felt obliged to afford them protection against competition from the Ivoirien planters. This, then, was the situation confronting returning veterans.

Did the *anciens combattants* return with ideas that one day their countries would become politically free? Had they heard the cry, "Africa for the Africans"? As early as December 1941, immediately after Pearl Harbor, American intelligence services began drawing up plans for possible landings, one of them at Dakar. Col. William Donovan, head of the Office of Strategic Services, received a feasibility study which addressed American long-term objectives. The author envisaged, with extraordinary foresight, the need for

> the organization of a new independent Africa, based on the federation of African states. Africa for the Africans! The present African situation is parallel to that in South America during the Napoleonic Wars. The African Bolivar is needed. [38]

The slogan "Africa for the Africans" did not, of course, pass into currency from this source. Yet nevertheless it did in time become one that African soldiers began increasingly to hear and use. Aoussi Eba, a teacher drafted in 1939, spoke of this:

> We never thought about independence—not even one day—in the future. We never imagined it. The French were everywhere. Assimilation was the goal. People wanted the same rights as the French—toward assimilation. It was after the Second World War—even then. There was a slogan everywhere—Africa for the Africans. Everywhere you heard it. We thought then that that was good. . . . I was a sergeant then. We heard that slogan everywhere—in the bars—everywhere. After the war, emancipation was simple. There was a new spirit of emancipation. The *tirailleurs* returned with that spirit. After all, it was inappropriate—the kind of life we lived here—with the whip over us. [39]

As the war drew to a close, the people of the Côte d'Ivoire demanded reform. In these early stages of protest it was not the philosophy behind France's assimilation policy that was being questioned but rather the constraints imposed on it by practical considerations. Yet this debate was eventually to lead to the transformation, if not dismantlement, of the entire colonial system. The experience of the soldiers, and their behavior following the conflict, mirrors the decolonization process. They, above all, expected recognition of their sacrifices and accomplishments. They felt, like *ancien combattant* Namble Silué, that "only the French know what we did for them. We liberated them. What greater thing could you do for them?"[40] To appreciate the role of the *anciens combattants*, and the part they played in the new politics of the Côte d'Ivoire, it is essential that the evolution of their new consciousness and the results of their often bitter anger toward all forms of inequality be taken fully into account. What follows is the story of the Ivoirien *Tirailleurs Sénégalais* of World War II.

Notes to Chapter One

1. F. J. Amon d'Aby, *La Côte d'Ivoire dans la cité africaine* (Paris: Editions Larose, 1951), 39–42.

2. Marc Michel, *L'Appel à l'Afrique: Contributions et réactions à l'effort de guerre en A.O.F., 1914–1919* (Paris: Publications de la Sorbonne, 1982). Recruitment figures for the AOF, 483.

3. Ibid., 117–33.

4. Ibid., 226–35.

5. Ibid. 233–34. See also Amon d'Aby, *La Côte d'Ivoire dans la cité africaine*, 37–38.

6. Myron Echenberg, *Colonial Conscripts: The Tirailleurs Sénégalais in French West Africa, 1857–1960* (Portsmouth, N.H.: Heinemann, 1991).

7. See especially Echenberg, " 'Faire du nègre': Military Aspects of Population Planning in French West Africa, 1920–1940" in D. D. Cordell and J. Gregory, eds., *African Population and Capitalism: Historical Perspectives* (Boulder, Colo. and London: Westview Press, 1987); "Slaves into Soldiers: Social Origins of the *Tirailleurs Sénégalais*," in Paul E. Lovejoy, ed., *Africans in Bondage* (Madison: University of Wisconsin Press, 1986), 311–33; "Morts pour la France: The African Soldier in France during the Second World War," *Journal of African History* 26:4, 1985, 373–80; "Paying the Blood Tax: Military Conscription in French West Africa, 1914–1929," *Canadian Journal of African Studies*, 9 no. 2, 1975, 171–92; and "Les Migrations militaires en Afrique Occidentale Français, 1900–1945," *Canadian Journal of African Studies*, 14 no. 3, 1980, 429–50. See also Echenberg's "Tragedy at Thiaroye: The Senegalese Soldiers' Uprising of 1944," in R. Cohen, J. Copans and P. Gutkind, eds., *African Labor History* (Beverly Hills, Calif.: Sage, 1978), 109–28.

8. Anthony Clayton, *France, Soldiers and Africa* (London: Brassey's, 1988).

9. Robert Paxton, *Parades and Politics at Vichy* (Princeton, N.J.: Princeton University Press, 1966).

10. "Le Soudan, Terre de Soldats," *Le Monde Colonial Illustré*, Paris, no. 203, (May 1940): 112.

11. Compare Paul Thompson, *The Voice of the Past. Oral History* (Oxford: Oxford University Press, 1978), 204.

12. Interview 102. See Appendix for a detailed list of all interviews conducted.

13. Interview 65.

14. General Douglas MacArthur, farewell address to a joint session of Congress, Washington, D.C., 19 April 1951.

15. Col. Emile Bombét, prefect of Korhogo, was indeed kind enough to issue me a virtual laissez-passer in the form of an open letter to all civilian and military officials in the department to cooperate in my inquiry. In fact, the good colonel will not, I hope, mind my saying that the only time I found it necessary to use the document was when I ran a stop sign in front of a police post. The document worked: my driving record remained unblemished.

16. The tapes of the interviews are on deposit at the Institut d'histoire, arts et archéologie africains, University of Abidjan, Côte d'Ivoire. A complete set of transcripts is on deposit at Africana Library, Northwestern University, Evanston, Illinois.

17. B. Holas, Les Senoùfo (y compris les Minianka) (Paris: Presses Universitaires de France, 1957), and see bibliography, 174–77.

18. Société d'études pour le développement économique et social, Région de Korhogo, vol. 1 (Abidjan, Côte d'Ivoire, 1965), 11.

19. Tiona Ouattara, "Les Tiembara de Korhogo; des origines à Péléforo Gbon Coulibaly (1962): évolution historique, politique, sociale et économique d'un tar Senoufo" (Ph.D. diss. Université de Paris I, 1977).

20. Senoufo informants, asked about "the war," assume first that the reference is to Samory's intrusion into the region. Gbon Coulibaly's response is widely quoted and used to explain why Gbon made a politically wise decision in supporting the Almamy.

21. Sinali Coulibaly, Le Paysan Senoufo (Abidjan: Nouvelles Editions Africaines, 1978).

22. W. C. Gunderson, "Village Elders and Regional Intermediaries: Differing Responses to Change in the Korhogo Region of the Ivory Coast" (Ph.D. diss. Indiana University, 1975).

23. Thomas J. Bassett, "Food, Peasantry and the State in the Northern Ivory Coast: 1898–1982" (Ph.D. diss. University of California, Berkeley, 1984).

24. Ibid., 250.

25. Compare Ivor Wilks, Wa and the Wala (Cambridge: Cambridge University Press, 1989), 25, 98–99, 202.

26. Robert Launay, Traders without Trade: Responses to Change in Two Dyula Communities (Cambridge: Cambridge University Press, 1982).

27. Cartes des Religions de l'Afrique Noire, Republique de la Côte d'Ivoire (Centre des hautes études administratives sur l'Afrique et l'Asie modernes, 1957). The pages of this report are unnumbered. The figures cited are from the tabulations at the end. The main text differs in giving the "population animiste" as 135,000. The population of the subdivision of Korhogo in 1954 was counted at 193,940. Why the total in the Carte (186,000 or 187,100) falls short of this figure is not explained.

28. Région de Korhogo 2 (1965): 22. The analyst remarks, cursorily it may be thought, that the conversion of Senoufo "did not mean that they had totally abandoned their traditional practices and beliefs, but had changed their names and adopted certain Islamic customs."

29. B. Holas, Les Toura: Esquisse d'une civilisation montagnarde de Côte

d'Ivoire (Paris: Presses Universitaires de France, 1962). A. Schwartz, *La Vie quotidienne dans un village Guéré* (Abidjan: Institut Africain pour le développement économique et social, 1975).

30. Jean-Noël Loucou, *Histoire de la Côte d'Ivoire*, vol. 1, *La Formation des peuples* (Abidjan: Centre d'Édition et de Diffusion Africaines, 1984), 61–65, 113–15.

31. G. Angoulvant, *La Pacification de la Côte d'Ivoire, 1908*–1915 (Paris: Editions Larose, 1916), 217, 252–55.

32. *Carte des religions*.

33. Interview 59. In fact, three of Yessongui's children have left the village to work in the towns.

34. G. Joseph, *Côte d'Ivoire* (Paris: Librairie Arthème Fayard, 1944), 66–67.

35. Albert Tevoedjre, *L'Afrique révoltée* (Paris: Présence Africaine, 1958), 33.

36. For AOF, see C. Coquery-Vidrovitch, "Vichy et l'industrialisation aux colonies," *Revue d'histoire de la deuxième guerre mondiale*, 29 (April 1979): 69–94. For the British Empire, Ronald Robinson confirms that similar ideas were floating around the Colonial Office in the mid-war period. Personal communication.

37. Service historique de l'armée de la terre (henceforth SHAT), Centre de documentation, Chateau de Vincennes. Photocopied extract from Lieutenant-Colonel Bernard and Captain Barjou, *Les Troupes africaines d'AOF et AEF* (Paris: Centre d'Études Asiatiques et Africaines, 1953).

38. OSS, Reports, microfilm, reel 1. Plan submitted to Colonel Donovan by Sherman Kent, chief of the medical section, 11 December 1941.

39. Interview 102.

40. Interview 64.

2

Before the Fall: The *Tirailleurs Sénégalais* in the Côte d'Ivoire

The Rise of *La Force Noire*

FRANCE DECLARED WAR ON GERMANY on 3 September 1939. While the British government entertained doubts about the wisdom of arming large numbers of Africans, the French, as we have seen, had long ago resolved this issue. Africans, whether *citoyens* or *sujets*, had the same right and the same duty as the people of the *métropole* to serve in the armed forces of France. The empire—Southeast Asia, the islands of the Pacific and the Caribbean, Madagascar, North Africa and sub-Saharan Africa—was expected to devote itself unstintingly to the fight for French liberty, French civilization, and French democracy against the forces of tyranny and darkness.

Black Africans had first been recruited rather than impressed into French military service in the 1830s in Senegal, then France's only sub-Saharan colony. This was a continuation of a practice, dating from the Napoleonic era, which had brought "men of color" from the French West Indies to serve alongside French troops in Senegal as officers, noncommissioned officers (NCOs), and ordinary troops. As early as 1816, the French had begun using Africans as auxiliaries. They were usually former slaves, whose freedom was purchased by the French and who were required in return—as a mark of gratitude to their liberators—to enlist for fourteen years in the *Bataillon du Sénégal* or its successors, the *Bataillon d'Afrique* and the *Bataillon de Gorée* (formed in 1819 and 1823, respectively).[1] These auxiliaries were sometimes given combat training but more often were utilized as service corps personnel. A decree of 1 April 1836 modified their conditions of service by specifying that

Tirailleur Sénégalais, *1905–12 era*   *LE MONDE COLONIAL ILLUSTRÉ,* AUGUST 1939

only volunteers would be taken for enlistments of seven or more years, but there were many who advocated a return to the earlier method of forced recruitment in order to solve France's chronic manpower shortage in her colonies. The problem was that Frenchmen were unenthusiastic about volunteering for duty in an area where the mortality rate for Europeans was, to say the least, alarming. Twenty percent of white soldiers serving in Africa between 1825 and 1828 had died there. [2] The mortality rate among African soldiers was not in fact much better, and early colonial administrators were dubious about the success of even a volunteer army.

Senegal's Governor Schmaltz wrote, while the decree of 1836 was still under discussion, that he had little faith in voluntary enlistments. He maintained that the best soldiers were men of servile origin from the interior rather than the Christian and Muslim recruits from Senegal's coastal enclaves preferred by Paris. [3] Schmaltz believed that men removed from their own environment, placed in service among strangers, and having to rely entirely on their new army companions for survival were less likely to desert than free men on their home ground. Nonetheless, volunteerism became officially established as the basis of recruitment.

On 21 July 1857, Napoleon III created by decree the first battalion of the *Tirailleurs Sénégalais*. [4] The brainchild of General Faidherbe, governor of Senegal since 1854 and principal architect of France's West African empire, the *Tirailleurs Sénégalais* would be used first in the conquest of the Western Sudan and later, in two World Wars, to defend the territorial integrity of France and her empire. Even before the turn of the century, however, the Senegalese—men born in the four communes created by Napoleon I and entitled to full French citizenship—were no longer a majority of the African soldiers recruited. [5] As the empire expanded, men from all the diverse populations south of the Sahara, but especially those from French Soudan (modern-day Mali) and Upper Volta (now Burkina Faso), were drawn into France's colonial army. They too were known as *Tirailleurs Sénégalais*.

The transformation of an elite force, attracting volunteers by enlistment bonuses, promises of adventure, and regular pay, into a large conscript army forming an integral part of the French military structure was brought about by the almost single-handed efforts of General Charles Mangin who, while still a captain in 1898, had served with Marchand in the Fashoda expedition. Clearly impressed by the fighting ability of the small force of 150 African soldiers who drove off more than 1,300 soldiers of the Mahdi, [6] Mangin subsequently campaigned vigorously to increase greatly the size, and broaden the role, of *La Force Noire*. Beginning in 1909, he launched a powerful public relations campaign, through the newspapers and journals of the colonial and military lobby, to advocate a massive recruitment of black troops. [7]

Many had misgivings about the scheme. The anticolonial bloc objected to the cost and underlying morality of the mass recruitment of black troops. French radicals feared that African soldiers, suddenly transported to the *métropole*, would be used to suppress political demonstrations and strikes. Despite the opposition, however, in 1912 the French Assembly endorsed Mangin's plan to recruit 7,000 West Africans for service outside the AOF. This was done with the clear intention of using them in combat, should France be once more engaged in war against Germany.[8]

When the "war to end all wars" did come in 1914, a total of ninety-four West African battalions containing 161,250 *Tirailleurs Sénégalais*, 3 percent of the five million French citizens and colonial subjects in uniform, served in it. Of them, 134,000 were engaged in battle. A little short of 30,000, or almost a quarter, died. This was approximately the same proportion of combat deaths suffered by all French troops.[9] Although in some military circles, the *tirailleurs* were criticized for not performing well under heavy artillery fire, the record of their military operations during the war generally preserved their favorable image among the French population: that of an immensely brave, bloodthirsty army of great warriors fiercely loyal to the cause of France.[10] Much publicity had already been afforded the news that fourteen sons and grandsons of France's greatest African adversary, the Almamy Samory, were serving as volunteers in France's army. It was seen as proof of the success of French colonization.[11] The image was one which would serve the French military well in the years ahead, when they sought and gained their government's approval for a large standing army of African soldiers.

There were those who did not share this image. Joost Van Vollenhoven, governor of the Côte d'Ivoire in 1917, was one. He was an opponent of *La Force Noire*. Indeed, he objected so strongly to the concept of a forcibly recruited mass African army that he resigned his post in January 1918, joined up, and died in the trenches. He was particularly troubled, it seems, by the impact of the African veteran, the *ancien combattant*, upon society, and had written on this in 1917:

> Upon being discharged, the ex-soldier can no longer count on anyone but himself; the military administration puts him on the road to his village, but he is no longer able to rely on his former chiefs; he leaves the society of the whites to enter the society of the blacks. . . . In the exclusive, closed and compartmentalized society of the native village, the ex-soldier is ignored, he is banished from the community. . . . He is a stranger for whom there is no place in any hut or family. . . . Consequently, either the former soldier becomes a poor wretch living a miserable or timid existence or, if he has acquired a vigorous mind of his own and the custom of speaking loudly, he does not hesitate to exploit those who surround him.[12]

Dianguina Coulibaly with the World War I helmet brought home by his brother.

Van Vollenhoven's perception of the ex-soldier as either a timid outcast or an unregenerate bully may have been unduly harsh. The men were, indeed, changed by their experiences but in more subtle ways. They were less likely to be intimidated by the dictates of traditional society, having tasted the delights of the outside world. Because they had lived among the white man, a species rarely seen and even less well understood in most Ivoirien villages, they were both honored and feared. In 1986, Dianguina Coulibaly spoke of the World War I veterans from his village:

> Three of them left and all three returned. . . . The village was very pleased, very pleased with them because they had been in a different culture. They knew many things. . . . They taught us how to do new things. . . . They came back in full uniform and the people had never seen a soldier before. They were proud to have returned from being there. They were chiefs now. Everyone listened to them, even the village chief. They were like judges. When anything was being discussed they always had the final word. [13]

Gmbale Soro, from a nearby village, expressed similar views:

> These were men who had *la force*. They could say to someone: Do this! And you were obliged to do it. In those days the whites com-

manded. When you left military service and returned—you had worked with whites. Thus *you* now had that force. . . . Then hardly anyone spoke French so when someone knew a little French, everyone was already afraid of him. They had no money, but because they had done military service, they were greatly respected because they knew French. [14]

World War I had decimated an entire generation of young men in a nation already concerned about its low birth rate. To many, over one million French dead conjured up the spectre of a nation, which, facing a decline in population, would someday be unable to protect itself against a future aggressor. The worries of a Van Vollenhoven and those of like mind had little impact. In 1919, Clemenceau decided to institute universal peacetime conscription in the colonies as in France, although not under identical conditions of service. [15] The financial havoc wrought by the war contributed to the decision not to return to a volunteer force, for conscripts could be paid much less. The passage of the Conscription Act of 1919 led to protests in several colonies. By the end of the 1920s, however, the system was well established or, as Myron Echenberg remarked, "institutionalized." [16] It had come to be regarded, as we have said, as yet another facet of the annual demands made upon the populace by the colonial administrations. Between 1919 and 1939, annual recruitment into the army from the AOF was to average ten to twelve thousand men.

Welcoming the War in Côte d'Ivoire

As early as January 1939, when war was still eight months away, the *Côte d'Ivoire Chrétienne* directed an editorial toward Ivoirien conscripts. It detailed the wonders awaiting them in the motherland, including the prospect of a visit to Lourdes and other shrines. It referred enthusiastically to the uniform they were to wear: "In this khaki dress, the color of the Baoulé savanna, you will become a defender of France." It exhorted the new recruit: "Promise me, my *petit noir*, my little Christian, that you won't be afraid. That France can count on you. You will be fighting for the noblest country on earth." [17]

The African's devotion to France became an increasingly frequent subject of self-congratulatory newspaper editorials in the early months of the war. No one appeared to doubt the absolute loyalty and fealty of the colonized peoples. *Le Progrès Colonial*, for example, was exultant: "For the second time in twenty-five years men of color have responded to France's appeal without complaints or murmurs but with enthusiasm which testifies to their loyalty." [18]

It was not only the editors who expressed such enthusiasm for the war: highly placed traditional leaders joined in the chorus. A dramatic assertion of loyalty came from Moro Naba Kom II, ruler of the Mossi of Ouagadougou. Two days after the declaration of war he volunteered two of his sons for the army, saying, "I have the great pleasure and honor of presenting my two sons, Djiba Naba and Doulougou Naba, two important canton chiefs. I place them at your complete disposal for the service of France."[19] A few months later Edmond Louveau, chief administrator of the Upper Côte d'Ivoire (Upper Volta)—who within eighteen months would find himself in a Vichy prison for supporting the Free French—reported to Governor Horace Crocicchia in Abidjan.[20] He was enthusiastic in announcing that as a result of the action of the Moro Naba, numerous of his chiefs and notables were enlisting. One of them, indeed, the Baloum Naba, had even demanded that the administration intervene with the military to accept his underage son. This, Louveau pointed out, this was a fine example of the love borne toward France by her subjects.[21] In point of fact, however, even in peacetime many notables had considered it wise to have at least one son in the army, to whom the local commandant's attention could be drawn when the time came to choose new village or canton chiefs.[22]

The Moro Naba was not alone in such expressions of devotion. In early September, three sons of Kouadio Adjoumani, chief of the Abron of the Bondoukou region, volunteered for the duration, although only one, Joseph Absale, was to pass the physical examination. Kouadio Adjoumani explained to the Governor:

Facing these inhuman creatures who are bloodying France a second time, we, her children, sons of the Abron, at this moment of the defense of our dear motherland, are ready to respond to her call and are happy to die for her, being certain of victory.[23]

The dispatch of congratulatory telegrams and letters, often ghost-written by local commandants, to the governor on important occasions was a well-established ritual. A declaration of war certainly fell in this category. The chiefs well knew that they would be expected to carry out new orders arising from the new situation, and many sought to give at least the impression that they welcomed with enthusiasm the role awaiting them. In fact, virtually all the provincial and more senior canton chiefs sent off encouraging messages to the governor and, if they had access to higher levels of the administration, to the governor-general of the AOF as well.

Among the Senoufo and Dyula of the north, enthusiasm was perhaps not as marked. Nevertheless, Gbon Coulibaly—province chief of the

Korhogo, member of the *Légion d'Honneur,* holder of the *Etoile du Bénin* and many other honors conferred upon him by an administration well aware of his services to the colonial system — did send one of thirty or so sons to the army. He preferred, however, to demonstrate his loyalty by having cousins and nephews volunteer. One of these, Bey Coulibaly, explained the situation:

> I enlisted voluntarily. Because our chief, old Gbon, said to us: You are obliged to sign up for four years. That's why I was a volunteer. I said, Good! My family. We all took four years. Yes, I'm the same family as Gbon, a cousin. My father and the father of Gbon — it is the same thing. He said we must enlist because it is wartime. He wanted the Africans to help France. I was glad to go. France — the French — were truly our cousins. [24]

Korhogo's commandant was well pleased with Gbon's support. The old province chief, he reported, had "a perfect attitude when war was declared. He advised calm and submission to the orders of France, the mother of blacks, an expression that he employs frequently." [25]

If it is difficult to take these various demonstrations of support for France strictly at face value, it would be unwise to dismiss them as being merely politic gestures designed to ingratiate the chiefs (and by association, the local commandants) with the higher echelons of the administration. The motives of the Ivoirien notables, and their sentiments toward France, were complex and multifaceted. The case of the Moro Naba bears further examination. There is no questioning the overt strength of his commitment to the French cause. Mossi volunteers underlined his contribution to the war effort by taking a special oath: "I pledge myself in the name of God and in the name of the Moro Naba to fight for the duration of the war." [26] The Moro Naba's later distress at the defeat of France, and the signing of the Armistice, has a genuine ring about it, suggesting there was more than expediency in his support for France. It was the occasion for him again to volunteer sons. "Here are my two sons, my eldest, to defend France," he told General Barraud, commander in chief of AOF troops. Nevertheless, it is clear that the Moro Naba expected a return on his investment. In 1932, the Colony of Upper Volta had been abolished. Most of it, including the relatively populous Mossi areas under the Moro Naba's control, were attached to the Côte d'Ivoire. This was done to reduce administrative costs in a time of world economic distress and to remove the last obstacles toward massive labor recruitment for the white-owned plantations and forestry concessions in the south. Thus, in 1939 the Moro Naba hoped that his people's willing participation in the war effort might be the decisive factor in restoring the former status of Upper Volta.

Not all supporters of France had such specific agendas. In the west, many canton chiefs were themselves veterans of World War I and remained firm believers in the invincibility of the French army. In the north Gbon Coulibaly, already heavily burdened by forced labor demands, reasoned that by offering his own kin to the army, he would set an example to his people and so minimize the difficulties in meeting the military quota for his province. Yet other notables—and these categories are not exclusive ones—wanted to continue reaping the rewards of collaboration, not least the medals and bounty with which they were periodically endowed and the occasional jaunts they enjoyed to the centers of power.

French residents of the Côte d'Ivoire appeared gratified by these manifestations of African goodwill. Even the most unbending advocates of the *mission civilisatrice* recognized the necessity of nurturing and preserving the cooperative spirit manifested by those as yet scarcely touched by that civilization. This is well exemplified in a patriotic letter sent to the Abidjan chamber of commerce by its Paris delegate, Alcide Delmont.

> The duty of those Frenchmen who magnificently created our empire
> is greater than ever before. The collaboration and the fidelity of the
> natives has never been more necessary than during this grave hour
> in the life of the nation. [27]

The Call to Arms

In 1937 the French High Command had already begun to consider the specific role to be played by the *Tirailleurs Sénégalais* should war break out. Not surprisingly, they were to defend West Africa, but more importantly, they were to be employed on a massive scale in France. It was envisaged that 162,000 men from the AOF should be deployed in France as rapidly as possible after the outbreak of war. [28] In June 1938, the first practical steps were taken. Rather than the normal 10,000 to 12,000 men, 25,000 were to be recruited from the "class" of 1939, that is, from those reckoned to have been born in 1919. The decision produced misgivings on the part of many civil administrators. They predicted the adverse effects of so massive a recruitment upon the production of food crops and anticipated the resentment of those not recruited but required to fill augmented quotas for forced labor. Even in the prime recruiting areas of Upper Côte d'Ivoire, commandants thought that these increased quotas, although they could be met, would

8 Soldiers of Misfortune

have detrimental effects upon the local economy and would lead many workers to evade both forced labor and military service by migrating to the Gold Coast, where the cocoa farms and mines were always in need of labor.

While the AOF was considered almost completely "pacified" in the 1930s, a few districts did remain under military control. No less than three of them were in the Côte d'Ivoire. Governor Crocicchia had fears that massive recruitment might lead to rebellion. The exigencies of mobilization, moreover, were stripping his administrative personnel to the bone, and he found himself attempting to govern a colony of four million Africans with only about a hundred Frenchmen. In the months immediately following the onset of war, Crocicchia bombarded both AOF Governor-General Jules de Coppet and General Schmitt, commander of the Ivoirien troops, with pleas not to remove more administrators. He urged them to remember the unrest that had flared up with the attempts to introduce conscription during World War I.[29] Schmitt, in particular, was unmoved. He considered such requests for exemptions as typical examples of civilian draft dodging.[30] As in all parts of the AOF, colonial officials from governors down to commandants felt themselves under a threat of dismissal should they fail to cooperate with the military authorities.

The High Command in Paris had anticipated opposition from the civilian administration in the colonies. It did not, however, expect the outcry from General Barraud of the AOF forces, who repeatedly expressed his belief that it would be logistically impossible to incorporate 25,000 raw recruits into the *tirailleurs* in the one year. Who would train them, he asked, when there was already a shortage of experienced officers and NCOs? Georges Mandel, the colonial minister, summoned Barraud to Paris to help him "understand" his orders. Bowing to the inevitable, the general agreed to comply; he would attempt to blend the new recruits into units of reservists.[31]

It is difficult to obtain any accurate figures for the buildup of the regiments of *Tirailleurs Sénégalais*. General Bührer of the French High Command showed the number of recruits from AOF as rising from 21,000 in September 1939, to 122,320 in June 1940. These figures refer, however, only to those serving outside their colonies of origin. The plan was to retain about 50,000 recruits for the defense of the West African colonies.[32] Another source indicates that 73,250 soldiers were recruited from the class of 1939 in AOF and 77,509 from the class of 1940: a total of 150,759 in the two years.[33] A third source gives a figure of 57,537 soldiers from the AOF serving in France, North Africa, and the Levant on 1 January 1940, and of 92,000 serving in AOF or elsewhere: a total of 149,537. Many of the latter category were, however, to be posted to France over the first five months of 1940. [34] Richard-Mollard estimates that at least 80,000 *tirailleurs* from West Africa "crossed the sea." [35] It will be seen that the High Command's projections of 1937 had not proved totally unrealistic. There can be little doubt that on the order of 150,000 West Africans were serving in the French army at the time of the collapse.

General mobilization in the AOF began on 2 September 1939, the day before the official declaration of war. In the Côte d'Ivoire, 8,000 European and African reservists were called up immediately to join the thousands already taken in the annual recruitment earlier that year. It was anticipated that only 600 reservists—presumably those resident in or near Abidjan—would appear on that very day, but according to one local newspaper, 6,000 turned up. [36] Whether this reflected enthusiasm for the war or simply confusion about reporting times is unclear. The next day, 3 September, official calls for volunteers were posted throughout the colony. Reports, whether true or not, began to flow in that many veterans of World War I were bringing their sons forward. One French journalist, writing of the AOF generally, observed that "crowds of natives were at the recruiting office claiming the honor of being able to bear arms for 'our country.'" [37]

War came as no surprise to the Europeans or the *évolués*, that relatively small class of literate Ivoiriens who worked, for the most part, in administration or business. In 1938 and 1939, throughout French West Africa, colonial administrators had conducted a modest publicity campaign which stressed Hitler's views on the inferiority of the African. The colonial minister Mandel, himself, quoted from *Mein Kampf* to the effect that Hitler regarded blacks as "born half-monkeys." [37] To the French, at least, the contrast with their "enlightened" racial policies seemed self-evident.

Such propaganda was delivered by newspaper and official bulletin, and the presumption is that the target was the *évolué*. It certainly reached Edmond N'Guetta of Abidjan, a clerk at the time.

> After school in Grand Bassam in 1938 I went to work for two years for [the commercial firm] *S.I.C.A.* until the war was declared. I was class of 1939. Drafted. . . . War was declared in September. We waited, then we left. Everyone was very enthusiastic. We were young. You know nothing about politics. We had read some speeches, but one knew nothing. You thought it would be easy—let's go to war. [39]

Mandel convinced himself that word of Hitler's beliefs reached not only the *évolué*, but was spread to every market and village. [40] This was obviously wishful thinking. In the Côte d'Ivoire in 1940 there were only a few hundred radios and two local newspapers with a combined circulation (mainly in Abidjan) of perhaps 3,000.[41] Official propaganda could have had little impact on the Ivoirien masses, whether rural or urban. Certainly the only real information available to most villagers came from those commandants and their subordinates who, while on tour in their *cercles*, chose to give talks heavily laced with anti-German propaganda. They hoped, thereby, to prepare village and canton chiefs for mobilization. The major propaganda effort in the Côte d'Ivoire, however, was directed into the army camps.

Echenberg has written on the nature of the propaganda aimed at the soldier. The most ambitious project was the production, by the AOF military command in Senegal, of a newspaper designed to inspire, reassure, and perhaps inform soldiers and their families of the just war in which they were now fully engaged. This was *La Gazette du Tirailleur*. Each issue included a comic strip, *Mamadou s'en va-t'en guerre*, which stressed not only the evils of Hitler and the threat he posed for Africa but the warm camaraderie between black and white soldiers and the fine reception awaiting the *Tirailleurs Sénégalais* in France.[42] It ran, however, only between January and June 1940 and appears not to have circulated in the Côte d'Ivoire. Nevertheless, the same rather crude approach, bordering on jingoism, was employed by both civilian and military authorities in the Côte d'Ivoire in their attempts to encourage reservists to report for duty and volunteers to come forward.

Veterans from the Korhogo region recalled the first few months of the war and testified to their confusion. Panafolo Tuo explained:

> I was mobilized again when the war started. Most of the *anciens combattants* were unhappy about being called up again. . . . The administrator summoned us to say: We need you—the *anciens combattants*. . . . They never discussed why there was a war, but we knew that the Germans were the enemy. They said we must help the whites and then they placed us where they wanted us. I knew nothing about the Germans. The French said that the Germans didn't like Africans. That made us very angry. We, we were with the French and if the French didn't like something, neither did we. We were with them.[43]

Another reservist, Nanlougo Soro, had recently been discharged from military service in France. After recall, he was subjected to a theological discourse on the war by his local commandant. In an interview, he laughingly recollected his skepticism:

> We did hear about Hitler who provoked the war. Hitler said that his God wanted war. The French wanted to stop the war, but Hitler said no: God wants war. It must have been another God; ours does not make war.[44]

Whatever his feelings toward the nature of European deities, Nanlougo decided to cultivate the local ones during his brief spell as a civilian:

I wasn't at all surprised. They had said war was coming. So I looked in the bush for all kinds of medicines to protect myself in war during the six months I was in the village. I had a small bulletproof shirt and I scoured the bush for medicines that would keep a bullet from going into my body. [45]

Mobilization 1939

The mobilization of reservists proceeded smoothly throughout the Côte d'Ivoire. In the Korhogo region, when called upon, the Senoufo or Dyula veteran put on his uniform and reported. Sekongo Yessongui described how the chief, Gbon Coulibaly, tried to ensure that "his" reservists would leave in good spirits:

Gbon sent the message. . . . So we all left. We went to the big marketplace and there they sent us all sorts of drink. Everything that's alcohol. They killed a cow and prepared all kinds of different foods. When we discovered we were going to eat we were very happy. Then they said to us: "Go back to your villages and wait for a message. Then come here. Make preparations. Be careful." . . . The canton chief of Napie made a list of all of us. One day the letter came calling us to Napie. He read the letter to us and told us we had to reenlist. It was a surprise. We had thought the party was compensation for our military service. After we had drunk so much we forgot everything, they told us. . . . That was in 1939. [46]

Sometimes official notification of mobilization came to the village through the commandant. Often, however, soldiers or *gardes de cercle* simply arrived by truck, as Founwo Yeo and Duondiana Yeo found out:

A truck came here. They called out our numbers. We got in the truck and left right away. They had gone to the canton chief and demanded his list of all the *anciens combattants*. We knew about that, but we never knew the exact day they might come for us. We had no time to arrange things. Hurry up! Everyone on the list went—no one ran away. This happened early in the morning. There were about forty of us from here. We didn't know anything about a war going on— nothing. We left in civilian clothes. . . . We spent one month in Bouaké to relearn military things, then went to Abidjan for two days. There was no time to write. No time. They didn't ask if we wanted to send money home. They were only *anciens combattants* at Bouaké. They knew about war already. No, they didn't tell us that we were going to war until we got to France. They said nothing. You can't tell people that they are going to war. [47]

The reservist roundup proceeded smoothly. Those few who attempted flight were quickly captured. For the most part, however, there was little overt resistance. The old fear of the family having to suffer imprisonment, fines, or other manifestations of colonial wrath made evasion virtually unthinkable. Soma Koné explained what could happen:

> We left so we would not create problems for our families left behind. If someone fled they would take the entire family to prison. I never saw this happen myself, but we all believed this to be true. I did see it happen to families whose son refused to do forced labor but not to those who ran from the army. One of my relatives who lived in the same courtyard—his name was Mori Bey—was sent to the *basse côte*, the south. He ran away. They took his two brothers, Soungli and Gbala, and sent them in his place. They put his father in jail. This was in 1940. [48]

Not only did the Senoufo fear retribution, but geography was a factor in their obedience. Korhogo's central location did not facilitate flight into the British Gold Coast or into Liberia. Djirigue Soro, a Senoufo of M'bala, had served in the Sixth RTS and was discharged in 1934. He was recalled, and described his experiences vividly:

> We were sent a notice in the village to come to Korhogo. It was sent to M. Yakinnigue, the leader of the *anciens combattants* in the village. He was an *adjutant-chef* who settled in M'bala, retired there with his pension. He was not the same class as I was, but he was the highest ranking soldier here. He is dead now. He, by himself, was not important in the village, but because he had been in Korhogo, he took on importance. My family gave me medicine [amulets] against bullets. My family thought I was going to die—that I would never return. Yes, there were other *anciens combattants* here—the first two went to the First World War, but they never said anything about it, no, even after we had received the order to go to Korhogo.

After reporting to Korhogo, Djirigue Soro returned to his village to await events. He continued:

> Without any warning, the French came to the village at night—they took us all away. There was no time to prepare for my absence. My family had to send the medicine to Korhogo. There was no time to give it to me in the village. . . . We didn't even spend one week in Korhogo. Less than a week in Bouaké. They [the officers] only told

us that those who had left before us were already dead, so we had to leave [for France] right away. I knew one of those who had gone before. It was the African NCOs who told us about the deaths. They said: "If you're lucky, you'll come back. If not, you'll die." There was no explanation. They only said that France and the Côte d'Ivoire were one family. Thus the war in France—between France and Germany—meant we had to help France. We, not even we, could discuss it. They said we were the same. At that time, we went into the French army. If they said we were the same as the French, we had to accept it. [49]

The Korhogolese recognized that there was little option but to accept recall, but this was not a reflection of their enthusiasm for war. Not one of the recalled reservists who were interviewed remembered feeling anything but unhappiness and resignation. They knew they had to go, and eventually they learned they would have to fight, but in no way did they conceive of the war as having anything to do with the defense of their homes or their colony. As many said, it had nothing to do with them. The war became their war only because the French ruled them and the French decided to send them to battle. But Senoufo and Dyula alike, after over forty years of French rule, had become accustomed to obeying, whether orders to do forced labor, or go to school, or serve in the army.

Soro Nougbo, a Senoufo, told his story. "I was a farmer before my military service," he said. "That was the worst period for forced labor. I was sent to a place behind Agboville—a small village, to work for M. Legorce." He was then recruited from the class of 1936 and served in France with the First RTS.

> Military service was harder than forced labor. We were used to that kind of work, but everything in the army was new—so it was much harder. I was not happy. I did not want to do military service. I wanted to work for my father.

Discharged and repatriated in 1939, Soro Nougbo spent four months and ten days—he was very specific about this—in his village before being recalled:

> They called all the *anciens combattants* to go to war. No, they had not told us anything in France about a war starting—but when the war came, they called us to Korhogo to say that the French and the Germans were at war and we must help the French. The meeting was at Old Gbon's house, the canton chief. He told us about it. It was forced—for all of us—we could not do anything else. They called everybody up from the class of 1925 to that day. [50]

Laqui Kondé and family

Laqui Kondé, like Djirigue Soro, was from M'bala. He had been drafted in 1928 and discharged in 1931. He, too, was recalled in 1939.

> The chief administrator summoned all the *anciens militaires* to come to Korhogo. He said to come quickly. Where could we go? We put our uniforms on. We knew there was a war. Circulars had come from Abidjan and were spread out everywhere in the area—all over. Someone came from Korhogo to tell the canton chief to call the *anciens combattants*. Four of us went from this village—two Senoufo and two Dyula. If someone called you to go fight a war—fire a rifle— would you be happy? We had to go. If you wouldn't leave, they would gather all your family together and put them in prison. If you go yourself, you may die, but it is only you. No, there were no volunteers, not even one from here. [51]

Once recalled, Korhogo reservists joined others from all over the colony. They were usually sent first to Bouaké or to Bobo-Dioulasso for reclassification. After retraining, for as little as a few weeks in some cases, many were then moved from Abidjan for posting to France, North Africa, or the Middle East. Often it was only at this late stage that they became aware that they were going to fight. Senoufo Samongo Soro, speaking of the time he was in camp awaiting transport to France:

In Abidjan, they told us there was war. The very day they informed us, many killed themselves. They hung themselves on trees. Many people. The governor's wife came to try to reconcile us to going. She said: "Yes, you are leaving for war. There should be no question of killing yourselves. You don't have to die in a war. Those of you who are going to have a long life will return here. Others will not. But nothing is certain. So go to war." After that there were no more deaths. Everyone was assembled on the parade ground. We listened to her because so many had already killed themselves and she was giving good advice. When you are born a man, you must act like a man. . . . After that speech it was better. We were calm now. [52]

Another Senoufo *ancien combattant*, Donipoho Sekongo, gave a similar account. "When we were ready to leave Bobo-Dioulasso," he said, "they couldn't hide it anymore—they had to tell us the truth. . . . There were Mossi soldiers who killed themselves because they had already seen war. Now they would be at peace." [53] Although such accounts undoubtedly exaggerate the number of suicides, they must be presumed to contain some truth. Unfortunately contemporary archival sources throw no light on this matter, for the official posture was always to stress the enormous enthusiasm of Africans for the war.

While the reservists were thus being mobilized in the Côte d'Ivoire, many other Ivoiriens were among those 30,000 *tirailleurs* already doing their military service in France, North Africa, or the Middle East. Even they lived with rumors rather than facts. In some cases they were officially notified that they should consider themselves in the army for the duration of the war. Others knew that war had been declared but seemed not to have realized that they would actually be expected to fight. There were also many who had served their full time and were expecting imminent repatriation and discharge. When told that they were to remain in the army, they reacted with anger, though interestingly enough, anger as often directed against the Germans as the French. Somongo Yeo, from the Korhogo area, spoke of how he and his comrades received the news:

We knew that the war had begun, but they never told us the purpose of the war. We had been forced to go into the army—forced to go to France, but now, because of the Germans—the enemy that had attacked the French, we could not go home. We had finished our service—we should have been able to come home, but we couldn't. And we were angry—with the enemy. They tried to explain why we had to stay and fight. The French were not happy; equally unhappy were the Africans. But we were brothers now—the same family— the same skin. We must go to war. Still, it was an obligation, even though they made those speeches to us. We were forced to go. [54]

Newspapers such as *Paris-Dakar* published impassioned letters, putatively written by serving soldiers, denouncing Germany:

> I have offered my country the sacrifice of my life to defend her against the German monster. I burn with desire to leave. This war concerns us as much as the metropolitan French. By fighting alongside our white brothers, we Africans, defend our own cause. [55]

The authenticity of such letters is obviously suspect. They were a kind of propaganda designed to bolster the morale of the civilian population. Philippe Yacé offered a much more realistic view of affairs. He was, at the time, one of the less than five hundred Ivoirien *citoyens*, and later became the first African president of the *Association des Anciens Combattants* in the Côte d'Ivoire.

> It was the law. There were no explanations. First, for the subjects, they did their service because everyone did it. Now, the French did not have to be told. They were French, and they had to serve. It was the law, having to serve in the army. Nineteen years old—the army! But between France and the African colonies it became a moral issue. There we were—we were in France to fight, but we were under-represented. Until 1945, only Senegal had a representative. . . . There are two ways to look at it. After all, if France had colonies she would use the people in them to fight for her as England did. French and Africans were equal in their duty to France. Thus there was no need for explanations of why you were fighting. For the African subjects and we citizens, there was of course frustration. After the war these things were fixed. But remember, no nineteen-year-old was ever told anything. [56]

There is no doubt whatsoever that West African soldiers did, as Yacé states, do their duty. Once under fire, a sense of identity with the French became strong. Tuo Ouna, a Senoufo, said:

> When you are on the battlefield, you are there to kill the enemy. We looked for them. We wanted to fight them. The enemy made trouble for the French. Because we left on behalf of the French, we were there to fight the enemies of the French. We were considered like the French, therefore we fought hard to kill the others." [57]

His viewpoint was close in spirit to that of a volunteer from Man. Corporal Guepleu had been stationed in France since 1937, with the Fourth Regiment of the *Tirailleurs Sénégalais*. When war was declared he was at Toulon.

The question of whether war was coming never arose. You work—
you are not warned—that's just how war is. General Mangin came
and announced it. He called each battalion by number: "You, the
10th, you will go there. You the – – –, will go here." . . . The war
was caused by riches. For example, there are two villages side by side.
One decides to come and take something important from the other.
If that village isn't happy about it—it's war. There it was the Germans
who had taken gold from the French and that is what provoked
the war. [58]

To young Ivoirien soldiers such as Corporal Geupleu and Tuo Ouna,
obedience came naturally. The fact that the first came from a society
with a strong warrior tradition, the second from one without, seems
singularly irrelevant to the situation in 1939. Regardless of background,
and however reluctant initially to serve in the army, few Ivoiriens failed
to do what they, just as surely as the French themselves, came in time
to see as their duty. This attitude, remarkable in itself, was to provide
the French with few doubts about the success they would have in the
greatly expanded recruiting drive awaiting the class of 1940.

Notes to Chapter Two

1. Pierre Gentil, *Les Troupes du Sénégal de 1816 à 1890,* vol. 1, *Soldats du
Sénégal du Colonel Schmaltz au Général Faidherbe* (Dakar, Senegal: Nouvelles
Editions Africaines, 1978), 16.
2. Ibid., 30.
3. Ibid.
4. Ibid., xi.
5. The four communes of *la vieille colonie* were Dakar, Gorée, St. Louis,
and Rufisque. These citizens would be classified in the military as *originaires*;
by World War II they had won the "privilege" of doing their military service
in the regular French army.
6. Charles John Balesi, *From Adversaries to Comrades-in-Arms; West Africans and the French Military, 1885–1918* (Waltham, MA: Crossroads Press,
1979), 21–22, 38.
7. Marc Michel, *L'Appel à l'Afrique: Contributions et réactions à l'effort de
guerre (1914–1919),* 7–12. This is the definitive work on both the creation of
the "modern" *Tirailleurs Sénégalais* and their activities in World War I.
8. Balesi, *From Adversaries to Comrades-in-Arms,* 75.
9. Ibid., 121; Similarly Myron Echenberg, "Morts pour la France," 363.
10. Balesi, *From Adversaries to Comrades-in-Arms,* 109–12; also Echenberg,
"Paying the Blood Tax," 173.

11. Shelby Cullom Davis, *Reservoirs of Men: A History of the Black Troops of French West Africa* (Geneva: Kundig, 1934), 156. Four were killed, four wounded, and two reported missing in action.

12. J. Van Vollenhoven, "Circulaires au sujet des tirailleurs réformés ou licenciés," *Journal officiel de la Côte d'Ivoire* (1917): 565.

13. Interview 42.

14. Interview 71.

15. Echenberg, "Paying the Blood Tax," 175. French citizens were conscripted for two years, while African subjects were required to serve three. For the antecedents to the 1919 Act, see Echenberg, "Slaves into Soldiers," 318–20.

16. Remark made during the session on West Africa at the "World War II and Africa" Conference at the School of Oriental and African Studies, University of London, June 1984.

17. *La Côte d'Ivoire Chrétienne* (Abidjan, January 1939). The November 1940 issue reported that 60 percent of the *tirailleurs* recruited from Basse Côte were Christians.

18. *Le Progrès colonial* (29 February 1940).

19. Albert Balima, *Genèse de la Haute-Volta* (Ouagadougou, Burkina Faso: Presses Africaines, 1969), 80.

20. For Louveau's own account of his downfall in 1940, see *"Au Bagne": Entre les griffes de Vichy et de la milice* (Bamako, Mali: Soudan Imprimerie, 1947).

21. ANCI, report dd. 16 February 1940. Carton 4018, Dossier VI–13/3.

22. Echenberg, "Paying the Blood Tax," 189.

23. ANCI, Carton 4018, Dossier VI–13/3.

24. Interview 20.

25. ANCI, Administrative assessment of Korhogo by Commandant Mondon, 1939, Carton 467, Dossier XII–54/14.

26. Balima, *Genèse de la Haute-Volta*, 80.

27. ACCCI, Alcide Delmont letter to Abidjan Chamber of Commerce, 24 December 1939, Dossier 22.

28. SHAT, "Rapport annuel de l'Etat Major, 3ème Bureau, Troupes du groupe de l'AOF, 1940," Carton 3, Dossier 02A2 (4 February 1941).

29. ANCI, Carton 719.

30. Ibid.

31. General X (Bührer), *Aux heures tragiques de l'empire (1938–1941)* (Paris: Office Colonial d'Edition, 1947), 54–55.

32. Ibid., 109–10.

33. SHAT, "Rapport annuel de l'Etat Major, 3ème Bureau, Troupes du groupe de l'AOF, 1940," op. cit.

34. SHAT, Centre de Documentation, letter dd. 4 June 1958. The figures were compiled by SHAT in response to a query from the Section d'Etudes et d'Information des Troupes d'Outre-Mer.

35. J. Richard-Molard, *Afrique Occidental Français* (Paris: Editions Berger-Levrault, 1952), 165.

36. *Le Progrès Colonial*, (Abidjan, 29 February–5 March, 1940).

37. Pierre Mille, "L'Empire Colonial et la Guerre," *Notre Combat*, 1, no. 8 (10 November 1939): 18.

38. John Summerscales, "The War Effort of the French Colonies," *African Affairs*, 39 (April 1940): 123.

39. Interview 3.

40. Summerscales, "The War Effort of the French Colonies," 123.

41. ANCI, Carton 2988, Dossier VI–146. Similarly, G. Roux, "La Presse Ivoirienne: Miroir d'une société" (Ph.D. diss. Université René Descartes, Paris, 1975), 18.

42. Echenberg, paper presented at African Studies Association meeting, Denver, Colo., 21 November 1987.

43. Interview 30.

44. Interview 35.

45. Interview 35.

46. Interview 59.

47. Interview 63.

48. Interview 9.

49. Interview 34.

50. Interview 28.

51. Interview 32.

52. Interview 69.

53. Interview 67.

54. Interview 38.

55. *Paris-Dakar,* letter from a Soudanese [Malian] *tirailleur* incorporated in an article denouncing German propaganda directed at African soldiers in the French army (24 January 1940).

56. Interview 49.

57. Interview 24.

58. Interview 87.

Seydou Nourou Tal with the sons of the Moro Naba

3

The Class of 1940

Quotas: Beating the Bush

THE ONLY WAR YEAR for which good statistics for the Côte d'Ivoire exist is 1940. From them it is possible to follow closely the actual process of raising and training large numbers of colonial soldiers for the French army. The recruiting campaign of 1940, launched in December 1939, was the first to take place under wartime conditions. The system in place since 1919 was retained more or less intact; only the numbers were changed. The target was to recruit 82,000 from the AOF as a whole. The 30,000 men of the *première portion* were to be incorporated immediately, and 52,000 were to be held as the *deuxième portion* for later induction. One-third of the recruits were to be Ivoiriens, thus more than tripling the 1939 recruitment quota. [1]

To launch the recruitment drive, the redoubtable Seydou Nourou Tal, *grand marabout* of French West Africa, was sent on a month-long tour of the Côte d'Ivoire, Guinea, Togo and French Congo (Brazzaville). He was to prepare Africans for the war effort. The administration regarded him as a very persuasive individual, without peer when it came to convincing Africans to accept unpopular directives. Everywhere he preached obedience to the authorities, proclaimed the justice of France's cause, and drew attention to the abundant economic opportunities available to all under the beneficent French regime. He delivered rousing speeches condemning Germany's racist doctrines. He had, in fact, made two earlier official tours of the Côte d'Ivoire extolling the rewards of cooperation with the French. Now he spread a new message throughout the colony.

Seydou Nourou Tal visited the army camps. He told the soldiers that they were fighting not only for the defense of the motherland but for humanity and the triumph of justice. Germany alone, he said, was to blame for the war. The men should have no fears, for they would be in combat only in the spring, when the weather was fine. They would, moreover, be fighting alongside three million Frenchmen. But he did not confine his message to the soldiers. He also addressed the farmers. He told them to persevere in their efforts, for things were now so much better under the French than ever before. Conveniently ignoring the annual administrative appropriation of a portion of each village's harvest, he assured his audiences that, thanks to the French, their harvests now belonged to them and not to their chiefs. "It is thus possible for everyone to get rich," he assured them. According to the official record, his speeches were greeted with tremendous applause and innumerable choruses of *Vive la France!* Administrators were delighted with the way the *marabout* had performed "his heavy and delicate task."[2]

The massive recruitment campaign extended over two months. The task was a heavy one by virtue of the sheer numbers involved. All men officially designated twenty years of age had to be assembled, medically examined, and classified. The statistics for the Côte d'Ivoire include, of course, the greater part of Upper Volta which was under its jurisdiction. By January 1940, 96,679 men had been told when to report to their recruitment centers (see Table 1). The procedures were well established, and for the most part, as remarked above, no organized resistance was encountered. At most, some individuals might attempt flight. A few sought anonymity in Abidjan. Others, living near the Liberian or Gold Coast frontiers, might cross them. Kangoute Katakie was formerly interpreter to the commandant of Bouna, which lay across the Black Volta from the Gold Coast. In that area, he commented,

> every year they [the people] knew the men would be called for the army. They knew when the recruitment was coming. . . . When you called for one hundred, you would get eighty. You had to go and search for the missing ones. Their relatives had to find them. The notice was addressed to the head of the family. If someone did not show up, the family chief was punished. He was the one responsible.[3]

By and large, however, flight was uncommon, and the entire recruitment process became accepted if not acceptable.

Each *cercle* was assigned a recruitment quota. Its commandant would then distribute the quota by divisions and subdivisions. The quotas were proportionate, in theory at least, to population. Censuses were taken in villages, occasionally by the commandant himself, but more usually by *gardes de cercle* assisted by the canton chiefs and their representatives. The accuracy of the counts varied enormously and depended, as was so often the case in the French colonial system, upon the zeal and efficiency of individual administrators. Energetic officers who traveled widely in their districts had a relatively clear idea of the pool of prospective soldiers. Others lacked the determination or ability to visit every village under their charge and often left the counting to the canton chiefs. In the Korhogo district, where we have seen that there was no marked enthusiasm for military service, an indolent commander passed over much of the work to his Malian interpreter, who developed a lucrative business out of negotiating with the canton chiefs over the exact quota they would receive. The numbers began to show less relationship to population, more to the nature of the "considerations" he received. "The power of Soumaré," it was reported, "is evident by the numerous sums of money and the important gifts which are given to him by those who find it necessary to make various requests, because *rien ne peut se faire sans l'intermédiaire de Soumaré.*"[4]

Once the quotas were established, by whatever means and on whatever basis, the commandant then delegated matters to the canton chiefs. They in turn distributed the quota among their villages chiefs, who finally had physically to round up the men. Their practices appear to have varied considerably. Depending upon the authority they exercised, some selected the men directly, others after consultation with the village elders or council. In some cases each head of family was required to produce one candidate. In others, a village might send all the young men of the approximate age to the induction center, for the selection to be made there.

Commandants routinely ignored one of the main provisions of the Universal Conscription Act of 1919. Men who already had a brother serving in the army or those who were the sole support of a widowed mother or grandmother or a sick or blind father were eligible for exemption from military service. As with most other aspects of African recruitment, little attention seems to have been paid to these exclusionary provisions of the Act. None of the men interviewed for this study was ever asked about such matters.[5] No Senoufo recruit, it seems, was aware that an appeal could be made even after the decision to induct him had been taken. Torna Sokongo, of the Guiembé subdivision of Korhogo, is a case in point:

> I cultivated for my father. I had an older brother and a younger one, too small to work in the fields. . . . Before I left for the army my older brother died. There was no one left to work in the field. My father was too old to cultivate—there was no one left. So my father died while I was in the army. You couldn't say that you couldn't go because your father had only one son. The canton chief didn't care about that. That wasn't his problem. When they asked him for a certain number of people—that was his problem.[8]

Some Ivoirien chiefs did, we have seen, conspicuously volunteer their own sons for military service. The great majority, however, used their privileged positions to keep close relatives out of the army. The inequity was recognized by informants. Many veterans confirmed Zie Coulibaly's statement that "not many chiefs' sons went to the army. . . . They were not called."[7]

Recruitment, Examination, and Selection

It was in the best interest of both canton and village chiefs to try to produce men of a quality such as not to bring down the wrath of the administration on their heads. Throughout most of the Côte d'Ivoire, educational standards were seldom an issue. Of the almost 12,000 Ivoiriens of the *première portion* taken into the army in 1940, only 294 were listed as literate.[8] Physical condition was more to the point. The administration expected the chiefs to provide a selection of healthy young men of the right age, and failure to do this could result in fines and removal from office. In some areas, however, the chiefs simply could not afford to send their fittest men to the army. They also had to meet the forced labor requirements while still producing enough food to sustain the community. It is not surprising, then, that chiefs frequently attempted to unload their less than prime men on the recruitment commission. This was relatively easy at a time when the sheer quantity of men required tended to deflect attention away from their quality. This kind of passive resistance, however, was not new in 1940. An eyewitness described the situation five years earlier, with general reference to the AOF.

> On the day of the assembly in the *chef-lieu*, the recruitment commissions see filing before them a strange assortment [of men] which is far from representing the elite of the native populations. Miraculously five or six times too many are there and the doctor first eliminates the most lice-infested, those with rickets, those too young and too old. They are left with three or four hundred who have the air of being between nineteen and twenty-one years old.[9]

The work of the recruitment commissions in 1940 is well documented for the Côte d'Ivoire. They usually included the local commandant, an army officer, and a doctor. They would spend from two to four days in any one district. Canton chiefs were expected to be present during the examination and selection process, whether to be castigated or congratulated on the contingent of men they had produced. The commission would utilize the services of *anciens combattants* to "inspire, help and encourage the chosen to volunteer."[10] The medical examination came first. Depending upon the facilities of the area and the diligence of the commission, it might involve thorough checks with x-rays at the one extreme, a perfunctory glance at the recruit's body at the other. Ditiemba Silué described his experiences:

> I was taken at Korhogo. The canton chief at Karakoro assembled all the village chiefs and told them the French needed soldiers. Twenty-one of us were chosen from our village. An African soldier did the first selection. After that we saw the doctor. Eleven of us were left. After the examination, I was the only one taken. They gave us an x-ray. The others were not taken because they were not healthy. Only me. They gave me the uniform right away. No, I was very unhappy. I even cried. But I thought I would be rejected when we got to Bouaké because of my weight—I was very thin. But when we got there, they never weighed us. [11]

Malaria was endemic and had to be ignored. Among the other diseases and disabilities commonly found were goiter, malnutrition, sleeping sickness, leprosy, heart conditions, and hernias. For the Côte d'Ivoire as a whole, 73 percent of the 96,679 called from the class of 1940 were rejected, whether for the first or second portions. For the *cercle* of Korhogo, 75 percent of the 10,360 called were rejected; and for that of Man, 83 percent of the 10,314 (Table 1). Presumably, the grounds for rejection were, most commonly, poor physique or sickness. This is borne out by the comments of members of the recruitment commissions. In the Man region, the physical condition of the Yacouba was described as mediocre; they were undernourished, and syphilis and sleeping sickness were rife. The Korhogolese were, in contrast, considered generally fit. [12]

A somewhat different aspect of the matter is revealed by the numbers of those selected for the first and second portions, expressed as a percentage of those actually given medical examinations in the course of the recruiting process. For Korhogo the figure is 26 percent; for Man, 34 percent; and for the Côte d'Ivoire as a whole, 34 percent (Table 1). Data for the entire AOF show that over the years 1930 to 1938 the proportion accepted of those examined varied in the range of 17 to 26 percent and averaged 19 percent. In 1939, however, the figure rose to 33 percent; and in 1940 to 35 percent. [13] The implication is that, with the outbreak of the war, the standard a man had to meet to be accepted for military service fell very significantly. The figures suggest that the practice in the Côte d'Ivoire was no exception to this trend.

Following the medical examinations, the commission announced its decision. Those selected for immediate induction—*le première portion*—were issued with uniforms, subject to availability, and had their own clothes taken away. Even the most reluctant of the Senoufo draftees inter-

Table One
Military Recruitment in the Côte d'Ivoire, 1940

Cercle	Total Men Called	Total Men Examined	No. of Conscripts/ Volunteers Taken		Percentage Taken		Percentage of Ivoirien Soldier by Cercle (First Portion)	
			First Portion	Second Portion	Of Men Called	Of Men Examined	Conscripts	Volunteers
Abidjan	12,301	8,134	633/0	3,040	29.86	45.16	6.64	0.00
Bobo-Dioulasso	5,752	5,432	826/74	1,051	33.92	35.92	8.67	3.48
Bouaké	14,487	12,515	1,425/0	2,293	25.66	29.71	14.95	0.00
Daloa	4,987	4,337	588/192	1,040	35.89	41.27	6.17	9.02
Dimbokro	3,547	2,932	336/64	628	28.98	35.06	3.53	3.01
Gaoua	4,416	3,721	251/449	316	23.01	27.31	2.63	21.10
Grand Bassam	2,976	2,385	107/43	200	11.76	14.68	1.12	2.02
Kaya	4,239	3,901	950/5	592	36.49	39.66	9.97	0.23
Korhogo	10,360	9,947	1,293/8	1,318	25.28	26.33	13.57	0.38
Lahou	2,065	1,791	421/35	559	49.15	56.67	4.42	1.64
Man	10,314	5,036	418/482	836	16.83	34.47	4.39	22.65
Ouagadougou	12,912	11,450	1,582/168	1,251	23.24	26.21	16.60	7.89
Sassandra	2,801	2,305	58/92	785	33.38	40.56	0.61	4.32
Seguela	3,083	2,765	396/12	122	17.19	19.17	4.16	0.56
Tenkodogo	2,439	2,408	246/504	962	70.19	71.10	2.58	23.68
TOTAL	96,679	79,059	9,530/2,128	14,993			100.00	100.00

SOURCE: ANCI, *Rapport Annuel de la Commission de Recrutement*, 1940. Carton 339, Dossier XIII –19–138/1085.

viewed took a considerable if ironic pride in his selection. Several were quite boastful. "Four of us left from this village," Gmbala Soro of Dossemekaha recalled. "They took only me. It was my body—I was the handsomest."[14] Silouenissougui Silué of Guiembé echoed this sentiment. "There were eight of us from my village, but I was the only one taken. Yes, I was pleased with myself at that moment."[15] Sekongo Yessongui felt that he had been chosen by an authority even higher than that of the recruiting commission:

> Three of us went from here, and I was the only one recruited. I do not know why they took me. I did know that God wanted me to do my military service. The white man had said that people with sores on them would not go, but then the white chose me even though I had sores. Then I was a handsome lad—I was pleased with myself.[16]

The issue of a uniform was of great significance for the Ivoirien recruit. It gave him an instant status. It set him apart. The recruits were not chiefs, but they had been lifted above the masses of commoners. Even in the Korhogo region, despite the unpopularity of military service, the symbolism of the French uniform was powerful. It testified that its wearer had been found fit to serve in the army, even if the recruit himself, like Tiorna Yeo, would rather not have had the honor:

> In my time they came to the village. Two persons, both Africans, and made a list of all of us. Then they gave us papers and told us when we had come to Korhogo with that paper. It was not possible to bribe them; we only gave them food. We went to Korhogo, where the nurses decided who was good. Those they kept, and the others were able to return to the village. Those who were taken were given their uniforms right away and did not get to go home. I wore the uniform. I was in uniform. I was not happy, but I had to do it. Things were not like they are today, before, you were forced to do everything. When they started talking about war, I was afraid. I knew it wasn't good—to go to war. The uniform was pretty, but we didn't know if we would come back.[17]

In the Yacouba country, the significance of the uniform was more dramatic and the men not at all ambivalent. Veteran Corporal Guepleu described his reactions:

> Right there in Man they gave me my uniform. I was happy about that and I signed up for six years. Volunteer! It was in my mind before I was taken. I first had this idea when I saw my first veteran. He had a fine bearing about him—a good way of life. Very respected.[18]

From the point of view of the recruiters the replacement of civilian clothes by uniforms had an additional, more practical outcome. It made it highly unlikely that any recruit would desert, for it was difficult to fade away into the bush when dressed in fez and khaki tunic.

Daouda Tuo-Donatoho described a typical enough experience when he was recruited from the class of 1937:

> I was forced to join. At that time everything was forced—forced labor. I was drafted. I was the only one taken that year from the village. . . . The village chief chose me. I had to go. First to Korhogo to have the medical exam—I passed, but many were in bad health—rejected. If you were fit they took your clothes and gave you the uniform right away. Then you went home and waited for the day to report. My parents were impressed by the uniform. They sent old soldiers—still in the army—to get us. Not even Senoufo—they were from the camp at Bouaké—spoke French or Bambara. We walked to Ferké to await the train. My family cried. They said we will never see him again. The canton chief at Ferké knew we were coming. They fed us and gave us lodging. I spoke no French then—some others did. [19]

The experience of those in the class of 1940 was often an even more abrupt one. Frequently those selected for service were kept at the recruiting center sometimes for a few hours only, sometimes for a day or two, and then sent to the camps at Bouaké, Bouna, or Bobo-Dioulasso. In many cases their families would only learn they had been taken when the rejected candidates returned to the village. Exceptionally, however, a relative might accompany the candidate to the commission. In the military district of Bouna, the commandant instructed all fathers to accompany their sons to the recruitment so that they would know who had been taken. This was a most unusual procedure, and appears to have been a personal decision of the commandant. [20] The induction of Yeo Tibeya of Napiedougou followed a much more standard pattern, though he himself was one of those few Senoufo to volunteer. "There were many of us in 1939," he said.

> The chief of the canton informed everyone in the village that there was going to be recruitment at Korhogo. All who were interested were to go there. We were numerous. There were many old soldiers in our village, even from the 14–18 war, but they never talked about the war. It was the canton chief who told us about the war—the recruitment. . . . They measured us, our size, if we were in good health—*apte*—[we were] taken. We left right away, from Korhogo to Bobo. [21]

Yeo Nabetegue

Twenty men went to the recruiting center from Napie on that occasion.

Few conscripts, who were usually only twenty years of age or there-abouts, were married. Some claimed to be, but there seems to have been a presumption that even so they were not "legally" married, that is, as recognized in French law. The payment of allowances to wives depended upon this factor, and many a recruit, such as Yeo Nabetegue of Korhogo, was surprised to find that his family received nothing. "They asked me if I had a wife," Yeo remembered:

> Yes, I said, I have a wife and one child. They put me in the bus to leave and I thought they asked me this so that they would send money to my wife, but she got nothing. They promised to send a bit of food to my family, but they did nothing for them. [22]

For the families of many of those recruited from the class of 1940, years would pass before they had any news of their sons, husbands, or brothers.

Volunteers and Conscripts

From the pool of chosen recruits, each *cercle* was expected to produce a specified number of volunteers, some of whom would in time become career soldiers. Routinely, during the first hours of their induction into the army, new recruits were encouraged to change their status from *appelé* to *engagé volontaire*. The commandant, with the aid of *anciens combattants* and African NCOs, would explain the benefits of signing on for an extra year. In exchange for a fourth year of military service, the volunteer would get higher pay. Those wishing to volunteer were then asked to step forward. Up to and including 1939, a 500-franc bonus was immediately paid them.

The Senoufo did not apparently find the inducements very attractive. According to *anciens combattants*, only one man from the class of 1939 truly volunteered, although others might have been "volunteered" by their chiefs. This man was Yeo Porio of Pangarikaha, who confirmed his status. "I volunteered to help the French," he insisted. "I went into Korhogo and volunteered." [23] Even so, others present teased him. He had left the village in a fury after a violent quarrel with his chief, they said, and that is why he volunteered. Nonetheless, his action was so remarkable—for a Korhogolese—that Porio acquired a certain fame.

No bonus was offered to those volunteering from the class of 1940. Presumably the honor of fighting for France was regarded as inducement enough. It was not, and later the bonus was reinstated. Nevertheless, a respectable number of men did volunteer, attracted by the higher

Yeo Porio, the Senoufo volunteer

rates of pay and the status carried with it. Reference to Table 1 shows that throughout the Côte d'Ivoire, 11,628 men were taken from the class of 1940 through the work of the regular recruitment commissions, and that 18 percent of them were volunteers. Percentages by region were, however, highly uneven. Of the 750 recruits from the Mossi *cercle* of Tenkodogo, for example, 67 percent were volunteers; from the 700 of the mixed Lobi and Kulango *cercle* of Gaoua, 64 percent; and from the 900 of the *cercle* of Man, 53 percent. In sharp contrast, of the 1,301 recruits from the *cercle* of Korhogo only 8 volunteered, less than 1 percent.

These statistics must, however, be used cautiously. The Mossie *cercle* of Ouagadougou shows less than 10 percent volunteers, but this reflects the fact that in 1939 the Moro Naba had "encouraged" many of his subjects to step forward without awaiting the arrival of the recruitment commission. In the *cercles* of Abidjan and Bouaké, recruiting offices had been opened in both towns, and those ready to volunteer had done so during the autumn of 1939. It is regrettable that no figures have been found for the total numbers of Ivoirien volunteers in 1939 or 1940. The statistics, furthermore, disguise the nature of this volunteerism. We have indicated that chiefs often produced volunteers by decidedly less than voluntary methods. Ouanlo Silué, who became a regular, reflected on this.

> When you are recruited for military service they do not tell you that you may go to war. It comes as a surprise when you get there. I was taken by force. Yes, I got a bonus of 500 francs and it [his military book] says EV *[engagé volontaire]* but when this war was hot, they just took people like that—*EV! EV!* It was really not voluntary enlistment. Everyone who was taken the same day as I was got 500 francs—everyone. We were all "volunteers."[24]

Military service by choice is still not seen as a true profession for a Senoufo. Although there were significant numbers of former soldiers in the Korhogo region, respected and a little feared as we have seen, few thereby acquired a status within their communities other than that determined by the circumstance of their birth. They might be utilized as interpreters by the village and canton chiefs, to explain and help execute orders from the administrative officers, but in traditional matters only traditional status counted. Administrators knew well that conditioned to obedience though the Senoufo might be, they were not men eager to volunteer their services. In 1940, Korhogo's commandant commented:

> The Senoufo accept military service without recriminations, like all other public services. They only enlist voluntarily if there is a direct, personal benefit such as the bonus, all of which is left with their family. Since the bonus was eliminated, there are virtually no volunteers.[25]

As we have seen, there were districts in the Côte d'Ivoire which produced volunteers much in excess of their quotas. There is an apparent correlation between a taste for the army and culture and history. Peoples such as the Yacouba and the Lobi, from highly segmented societies, had long traditions of opposition to strangers and had resisted pacification for decades. But the Mossi also responded to the call for volunteers. They, by contrast, belonged to centralized kingdoms which had indigenous military institutions, armies of cavalry and archers. The Yacouba,

Lobi, and Mossi, for different reasons, seem positively to have welcomed the idea of military service, though this is not to say that they necessarily sought the glory of actual combat. There is no doubt that they saw the army as providing them with a better life—good pay, regular food, travel, even a modicum of education—rather than a heroic death. They doubtless also anticipated returning as *anciens militaires* to their villages, with money, pensions, and some degree of literacy in French, thereby to receive the deference of those they had left behind. Ex-soldiers could fire the imagination of many a young man. Denis Yacé, who later went to the prestigious William Ponty College in Senegal, remembers being inspired by them as a young man.

> Some of them were volunteers. Especially after they would see the *anciens combattants* return to their villages—or at the recruitment centers with their uniforms on—speaking French—with their pretty medals and decorations. I remember when my older brother, class of 1932, came back dressed in his uniform. I said: This is great! But of course, none of us thought about war itself. We had no idea of what it was like. [26]

The Senoufo veteran, by contrast, treated his military service as a private experience. He neither entranced the young with his war stories, nor returned with evident material gain. This doubtless contributed to the extremely low number of volunteers from the Korhogo region, but even more important was the strong opposition by Senoufo families to having their sons either volunteer for the army or, if conscripted, serve more than the minimum time necessary. Some Senoufo, however, did grow to like the army. But for their desire to respect the wishes of their elders, they said, in peacetime at least they would gladly have reenlisted and tried to complete the full fifteen years of a regular. Tuo Ouana was originally recruited from the class of 1925.

> The French said, "Send your young men for the army." One was not happy but we went. It was forced, but once we got there it was fun. Yes, I was the only one from Kolokaha to get taken. Many left, but the others came back. Why me? Because they liked me. Yes, there was a medical examination—you had to get completely undressed for it.

Recalled in 1940, he rather regretted that he was discharged after a few months because of age. "When I had to leave the army," he commented, "I was not happy. While I was in the army I was happy. Now, I will be very happy if I can get the pension." [27] Djomopine Yeo of Guiembé was repatriated in 1941. He had enjoyed the pay of 30 francs every fifteen days.

I saved a bit. I couldn't spend it all because I had to think of the peo-
ple in the village. I bought bread, wine, meat, and some shirts. . . .
It was good earning money. I liked it. If I had done the fifteen years
I would have had money. But I did not miss anything else about the
army, the beatings especially. Why didn't I stay in? Are you kidding?
There was a war on now. Who would enlist for fifteen years?[28]

Before the declaration of war, but when war appeared inevitable,
France had already proposed giving its African soldiers certain privileges.
All combat soldiers were promised voting rights and, after discharge,
were to be entitled to use the French rather than the "native" legal system
(the *Indigénat*). This was not exactly equivalent to full citizenship, but
it extended to all such veterans concessions formerly made only to career
men. This unaccustomed benevolence, designed to encourage volunteers,
probably made no great impression on the Senoufo if, indeed, they even
knew of it. Yet even in the Korhogo region, the conscript realized certain tangible benefits resulted from military service. Far more important than any change in legal status, however, was the unofficial policy
of never requiring *anciens militaires* henceforth to do forced labor. This
was seen as the one real benefit conferred by army service. Yeo Tibeya,
who volunteered in 1939 on the orders of the Napiedougou canton chief,
remembered listening to a speech by the commandant.

After that I was the most eager of all to volunteer. Why? If I stayed
in the village, there was forced labor. The canton chief could send
me there—that was *la force*. When you did your military service and
if you came back, you were left alone, tranquil—you never had to
do forced labor. Many, many were taken from here to haul wood. My
mother was very happy—not opposed at all. My father was dead.[29]

The actual inducements and methods used to acquire volunteers were
not ones that the French always wanted to have exposed. The important thing was to have statistics which showed colonial subjects
"volunteering" to serve France. This had definite political allure since
it could be seen as a measure of the success of the *mission civilisatrice*
and was a concrete means of demonstrating the devotion of the colonized to France. The Germans responded. In 1940, a barrage of Nazi
propaganda, directed at Africa, accused France of subjecting her black
troops to adverse climatic conditions and denounced the use of forcibly
impressed African soldiers. The French government countered the
German charges by reemphasizing the voluntary nature of recruitment.[30]

The Germans may have had a point. Whatever the truth of the matter,
however, the great majority of French officers, administrators, and
residents generally, in the Côte d'Ivoire as throughout the AOF, were

genuinely convinced of the unquestioned loyalty of *their* Africans, and of the desire of these colonial subjects to come voluntarily to the aid of the motherland. The *Tirailleurs Sénégalais* occupied a special place in French colonial mythology, and most whites, reassured by the outward similarity between the recruitment process in France and that in Africa, truly believed that the men wanted to serve. This mythology remains firmly entrenched in France, two generations after the war and some three decades after the end of empire. A French officer who fought alongside colonial soldiers in World War II, in Indochina, and in Algeria remains deeply convinced of the loyalty of the African *ancien combattant*. Col. Henry Boileau observed:

> There is a great difference between Arab and African former soldiers. The black *ancien combattant*, even if he returned home, stayed loyal to France. Not the Arab. After Indochina there was the Algerian war. The Arab *ancien combattant* was then on the other side. There were a few who stayed loyal to France, but after it was over they had to leave our army. They came back with us to France. Once an African is on your side, he stays there. [31]

Even today, French residents in an independent Côte d'Ivoire like to believe that former African soldiers regret the end of the empire. The sentiment is expressed in the words of a Michel Sardou song popular in Abidjan bars.

Moi, Monsieur	Me, Mister,
j'ai fait la colo	I've done the colonies
Dakar, Conakry, Bamako.	Dakar, Conakry, Bamako.
Moi, Monsieur,	Me, Mister,
j'ai eu la belle vie	I had a great life
Au temps bénit des colonies.	In the blessed time of colonies.
Les Guerriers, m'appelaient	Warriors called me
—Grand Chef!	Great Chief!
Au temps glorieux de l'AOF.	In the glorious times of the AOF.
J'avais des ficelles au képi,	I had ribbons on my hat
Au temps bénit des colonies.	In the blessed time of colonies.
On pense encore à toi	We still think of you,
O Bwana	O Bwana
Dis nous ce que t'as pas on en a.	Tell us what you do not have.
Y'a pas d'café, pas d'coton,	There's no coffee, cotton,
Pas d'essence, en France.	gas, in France.
Mais des idées nous on en a.	But we have ideas
On pense encore à toi,	We still think of you,
O Bwana.	O Bwana.

Moi, Monsieur,	Me, Mister,
j'ai tué des panthères	I've killed panthers
A Tombouctou dans le Niger.	in Timbuktu in Niger.
Et des hyppos dans l'Oubangui	And hippos in Oubangi
Au temps béni des colonies.	In the blessed time of colonies.
Autrefois à Colomb-Bechar	Once, in Colomb-Bechar,
J'avais plein	I had lots
de serviteurs noirs	of black servants and
Et quatre filles dans mon lit.	four girls in my bed.
Au temps béni des colonies.	In the blessed time of colonies.
On pense encore à toi	We still think of you,
O Bwana![32]	O Bwana!

Training the *Ivoirien Tirailleur*

In 1939, army authorities had learned the danger of making "massive levies. . . . with no thought of how to train them."[33] On purely military grounds, given the enormous difficulties experienced in the training camps due to the scarcity of officers and NCOs, induction of the *première portion* of the class of 1940 by gradual stages would have been rational. Any such procedure was rejected due to the fear that those to be recruited might return to their villages and fail to appear when actually called. It was rather a case of a *tirailleur* in the hand being worth more than two in the bush.

The 1940 contingent selected, the process of turning a Senoufo, Yacouba, or whoever into a *Tirailleur Sénégalais* began in earnest. It involved not only teaching a recruit the skills of warfare, but creating for him a new identity—that of a soldier of France—transcending older loyalties and allegiances. A preliminary step had already been taken by the recruitment commission when those selected for service were issued with a new and "uniform" uniform. Then, by truck or train or occasionally on foot, the men were sent to the camps of Bouaké, Bouna, or Bobo-Dioulasso. They were immediately given a hearty meal. It was their introduction to the "uniform" cuisine that they would encounter for the duration of their service. For most, the regularity, quantity, and quality of army food, and especially the abundance of meat, remains the best memory of the war. The only divergent opinions were expressed by the *évolués*, the educated conscripts. Guy Ahizi-Eliam, now a judge on the Ivoirien Appeals Court, recalled that "the food was difficult." It was, he said, "Rice and sauce—like prison food. For those that were used to it or those that had never eaten enough, it was all right."[34] Other *évolués* objected bitterly to the company they were forced to keep. "We

Tirailleurs Sénégalais *training with the machine gun.*

are mixed in with the rest," one citizen wrote, "and treated like them. What does my status as *assimilé* serve me if I must sleep no matter where and with no matter who? One eats good things, but under deplorable hygienic conditions."[35]

Housing was another matter. Even before the war, when far fewer Ivoiriens were conscripted, the usual introduction to basic training was the construction of barracks units built to house twelve men. This activity gave them an immediate taste of military discipline. Ditiemba Silué described the literally down-to-earth construction methods:

> The African NCOs were Baoulé. They spoke Dyula to us. It was very hard at Bouaké. When we got there we were given gourds to get our own water to build our houses. Then we had to use our helmets to carry the dirt. If the gourd developed a hole in it after a while, then we had to use our helmets for that too. "Quickly! Quickly!" We were always being beaten. We were whipped if we were not fast enough.[36]

The first month of basic training was bewildering to men many of whom had never been more than a few kilometers from their villages. The new equipment, the training exercises, the orders given more and more in French as language lessons progressed, and the suddenness of finding themselves shoulder to shoulder with men from other cultures and regions, all combined to disorient the recruits. Bouaké was the largest camp in the colony. Soma Koné, a trader from Korhogo, remembered his introduction to army life there:

> There were all the races of the Côte d'Ivoire at Bouaké. I had never had contact with any Beté, Baoulé—I hadn't even been to Ferké [fifty kilometers from Korhogo]. There was a barrier—the language. We worked much harder than those from the south. . . . The food was very good. The training was difficult. If you didn't do it right, they would beat you. If you ran away, they would take your father. [37]

After a few months, most grew accustomed to their new routine. Mornings were spent learning how to use and care for their new weapons, in physical training and conditioning, and in drill and general combat techniques. Afternoons were devoted to general maintenance of the camp and cultivation of the yam and vegetable fields which provided much of their sustenance. Panafolo Tuo described the rudimentary French lessons, usually given in the evenings. "First they would question you. They would point to something—a head—a finger— and tell you the name first in French, then in Dyula. If you didn't learn, you were in trouble." [38]

The "trouble" often took the form of blows. Corporal punishment for minor transgressions was standard and remains, by contrast with the food, one of the veterans' most bitter memories. Punishments were invariably dealt out by the African NCOs. The French NCOs in the training units never laid a hand on the recruits. This was the subject of an interesting comment by Fonon Gano, a retired Senoufo sergeant from Boundiali. "There were Wolof, men from Upper Volta, Dahomey, and Guinea—all NCOs," he said. He was speaking of Bouaké Camp:

> The Mossi were the best. Disciplined. The Wolof are good soldiers, but not disciplined. Same for the Dahomians. Very few of the soldiers had gone to school. They were mostly the kind who would run into the bush at the sight of white skin. They were scared. They never saw this color before. Just ran into the bush. We thought their skin was soft, not like ours. Now of course we know that black skin and white skin are the same—equal. We were afraid of the color. It had nothing to do with them whipping or anything like that. That did not happen. New recruits were afraid of them at first. But you see, the Europeans didn't beat us—it was between ourselves. It was the Africans who beat the soldiers. If you did something wrong, they [the Europeans] just put you in prison. They didn't beat you. [39]

One thing is clear, that as training progressed men did indeed begin to think of themselves more and more as *les Sénégalais,* that is, not

Senegalese as such, but rather French soldiers who happened to be Ivoirien but were becoming cosmopolitans, accustomed to spending their waking hours with men from all over West Africa and even France. The process gained momentum once they were transferred to North Africa, the Middle East, or France. The experience of the Daouda Tuo-Donatoho was in no way atypical:

> After six months in Bouaké, we were sent to Marseille, then to Libourne. I was in the First RAC (*Régiment d'Artillerie Coloniale*). There were many, many battalions—French, African, Malagache. France was cleaner than here. I began to learn to speak French. Among our group, we each chose a comrade. There were Africans from all over, but we all wore the same uniforms. Some had different tribal scars—a bit different—but we all wore the same uniform. If someone asked me where I was from, I'd say the Côte d'Ivoire. Before, at home, I would have said Korhogo. [40]

Officers, NCOs, and *Evolués*

The Ivoirien *évolué* enjoyed no special status during basic training. His prospects of later promotion, however, were much brighter than those of his less privileged comrades. The use of the term *évolué* in the colonial literature included those on the one hand who had a few years of primary education, to those on the other who had graduated from the elite William Ponty College in Senegal as doctors, veterinarians, teachers, and administrators. Very few graduates were Ivoirien. Between 1930 and 1950, only 260 had passed through the college, 80 percent of them from the southern regions. [41] With these few exceptions, the highest level of education attained by the *évolué* in the colony was the teacher training college. It has proved impossible to obtain any realistic estimate of their number in 1940. Outside Abidjan, most of the recruitment commissions virtually ignored the *évolué* factor. The standard practice was routinely to stamp "*illettré*" on the soldiers' papers. Handwritten notebooks kept by commandants during the 1940 recruitment campaign reveal that out of nearly 12,000 Ivoiriens taken for the first portion, less than 300 were listed as being literate. [42] This was an impossibly low figure even for a colony not particularly well endowed with schools. Clearly, many who for years had been encouraged by the civil administration to think of themselves as members of an elite, perhaps even destined for that highest of all privileges—French citizenship—suddenly found themselves lumped with those they regarded as peasants. For them, the first weeks of basic training were excruciating. Aoussi Eba, then a teacher in Bondoukou, later a deputy in the Ivoirien Parliament, describes his experience on induction:

> They made us walk to Bouaké—on foot. My feet were completely torn up. Walking from Bondoukou to Bouaké. Exhausted. We got there and ate something. They sounded the assembly at two in the afternoon. I said, No! I can't stand up. I saw some comrades from my teachers college in Dabou. They were on the roof of a building— thatching it. My feet were incredibly sore—in those days you needed permission to wear shoes in the *tirailleurs*.
>
> They came to get me and I said, no, I refuse to go. They came and pointed to me and said, there's the *tirailleur* who does nothing. I said, I can't. I am a teacher. They asked me what I taught. I answered the captain and said I taught mathematics. The captain said, then you can write. Write *Vive la France!* I did it and said, you know, I can do a lot more than that. They told me to sit down. They looked at my papers: "Illiterate." They put that in everyone's book. Then the captain called out, are there any more teachers here? There were thirty-five of us. The captain said we were imbeciles. He put us in the offices and we had authorization to wear shoes. . . . There were some problems with the NCOs, but the others [nonliterate soldiers] knew we had been to school and understood. [43]

Aoussi Eba was not alone in believing that the special treatment afforded the educated conscript was "understood" by the illiterates, but this takes a somewhat rosy view of the situation. Some *tirailleurs* were downright angry about what they viewed as discrimination, among them Siliouenissougui Silué, a Senoufo farmer:

> There were some in my unit who could read and write—who had been to school. They worked in the office. Those who didn't know the alphabet built houses. They thought they were better than we were. We were very angry with them. They were profiting from their training. There was no school in Tiegano then. [44]

Whether it was policy or indifference that led to an initial common training for literates and illiterates alike, the desperate shortage of officers and NCOs in African regiments in 1939 and 1940 compelled a more careful scrutiny of the members of each recruitment class in terms of identifying candidates for promotion. By 1942, the situation, at least for Ponty graduates, had changed considerably. "All of us," said Denis Yacé,

> in the colonial era were obligated to serve. Some people volunteered, especially those from Man. They love war—fighting. I was at Ponty—

in the teachers college. After I finished, because I was a subject, not a citizen, I had to serve three years. I returned to the Côte d'Ivoire. We were given fifteen days leave before we were to join the Seventh RTS in St. Louis [Senegal]. After our leave we would have, should have, reported to the camp at Bouaké. Because we were special, educated, the general in the Côte d'Ivoire wanted us to stay here rather than go to St. Louis. But because we were the elite, we would need only six months to become NCOs.[45]

In 1939, throughout the AOF, the shortage of officers and NCOs was already acute. The army estimated that it needed 4,759 officers and NCOs to supplement the 3,960 already assigned to the command.[46] Obviously, the pool of Frenchmen involved was quite inadequate for the purpose and the 1940 recruitment only exacerbated the problem. In the light of these staffing problems, one understands why General Schmitt, commander of Ivoirien troops, had strenuous objections to the posting of educated recruits out of the colony. Early in 1940, he wrote a strong letter to Governor Crocicchia, complaining bitterly that he now had 22,000 men in Ivoirien camps with no corresponding increase in officers and NCOs.[47] The master plan of mobilization had called for a ratio of five officers and ten NCOs for each 1,000 men. Currently, Schmitt pointed out, some battalions had as many as 12,000 men and five rather than three companies. Some individual officers had no less than 1,500 men under their direct command. There were French NCOs who were each attempting to train between 200 and 250 soldiers at the same time.[48] Even allowing for some exaggeration on Schmitt's part, the situation was clearly less than satisfactory.

Colonial regiments were expected to use their own resources to fill the gaps. Few were able to do so. African *sujets* were permitted to rise to the rank of captain, but no higher. They were designated *officiers indigènes*. The army seems to have been reluctant, to say the least, to take advantage of this means to alleviate the shortage. As of 31 December 1940, only 1 of the 479 infantry officers stationed in the AOF was an African subject. In the Côte d'Ivoire, there were none. Other than *évolués*, few possessed the education necessary to meet the rigorous entrance requirements for officer training.[49] As a result, the shortage of officers remained chronic. Many reported cases of undisciplined behavior toward the civilian population in the Côte d'Ivoire were believed to result from it.[50]

If few Africans rose to officer rank, considerable efforts were made to train them as NCOs. Virtually all Ivoiriens classified as *instruits* were offered promotion. *Instruits* were defined as "all those who reenlisted and among those signed up as volunteers, chosen by the commanders, without any obligation for a minimum time of service."[51] As a result of this policy, the proportion of African to French NCOs, two to one at the beginning of 1940, presumably changed greatly in the course of that year, although no reliable statistics have been found to demonstrate this.

Although two-thirds of the NCOs who trained the class of 1940 were African, their officers were white. The army had always considered, on paper at least, the quality of European officers serving in *tirailleur* units to be of paramount importance. New officers were told it was essential to establish a relationship of trust with the African. They were advised to have "a great deal of individual personal contact with them," and to "give the men aid and counsel." Not surprisingly, however, a major charge was to "know how best to use the native officers," that is the NCOs. [52]

In 1939, the Special Recruitment Bureau in Paris seemed virtually to promise any young man who was single, over eighteen, and of good moral character a commission in the African regiments. [53] In practice, however, it does appear that wherever possible old "Africa hands" were sought to fill the officer ranks of the *tirailleurs*. Gerard Faivre, a former French private who served with the Eighth Regiment of the *tirailleurs*, spoke of this:

> Most of the officers were men who knew Africa. They'd spent twenty-five years there. They understood the men. One of them spoke many dialects, especially Bambara. Bambara was the main language in the Eighth. Our captain knew all the names of all the men and even their tribes. I didn't know a single officer who hadn't had an African background. For all the festivals—Muslim, tribal, Christian—they knew what should be done. At the Tabaski [celebration] they found the sheep. They always found the right thing. [54]

Whether experienced or new to Africa, these officers and their NCOs prepared the class of 1940 for war. Some *tirailleurs* took a minimalist view of their training. "They put up a target with a black point on it," said one Senoufo veteran,

> you lay down, at a distance, closed one eye, fired when you could see the black point clearly. That's what we did. If war came, no problem, if I knew how to shoot at the black point. If my bullet hits it, then I am well trained for war. [55]

There was, one truly hopes, more to it than that, for after a few months, recalled reservists and new recruits alike were regularly transported to France on packed ships. There, alongside the thousands of *Tirailleurs Sénégalais* already at the front, they would face the German army and witness the fall of France.

NOTES TO CHAPTER THREE

1. SHAT, "Rapport annuel de l'Etat Major, 3ème Bureau, Troupes du groupe de l'AOF, 1940," op. cit.
2. ANCI, Carton 4363, Dossier XXIII–3–8.
3. Interview 92.
4. ANCI, Report no. 10992, Police et Sûreté, Inspector Jean Coustere to Commissioner of Police, dd. 26 November 1943. Soumaré Souleymane had served as interpreter in Korhogo for twenty years. He could well have been the model for Hampaté Bâ's highly entrepreneurial interpreter, Wangrin. See *L'Etrange Destin de Wangrin* (Paris: Union Générale d'Éditions, 1973.)
5. Raymond Buell, *The Native Problem in Africa*, vol. 2 (London: Macmillan, 1965), 176.
6. Interview 51.
7. Interview 4.
8. ANCI, "Rapport annuel de la commission de recrutement 1940," Carton 339, Dossier XIII–19–138/1085.
9. E. de Martonne, "La Vérité sur les Tirailleurs Sénégalais," *Outre-Mer*, 7, no. 1 (March 1935): 36.
10. ANCI, Carton 339, Dossier XIII–19–138/1085.
11. Interview 15.
12. ANCI, "Rapport annuel de la commission de recrutement 1940," op. cit.
13. For pre-war figures, see Shelby Cullom Davis, *Reservoirs of Men: A History of the Black Troops of French West Africa*, 178. For 1939–40, see SHAT, "Rapport annuel de l'Etat Major, 3ème Bureau, Troupes du groupe de l'AOF, 1940," op. cit.
14. Interview 71.
15. Interview 62.
16. Interview 59.
17. Interview 44.
18. Interview 87.
19. Interview 5.
20. Interview 90.
21. Interview 36.
22. Interview 76.
23. Interview 18.
24. Interview 55.
25. ANCI, "Rapport annuel de la commission de recrutement 1940," op. cit.
26. Interview 2.
27. Interview 24.
28. Interview 47.
29. Interview 36.
30. *Paris-Dakar* (30 January 1940).
31. Interview 40.
32. Michel Sardou, *Le Temps bénit des colonies*, score dated 1974.

33. SHAT, "Rapport annuel de l'Etat Major, 3ème Bureau, Troupes du groupe de l'AOF, 1940," op. cit.

34. Interview 1.

35. ANCI, Dossier 2234.

36. Interview 15.

37. Interview 9.

38. Interview 30.

39. Interview 39.

40. Interview 5.

41. Bakary Diawara, "L'Ecole William Ponty de 1930 à 1950; La Formation d'une élite nouvelle Ivoirienne," *Annales Université d'Abidjan*, series 1–10, (Abidjan, 1982): 177.

42. ANCI, "Rapport annuel de la commission de recrutement 1940," op. cit.

43. Interview 102.

44. Interview 62.

45. Interview 2.

46. SHAT, AOF Carton 3, Dossier 02A2, Défense Générale de l'AOF.

47. ANCI, letter from General Schmitt dd. 6 February 1940, Carton 719.

48. SHAT, "Rapport annuel de l'Etat Major, 3ème Bureau, Troupes du groupe de l'AOF, 1940," op. cit.

49. The six to seven hour entrance examination required a knowledge of the history and geography of France, arithmetic and geometry, and physics and chemistry. See SHAT, Carton 9n268, Dossier 4.

50. ANCI, Report on the morale of the troops in the Côte d'Ivoire , Carton 1440–XVIII–15–24, April 1940.

51. Ibid., Dossier 1.

52. SHAT, Order of the Directeur Général des Troupes Coloniales, 19 September 1938, Carton 9n270, Dossier 12.

53. *France d'outremer. La Vie de l'empire français: Guide colonial à l'usage des parents et des leurs enfants* (Paris: Sarazin, 1939), 303–4.

54. Interview 108.

55. Interview 53.

4

The Battle of France

Soyez les Bienvenus!

IN 1939 AND 1940, UNIT BY UNIT, over 100,000 West African *tirailleurs* embarked for France. From the camps in the Côte d'Ivoire, trained men were sent to Abidjan and Grand Bassam to await their ships. The two- to three-week voyage in the cramped troop carriers was unpleasant, often frightening. Even worse was the sense of being totally cut off from their homes and families. Most had no idea of where they were going and feared that they would never return. It was strangest of all to those men from the north, few of whom had ever seen the ocean before. "We left for Abidjan," Ditiemba Silué remembered.

> They never said why. We went by train. At the station, soldiers surrounded the train. No one could get out or leave. The next day they took us right to the boat without knowing where we were going or why. It was terrible on the boat. We were seasick for days. For four days we could not eat a thing. I never had even heard of Dakar. There was nothing to eat there. All we got were peanuts, kola nuts, and wine. They said that rice came from Indochina and the boat had not come in. There was not much in Dakar. In Dakar we were told we were going to France to go to war. I felt all right about it. Why not? If I fight for them, maybe then I can go back to the village. [1]

Panafolo Tuo, a fellow Korhogolese, found comfort in having white comrades on board:

> I was at Bouaké for four months, then to Abidjan for eight days. They told us to rest up; we were going to take the boat to Marseille. I did not like it at all. We were fifteen days on the water. There were huge waves. When you ate you vomited. They told us to eat hot

Parading in Dakar before embarking for France　　LE MONDE COLONIAL ILLUSTRÉ,
NOVEMBER 1939

peppers—that it would help. They were wrong. . . . When I first saw Marseille all I could think of was how would I ever get back to my village. I was very worried—will they take us home? But then I knew that on the boat there were whites, so I was not so fearful because they were on the same boat. [2]

Despite the rigors of the trip and the uncertainty of what lay ahead, many *tirailleurs* were excited at the prospect of finally seeing France. This was fueled by what they knew of the experiences of the reservists among them who had served in prewar France. Almost fifty years later those who had served in a France at peace could recall with enthusiasm the time spent there. Donipoho Sekongo, three years in the army before being recalled from his Senoufo farm for the war, remarked, "If you're not at war, the French army is not difficult. Life in Africa is harder— much harder." [3] A countryman of his, Sekongo Yessongui, looked back on his experiences with nostalgia.

I was very pleased to see France because it was the French who had recruited us. I found a beautiful life there. It was better than staying here. Compared to the work we did in Bouaké and Abidjan, we did nothing there. Why, I had a rest in France! Here [in Côte d'Ivoire] one of the *chefs* would take some of us to work on his house—to do hard work, not army work. . . . They could whip you—they could do anything with you. . . . In France there was only one job—army. We did the same work all together. . . . That's why I preferred France. It was different—I discovered they didn't have forced labor, and we, the soldiers only did army work. . . . They told us that we brought you here in case of a war to save France. Thus there is no other work than that of the army. [4]

France left an indelible impression on such men from the north. They could not avoid contrasting its beauty and abundance with the starkness of their savanna homeland. Their sense of wonder might, however, be tempered by an instinctive feeling of resentment at the contrast. "France is much richer than the Côte d'Ivoire," observed Tuo Mahan, who had arrived there in 1938.

I found all their houses were made of brick and stone. . . . You could not spit in those buildings. What would stop you from spitting in my house? . . . We talked about what we were seeing . . . especially about the things they used to make wine. . . . We were very interested in it. We never talked about why the French didn't have to give up their livestock, their chickens, or their labor as we did. We could not ask the whites. We understood that we were angry in our hearts, but there was no way of expressing our anger. [5]

His sentiments were much like those of Tuo Ouana, another Senoufo:

> The cities are more beautiful than here, but I could not carry it back.
> The French—the old ones—were all right. But we had to accept their
> behavior. They had sent us over here, we could but follow them. You
> could not say no. . . . We were the same as them [white soldiers],
> but the whites could not accept the fact that Africans were equal
> to them. We could not show this—but we knew. [6]

The resentment, uneasily combined with admiration, of those who saw
prewar France, manifested itself only much later, in retrospect. In 1939
and 1940, their overall attitude was such as to raise, rather than lower,
the morale of those setting foot on French soil for the first time. These
new arrivals, moreover, would also find that the French were prepared
to give them aid and comfort.

All over France, a well-oiled system of support for the *Tirailleurs
Sénégalais* had long existed. The role of military service in the *mission
civilisatrice* had been recognized for many years. "As it is impossible to
organize caravans of Senegalese to visit France," it was remarked in 1935,
"the benefit of military service is that it is the only means to allow a
certain proportion of those we administer to leave their small corners." [7]
The Catholic church worked especially closely with the military authorities to make the *tirailleurs* feel at home. It was not, of course, a totally
disinterested effort. There was the prospect of gaining converts. Chaplains
were attached to *tirailleur* regiments, as to all army units. However, the
auxiliary bishop of Paris, writing in 1936 of the chaplains' special role
in African units, issued a warning about conversion:

> Their admission to the Catholic Church must follow the rules of
> missions in Africa. Actually the problem is not getting them in—for
> the fetishists at least, entrance into the Church constitutes a social
> advance. The missionary must emphasize this. He need not be too
> zealous to get converts. He must be careful not to make false
> promises. [8]

Whatever promises were or were not made, Christianity apparently
had little impact on "fetishists," those followers of traditional religions,
and least of all on those who were conscripts serving limited terms.
Among the Senoufo *tirailleurs*, Islam fared little better. In contrast with
the British West African forces, in which there were strong pressures
for recruits to convert and regimental imams were officially recognized,
there was little to induce the *tirailleur* to adopt Islam. Even devout Muslim
soldiers made little effort to proselytize. Toleration prevailed, as Dianguina
Coulibaly indicated:

[We were] about half and half. Nobody prevented you from pray-
ing. When the hour for prayer came, we were allowed to pray, even
in the middle of a training exercise. No one changed their religion.
The fetishists stayed fetishist.[9]

The French army was traditionally anticlerical. It was also eternally
suspicious of pan-Islamic movements, seeing them as a threat to the
undivided loyalty of the soldiers. Certainly the military authorities would
not view conversion as in their interests. In this regard the men were
left in peace, to follow whatever were their chosen faiths. Even at home
the Senoufo had not been aware of a need to choose between traditional
observances and those of the Christians or Muslims. Few material gains
resulted from conversion, whether in the civilian or military spheres.
Therefore, many reasoned, why bother to change? Today, notwithstanding reports of the growing strength of Islam in the northern Côte d'Ivoire,
Senoufo *anciens combattants* remain relatively unaffected, although many
may put on Muslim dress for special occasions.

The issue of conversion aside, in 1939 special efforts were made to
have the first Christmas of the *Tirailleurs Sénégalais* in France a warm
and memorable one. Charitable organizations established close ties with
colonial regiments. One, the *Jeunesse de l'Empire Français*, adopted a
tirailleur battalion and sent gift parcels to those they rightly assumed
to be "a bit disoriented upon their arrival."[10] Immediately after the outbreak of war, a hostel was opened in Paris, at the Seminary of the Holy
Ghost Fathers in Chevilly, for *tirailleurs* on leave. They were given private
and heated rooms, food, entertainment, and sightseeing tours of the
capital. French civilians provided them with warm clothes. *Paris-Dakar*
reported that families also were inviting lonely *tirailleurs* to their homes
for Christmas.[11] Even the army did its share on the social front. *Marraines*, literally "godmothers," were signed on to look after individual
soldiers. They wrote to them, invited them to their homes, and again
gave them gifts.

All Men Are Equal, But . . .

The style of the press coverage of the *Tirailleurs Sénégalais* during
this phase of the war closely parallels that so favored by American and
British newspapers and newsreels throughout World War II. It was a
style designed to reassure the folks at home that "their boys" were happy
and well cared for, but a style that at the same time ignored wherever
possible the fact that these same "boys" were facing brutal combat. In

Tirailleurs on leave at the seminary of the Holy Ghost Fathers

LE MONDE COLONIAL ILLUSTRÉ, NOVEMBER 1939

the many Christmas features printed by AOF newspapers in the first year of the war, the fact that the majority of the "Senegalese" were not Christians seems to have escaped the otherwise sharp eyes of journalists bent on assuring their readers that "the boys" were being given preferential treatment in France.

At regular intervals, especially during the early months of the war, the Catholic church and colonial army authorities showed a concern with the state of religion and politics among the African troops. Besides the ever-present fear of Islam and especially of pan-Arabism, both church and army perceived a newer threat of world communism as also likely to subvert the loyalty of the *tirailleurs*. The church may have seen the latter as the more serious threat, if only because it was newer. The army remained more concerned with Islam. A military report of 1937 on the effects of "subversive" communist propaganda upon the men of the Thirteenth RTS concluded that it was having little effect upon them. Muslim propaganda was thought to be much more dangerous, "its mask of religion . . . more adapted to their mentality."[12] The report concludes,

> Up to now, their loyalty, their devotion, their goodwill have not been penetrated, but it must be feared that the idea of a common religion brings the black element closer together with the Arab element than is desirable. . . . We must strive to conserve the fetishism that alone guarantees us the absolute fidelity of our native troops. [13]

One Senoufo *ancien combattant*, Sekongo Yessongui of Kakalogo, spoke of efforts to convert him by both Catholics and Protestants while he was stationed in France.

> I started to pray for three months, but then the war took me. I liked the Christian religion because the priest told me they do not forbid the customs that our fathers practice. But the Protestants said: "No! No! No! Drop all of that." The priest said it was fine; we just had to pray on Sunday. One wife? Yes, they did say that.

Yessongui reverted to his traditional beliefs once home.

> The priest that I knew in France came to Napie and came here several times to get me to keep praying, but I said no. I could not accept it any-more. I had taken again the customs of my father and my uncle. I would have had to drop all of that and you never know what is going to hap-pen. I realized this myself—that I could not do the two together. [14]

Few other of the Korhogolese veterans recalled any attempts to make them Christians. As Ouattama Soro commented,

No one tried to convert you to another religion. You practiced the same religion as in the village. . . . When you need your fetish you take it out—hide it in your pocket so the commandant won't see it. My father took a fetish—to keep me out of the army. I did too, but it was not strong enough. They took me. [15]

French sympathy for the African soldiers was clearly not predicated upon their being Christian. The majority of the *anciens combattants*— Muslim, Christian, or neither—denied encountering in France the prejudice and discrimination so much a part of life in the Côte d'Ivoire. "We experienced no racism in France," said Phillipe Yacé:

Racism only existed in the colonies—among the whites who were educated to believe that they were superior. In France, the French saw what we were doing—what we had come to do and they accepted the African. . . . There was never any discrimination. It is different now in France because those that come from Algeria, Spain, etc., are coming to work—to take jobs away from the French, not to fight for them as we did. [16]

Such observations are not, of course, free of hindsight. While few veterans recollected having had any specifically *racial* problems with either French civilians or fellow soldiers, they were well aware that black and white were treated differently and unequally. In the mess hall, African *tirailleurs* found themselves distanced from their European comrades not only physically but also gastronomically. The military authorities had decided that Africans would prefer their "own" kind of food while in camp. It was also the case that the cost of African rations was half that of European. Many *tirailleurs* did not understand why this was so, and resented the assumption that they would not thrive on European fare. They objected, even more strongly, to the fact that, unlike their French counterparts, they did not receive a wine ration. One Senoufo, Tafolotien Soro, was understandably appalled. "We got meat at every meal," he remarked, "but the French got wine with their dinner. When we asked why we didn't get it, they said it is because you are slaves—that is why you don't get wine."

Tafolotien Soro had a further complaint. "The French soldier," he said, "got much more money than we did. . . . Why? Because they were white and we were black. The French paid the canton chiefs, that's why there was no money for us." [17] In fact, the pay of the ordinary white soldier in a *tirailleur* regiment was several times that of his African comrade. Many Ivoirien *anciens combattants* long remembered this unequal treatment. Tafolotien was unusual only in the bitterness he felt. "If you started trouble with a white," he added to his testimony, they would put you in prison. In a war, you can kill them. If you don't kill them, then after the war they can cause trouble for you. No, there was no friendship between us. Their food was different—it was always varied. We, we just ate rice. When we changed, when we were with the Americans, it was only then that we got good food—even boxes of cigarettes. The French are too bad.

Ve Sabh, a veteran from Man who became active early in the nationalist movement, expressed rather similar sentiments:

The mess hall there was an African and a European one. We asked why. If you say those sort of things, you're a bad soldier. I think it's because of questions like those that my advancement was stopped. Here's another example. You are a sergeant. So is he. You do the same work. He, the white, is afraid. You advance. He follows you. Then when you get there, he starts giving the orders. He's the same rank. He had more paper [qualifications], but it is not paper that fights war. . . . No, we were not equal. That is why we got our independence. If we had all been equal, we would not have needed it. There were those French who said among themselves: "See that guy over there. He is less civilized than we are." [18]

Life in camp was one thing. The *tirailleur* also had a life outside camp. Social relations between French civilians and African soldiers varied greatly. Most of the Senoufo *anciens combattants* interviewed said they had never visited a French home but had spent quite a lot of time in local bars drinking and talking with Europeans. How much talking they did was determined by how much French they possessed, over and above military argot—and doubtless also by how much alcohol they consumed. Some African soldiers found French girlfriends, but most *say* that they dared not enter into too close a relationship with local women. Nanlougo Soro commented on this:

Yes, I had French friends. I would go into town with my French comrades to drink. No, no, I never went out with French women. There were a great number of them, but I was afraid to talk to them. I had no idea how to treat a French girl. [19]

For those more daring, however, there seemed little difficulty in finding French women eager to make their acquaintance and in some cases, apparently, much more. Marriages were contracted. If these were certainly not forbidden by the army, they were not enthusiastically welcomed. Paternalism rather than racial prejudice seems to have been the issue. French officers suspected that many of the women the *tirailleurs*

Lunchtime at the seminary   LE MONDE COLONIAL ILLUSTRÉ, NOVEMBER 1939

met outside the camp were prostitutes, interested only in taking their money.
The army warned the *tirailleurs* of the danger. Cautionary tales of unsuspect-
ing men being tricked into marriage by unscrupulous women were circulated,
though given the pay levels of African soldiers, it is difficult to believe that
French women wanted to marry them in order to secure wives' allowances.
Ex-corporal Tuo Nahon spoke vividly about such matters. While clearly he
did not share the shyness of Nanlougo Soro, he certainly exercised caution.

> When a French girl met an African that she liked, she invited him
> to have a drink in a bar. When the guy was drunk, she asked to see
> his papers. He gave them to her, and they ended up getting married
> before the Mayor. He did not understand that they were getting
> married. The intelligent ones did not do those things. I noticed what
> was going on—I saw one of the men getting married. That's why
> I always kept my papers in camp when I went out.
>   There was no lack of girls to go out with who didn't care about
> getting married. I had many girlfriends who didn't need marriage.
> No problem. I came home with many pictures of them, but my house
> burned down and they were all burnt up. You know, those that were
> married and stayed in France have families here who think they died
> in the war. But it's false. They are living there—in France—with their
> wives. If my mother and father had been dead before I left for the
> army, I would have done fifteen years, but marry a French woman
> and stay there—No![20]

Different again was the experience of those with *marraines*, god-mothers. "I had a girlfriend in France," said Gmbale Soro, with reference to his *marraine*.

> .She went to the office and took my name and number. At the end of each month she would send me a little package—with a shirt and some biscuits. After the war I saw her. I arranged it myself. . . . I showed her my name and number and then she knew it was me. She was very pleased to see me. I sent her letters. I still have her photograph. [21]

From Sitzkrieg to Blitzkrieg

On 7 September 1939, four days after the declaration of war, French units crossed the German frontier in the Saarbrücken region. Two regiments of the *Tirailleurs Sénégalais*, the Sixteenth and Twenty-fourth, took part in the operations (see Table 2). There was virtually no fighting. The so-called phony war, the Sitzkrieg, had begun. It was to end when the Germans crossed the frontiers of Holland, Belgium, and Luxembourg on 10 May 1940. During the eight months which intervened, the French army built up its strength not least by drawing troops from the colonies. Sixty-four new *tirailleur* battalions containing 38,000 men, and seven new Colonial Mixed Divisions, were formed during the winter. [22] By the beginning of June 1940, there were almost half a million colonial soldiers under arms in France, including something of the order of 100,000 *Tirailleurs Sénégalais* newly arrived from the AOF. [23]

Africans were assigned to infantry or artillery units and sent off to the *tirailleur* camps, principally Fréjus and Souges both near Bordeaux, and Rivesaltes near Perpignan. Fréjus was the largest and oldest of these. Many retired *tirailleurs* remained there after completion of their fifteen years of service. In 1934, its mayor had complained to the minister of war about the numbers of retired African soldiers whose French wives were on public aid. The army, he complained, would only offer the ex-*tirailleurs* a fare home, refusing to make provision for their wives. [24] By the autumn of 1939, however, Fréjus had other and more pressing concerns. The camp was in the process of being rebuilt and expanded in order to house, feed, and train 40,000 *tirailleurs*, far above its prewar capacity. Henri Winckler, a career sergeant from Madagascar who served eighteen years with the *tirailleurs*, recalls the time he spent in both Souges and Fréjus:

> In 1939 we were transferred to the camp at Souges. We were very unhappy there. To come from a warm country to Souges—it was

Table Two
Combat Periods of the *Tirailleurs Sénégalais*

Unit	Dates	No. of Division
4th RTS*	14 Jun 40–25 Jun 40	2nd
8th RTS	14 Jun 40–25 Jun 40	2nd
12th RTS	10 May 40–21 Jun 40	1st
14th RTS	10 May 40–21 Jun 40	1st
16th RTS	7 Sep 39–21 Sep 39	1st
	9 Apr 40–9 May 40	
	20 May 40–20 Jun 40	
24th RTS	7 Sep 39–21 Sep 39	4th
	20 May 40–20 Jun 40	
25th RTS	15 Jun 40–25 Jun 40	8th
26th RTS	12 Jun 40–25 Jun 40	8th
27th RICMS†	18 Jun 40–25 Jun 40	9th (DICL)‡
28th RICMS	18 Jun 40–25 Jun 40	9th (DICL)
17th BATS§	1 Jun 40–20 Jun 40	General Reserve
19th BATS	1 Jun 40–20 Jun 40	General Reserve
64th BATS	1 Jun 40–20 Jun 40	General Reserve
66th BATS	1 Jun 40–20 Jun 40	General Reserve

SOURCE: Bulletin Officiel du Ministère de la Guerre. *Unités Combattantes des Campagnes 1939–1945: Période du 3 septembre 1939 au 8 mai 1945.*

*RTS=*Régiment des Tirailleurs Sénégalais*

†RICMS=*Régiment d'Infanterie Coloniale Mixtes Sénégalais*

‡DICL=*Division d'Infanterie Coloniale Légère*

§BATS=*Bataillon Autonome des Tirailleurs Sénégalais*

so cold. They gave us coal for our stoves. Many *tirailleurs* died—
asphyxiated. They would pile on the coal and did not watch the
ventilation. We were assigned to the *centre de transit des tirailleurs
coloniaux.* We had no rifles. Then finally we got old ones. My job
was to show the men how to use them. Contingents were continually arriving. There weren't enough officers and NCOs. It was our job
to train and equip them. There wasn't enough time. . . . We left Souges
to go to the front. [There was] no shooting. Then [in 1940] we went
to Fréjus. Bordeaux was full, with the exodus. Everyone was leaving. They would be pushing prams—they did not even know if the
baby was still alive. People would give them food from the side of
the road as they went by. It was astonishing—horrible. [25]

Many *tirailleurs* were assigned to a *Régiment d'Artillerie Coloniale*
(RAC). Prior to the war Africans serving in them had been trained as
grooms, drivers of the horse-drawn wagons, ammunition loaders, and
spotters, but seldom as gunners. Only one RAC, the Tenth, was motor-
ized. [26] Senoufo artillerymen talked of being taught to ride and given
responsibility for the horses. They took pride in this, for the possession
of a horse in their homeland was a powerful symbol of wealth and
prestige, associated with chieftaincy. With the outbreak of war, however,
for the first time they were also trained to man the guns. The RAC direc-
tive of 9 September 1939 provided the rationale:

> Experience has demonstrated sufficiently that credence should not
> be given to the opinion that the native gunner is not competent to
> take on any function other than driver or scout; the native NCOs
> only to have the functions of interpreter or of junior instructor. But
> they must be better employed. All natives must be trained in artillery,
> not just as ammunition carriers or loaders, but to have the greatest
> possible number of gunners. . . . Natives frequently have physical
> qualities remarkably developed and often make better scouts and
> listeners than Europeans. Use these real gifts. Do not waste them. [27]

The transformation from groom to gunner was not always regarded
as an improvement in status. "I was a groom. I took care of the horses.
It was good," said Daouda Tuo-Donatoho, adding ruefully, "but the war
changed everything." [28]

The majority of *Tirailleurs Sénégalais* were assigned to the infantry.
Although West Africans had served as foot soldiers in the French army
for over eighty years, at the beginning of World War II many French
officers still had reservations about their reliability under fire. A *tirailleur*
battalion, trained in the Côte d'Ivoire, arrived in Courneau, in Bordeaux,
in the autumn of 1939. Morale was low, and many soldiers were physi-

cally weakened by the voyage and the change of climate. The battalion had to be disbanded. This was seen as lending support to those skeptical of the fighting abilities of the Africans. Not so, however, according to A. Duboc, an experienced colonial officer and member of the High Command. He had no hesitation in laying the blame squarely upon bad training and inexperienced officers. [29] As it happens, Duboc was a great admirer of the Senoufo and Dyula. He described them as "vigorous and intelligent," and thought they would make excellent soldiers. [30] This was not, however, to be put to the test until the phony war had ended.

Most of the *tirailleurs* at the front dug trenches, built fortifications, and waited—as all Europe waited. Ehouman Adou was among them.

> The declaration of war? In 1939, when they told us, we didn't believe them. How do you fight? When we got to the front, we knew it was the truth. We were with the First *Division d'Infanterie Coloniale* [DIC]. We passed through Verdun, transferred to Pont de Kehl, in the Lorraine. There was no shooting. We were sent back to Marseille in winter because nothing had happened there for three months. We always had news of the war; we thought we were going to win. [31]

His unit benefited from the official policy, in force since World War I, of withdrawing all African troops into southern France during the winter. This was based on the belief that Africans could not stand cold weather and were particularly susceptible to tuberculosis. By the end of November 1939, all *tirailleurs* had been withdrawn from the front. A number of battalions were transferred to the Levant to reinforce the West and North African troops already stationed in the French protectorates of Syria and Lebanon. Their fortunes will be followed in a later chapter. For the great majority of African soldiers remaining in France, and being strengthened daily by new arrivals from the AOF, rigorous training continued throughout the winter months. When the great German offensive began in May, there was no more time for doubt. Ready or not, the *Tirailleurs Sénégalais* were thrown into the fray as part of the massive effort to try to stem the tide of the invading forces.

The Battle of France

When the German armies thrust into Holland, Belgium, and Luxembourg on 10 May 1940, *Tirailleurs Sénégalais* were to be found in five of the *Divisions d'Infanterie Coloniale*, namely, in the First, Second, Fourth, Eighth, and Ninth, the last being light infantry. The West

Africans belonged to eight *Régiments Tirailleurs Sénégalais* (RTS), and two *Régiments d'Infanterie Coloniale Mixtes Sénégalais* (RICMS). In addition, there were four detached battalions of *Tirailleurs Sénégalais* (BATS), which were held in the General Reserve (Table 2). [32] Some of these regiments, notably the 12th and 15th, were in the right (or wrong) place and were thrown immediately into combat. Others, because they had spent the winter in the south of France, were among the last to be deployed, throughout the first three weeks of June. [33] Because they were among the freshest troops brought up to the front, they found themselves covering the retreat of French soldiers who, having wintered on the front, had seen constant combat since 10 May.

Given the nature of the official sources for the period, it is impossible to follow the movements of the Ivoirien *tirailleurs* as such. One can, however, trace the broad pattern of deployment of the AOF troops. West African units were in the First and Seventh Armies on the Somme, and in the Ninth Army on the Meuse. They fought in the disastrous campaign to save Belgium and were among the last troops left to protect the rear of the British and French forces retreating to Dunkirk. They defended the Maginot Line until it proved both useless and indefensible. The Twenty-fifth RTS fought to the end at Lyon; 115 of them were finally defeated, with heavy casualties, in their last stronghold at the Convent of Montluzin. [34] The Nineteenth BATS first fought in and then retreated from Alsace. [35] Between 14 and 24 June 1940, the Fourth and Eighth RTS, forming part of the Second DIC, battled successively and unsuccessfully at Moret, Montereau, St. Gordon sur Loire, Vierzon, Chasseneuil, Argentan, Bellac, and Sereilhac; 514 *tirailleurs* of the Eighth were killed, lost, or captured during the retreat. [36]

Many of those interviewed vividly described their part in these events. Tuo Lielourou of Napiedougou, who had been first called up in 1936, was discharged in 1939 and then almost immediately recalled. "A letter came from the *commandant de cercle* to the chefs of the cantons to get all the *anciens militaires*," he recounted. "I was very angry. Of course you are angry if you are going to your death. I hadn't heard anything about the war coming." When the German breakthrough occurred, he was with his regiment in the south of France.

> We left from Toulon for the war, to the Somme. In the Somme area—the place where they had ended the 1914–1918 War. There was a great deal of iron there—we had to remove all sorts of old iron—trucks, guns, everything, before we could make our camp. We marched to the Somme, section by section, carrying our backpacks. We were ready for them, but we didn't know until the war started who was stronger. Fighting began at 5 in the evening and continued until 7

in the morning. Then we rested. Yes, the Germans stopped too. We could not see them, just their battery—the ends of their cannons. There were black and white soldiers mixed together. They [the French] had better be there—it was the whites who sent us. The war lasted nearly two months at the Somme. It was there that they took us. They were stronger than we were. They dropped bombs on us. We were in retreat, toward Paris. On the road they took us. They sent us to Germany. We were captured along with the Tonkinese, French, and English. We were all taken. Yes, there were civilians on the road too. Everyone was running because they had bombed the city. You know, war only kills men, but when you drop bombs, everyone, including women, gets burned. [37]

Although the actual combat period was short, it seemed an eternity to some survivors. Laqui Kondé, a Senoufo who served in the Eighth RTS, was in action from 14 to 25 June and remembered the last days of battle.

We took our machine guns, our cannons, our tanks and left for the bush—on foot—right away. . . . It was miserable. When we went to sleep and woke up again, we thanked God. The war [i.e., the firing] started. . . . It was very confused—people were running. We were trying to find a place to shoot from that would be safe. Bombs were dropping. Everyone was for himself. There was no one in charge then. . . . We were like that for one year [*sic*]. We were always on the move. Sometimes we were stronger—sometimes they were and we ran. . . . It was a bullet that broke off my tooth—not a peanut you know. Yes, we were with the French all the time. We were stronger than the whites. That bullet which hit my tooth would have killed a white. When the shooting came, the whites ran. They knew the area and we did not—so we stayed. Our officers? They were behind us. I didn't know or think about anything except life or death. We were between the two. The officers said: "Stand. We will win." But it was the Germans who were stronger, so we forgot what they said. [38]

An eternity it might seem, although it lasted only a few weeks. Ironically, this was to prove a problem for many Ivoirien veterans like Laqui Kondé who, forty years later, would discover that, despite the fierceness of the fighting, they did not qualify for the small *pension du combattant*. It was paid only to those in combat for more than 90 days. Paradoxically, of all West Africans who fought in the battle of France, it was those captured by the Germans, to spend years in the prisoner of war camps, who would form the great majority of those eligible for this pension.

Laqui Kondé's recollections of the Battle of France exemplify certain beliefs commonly held by many Ivoirien *anciens combattants*. First and foremost is the strong conviction that the African was a braver and better soldier than his white counterpart; second, that great confusion reigned in these last two weeks of battle and retreat, retreat and battle; and third, that the *tirailleur* fought tenaciously at the front until either ordered to retreat or forced into flight by overwhelming enemy numbers. On the last point, they readily admitted that their tenacity was reinforced by the fact that they had no clear idea of where they were or which way to flee. *"Nous avons dû rester sur place. Nous ne connaissons pas le coin,"* as several veterans said. Some officers, in the last desperate hours of the Battle of France, appeared relieved that their African soldiers were unaware of the geographical dimensions of the rapid German advance. One, on the very day that Holland fell, wrote in his diary: "Fortunately our *poilus* have no more idea where Rotterdam is than Pekin, so this news does not worry them."[39]

The archival materials on the fall of France give substantial support to the memories of the veterans. Reports written by officers and NCOs with the Eighth RTS, during those terrible weeks in May and June, lend credence to the account of Laqui Kondé. Captain Rousset described the harrowing effects of the constant retreats:

> The 8th RTS, along with the 4th RTS and RICM remained in the Grasse-Nice area until May 1940, for the defense of the Var. At the end of May they were called away—on the day that Italy declared war. They were always on the defensive—they only knew retreat and collapse. All along the sad series of retreats which led them from the Seine to the Loire, from the Loire to Cher, from Cher to the Creuse, the admirable and legendary fidelity of the *Tirailleurs Sénégalais* was not belied for an instant.[40]

A Sergeant Moret of the Eighth confirmed the courage of the West Africans. Under bombardment and heavy machine-gun fire, he wrote, with "houses burning all around us and the heat being very powerful, despite all that, my brave *tirailleurs* kept in good spirits."[41] A second lieutenant referred to 16 June, when his unit was in the region of Montereau. He wrote,

> It was a day of chaos—retreat, with the *Tirailleurs Sénégalais* covering the retreat of others. My various battles have attracted the admiration of many people and the local press which wrote—in a long article—that one section of *Sénégalais* had put a German company to flight—[the Germans] having suffered many losses.[42]

On that same day Rousset added an interesting detail:

On 16 June 1940, a cavalry officer dressed in an impeccable fashion in his motorcyclist's garb, a monocle in his eye, after having given us information on the enemy advance to the edge of the woods of Champigny and of Chatillon, concluded with these words: "Monsieur, the Teuton comes. It will be necessary to cross swords with him again."[43]

In the extremely confusing situation that prevailed in May and June 1940, it is not surprising that some *tirailleurs* had distorted impressions of events. Sekongo Yessongui gave a description of the period which, obviously a strange admixture of understanding and misunderstanding, is none the less informative:

We arrived at the front. . . . We got off the train and went into the bush at the front. We got practically to the German border. Near six o'clock we started to dig holes. . . . That same night the Germans killed forty people. Then we retreated into France. They pushed us back. In the morning the commander called to say that we can't move forward into Germany. The route is blocked and we are being pushed back. We don't know if the Germans will push us back any farther into the interior. We, the *Tirailleurs Sénégalais*, said, "It's serious now. They pushed us back last night. Now it's daytime. We're going to see them today. . . ." That morning we were ready and our officer said, "Hold your fire. Dig foxholes, we will find the soldiers. No one is to fire. Stay here." The commander said that we had been sent here to fight a war. "You have the experience and now we are going to use it to push the Germans back." There, in our strength, we pushed back the Germans. We took back everything they had taken. We pushed them back and captured them. We started at noon. We killed sixty of them and got back everything. The commander had said, "We colonized Africa. You pay taxes to us. So we want you to help us fight against the Germans so they'll pay taxes as well. We'll make the Germans be like you. . . ." Seven days of fighting. We pushed them all the way into Germany to the interior of their country. But our *chef* tricked us.[44]

The *chef* referred to by Sekongo Yessongui was Gen. Maurice Gamelin, whose defeatist attitude led to his being relieved of duty on 19 May 1940, when he was replaced by Gen. Maxime Weygand as commander in chief of land forces. Many of the Ivoirien veterans interviewed remembered Gamelin with great bitterness. Some Senoufo were convinced that he himself must have been one of the enemy. "General Gamelin," argued Tionnina Soro, "was with us on the battlefield and Pétain was the leader of France. Gamelin was a German. He cut the telephone line between us and the French." [45] Sekongo Yessongui was even more specific.

> Gamelin had been captured in an old war and stayed in France. He was a German. He became a great soldier in France. The day we were ready to capture all the Germans, he told us to stop firing. . . . It was the French who told us about him. "Our commander was a German. We were wrong to make a German our leader." It was too late. [46]

Another informant, Peleguitamnadio Yeo, had had the time as a prisoner of war to talk and brood over the matter. He offered the same conclusion:

> The Germans retreated and we followed them. Then General Gamelin said we could not continue capturing Germans because politics had entered the war. General Gamelin had made the French soldiers all gather in one place. . . . So the Germans encircled us and captured us. He was a German who was doing his military service in France. We didn't know that before this happened, but afterward a captain of the *gendarmerie* discovered his secret and told us. They sent Gamelin to Paris and de Gaulle took over as our leader and ten days later we were taken. [47]

The tradition of a "German" Gamelin is particularly strong among those, like Peleguitamnadio Yeo, who were in the Ninth Army on the Meuse and were captured. Perhaps the *tirailleurs* borrowed the idea from French soldiers trying to find an explanation for the ignominious collapse. As Gen. Sir Edward Spears commented of the French nation as a whole, "the cry *'nous sommes trahis'* comes easily to French lips in an emergency." [48] Spears's viewpoint might well have been colored by his subsequent ordeal as Churchill's man in de Gaulle's camp. Panafolo Tuo was more charitable. "It was hot at the front," he remembered.

> We spent eighteen days on the Line. When it was over, practically everyone was dead—all but a few of us. Then Pétain lowered the flag. But we stayed on the Line. General Gamelin had been sent by old Pétain to take us back, but he did not know the way. That is why we were taken. It was General Gamelin's fault. He was supposed to send reinforcements, but he never did. We could not retreat because we had no orders to do so. They were shooting at us from all sides now. We couldn't even orient ourselves. They had told us to orient ourselves by the sun, but the sun is not on the same side here as in Africa. They said Africa was where the sun rose, but we knew from the boat ride that there was only water there. We could not walk on water to get home. A plane sounded its bell and told

us to stop the war. We had no more cartridges, so we couldn't shoot anyway. It was finished. Pétain told us to surrender. The Germans took us—we were their slaves now. Their prisoners. We were their horses now. [49]

Whatever the case, the view of the *tirailleurs* was not one shared by either the Vichy regime or the Germans. Gamelin was imprisoned, along with other former leaders of the Third Republic, in 1942; he was held first in unoccupied France and then in Germany itself. [50]

The strange case of General Gamelin aside, some veterans more reasonably blamed the entire French High Command for the defeat, and specifically for not sending further reinforcements to the front in May and June 1940. Nambilogo Silué was a member of an artillery regiment which made a precipitate flight from the Seine to the Loire. While he may not have understood the political or strategic reasoning which resulted in the collapse of the French army, he and his comrades were very well aware of the underlying reality—that they were totally outgunned on the ground as in the air:

They said that France had been given to the Germans. . . . When we found out about the end we said, "Bravo! It's over!" We were ashamed, but it was not our fault. . . . They did not send us planes. It was not our shame. I retreated from that town. . . . After that first town was bombed, civilians, officers, everyone ran away on the roads. We followed them. We had the cannon, but they took it away. We had nothing left. . . . Each time we passed another town, more people joined us. It was like that for nearly one month. We did not eat anything. There was nothing to eat. You couldn't stop and look for food. We just went on. . . . We finally got to a new town. . . . Then we found practically all of our *Tirailleurs Sénégalais*. The commandant who had fled was there too. We found him. It was in this town that he gave us the paper [a regimental citation]. Everyone got one—in that last town. Those who had been taken to prison got nothing. . . . We talked, but it was not a true conversation. We were very hungry. . . . We slept. We were so tired. We talked very little. "I ran from this place." "I saw that." We were practically invalids. . . . All the French had been taken prisoner. Only the commandant escaped. . . . He was a good man—kind—but a bandit because he left his brothers behind and ran away. [51]

On 15 June 1940, troops of the Nineteenth BATS were ordered to defend a bridge that was quite clearly indefensible. Their spirit, wrote one of the officers, was "excellent, because not one of us can admit that the war is already lost, it must not even be suspected—we are going to fight." [52] But if the troops in the field were kept in ignorance, the High

Command knew that the war was virtually over. On 16 June 1940, Deputy Premier Marshal Pétain called for an armistice. He threatened to resign should the cabinet not agree. The next day Pétain, now Premier, went on the radio to announce that negotiations with the Germans had begun. On 21 June, in the same railway car in which the Allies had accepted the surrender of the German Imperial Forces in World War I, Hitler met a French delegation headed by General Huntziger. No discussion of the terms of capitulation was permitted. The Battle of France was over; France had fallen.

On 25 June, General Order 117 reached the soldiers. *"L'heure de cesser le combat a sonné,"* General Besson, Commander of the Third Army, announced.

> By our heroism, by our spirit of sacrifice, by our willingness to hold, cost what it might cost, we have saved the honor of the French Army by fighting to the end.
> You have understood that it is better to die than to abandon one's position, one's arms, one's commanders.
> From the <u>Somme</u>, along the <u>Oise</u>, on the <u>Marne</u>, on the <u>Seine</u>, after the <u>Loire</u>, until the end, despite our suffering and our exhaustion, we have given a most splendid example of what might serve as the watchword of the French, exhausted perhaps, defeated, never.
> In the name of France
> In the name of the Commander in Chief
> In my own name,
> I congratulate you on your magnificent conduct and I thank you.

Each soldier received a copy of the Order, to which was appended the following: "This citation confers the *Croix de Guerre* with bronze star." The above is translated from that handed to Soro Nougbo of Noubougnonka. A reservist, recalled to war in 1939, Soro was further commended for "having done his duty until the last day of his position in the army."[53] He returned home in 1941 and became an active supporter of Félix Houphouët-Boigny and the RDA after the war.[54]

For the *tirailleurs*, General Order 117 probably compounded rather than dispelled the chaos of June 1940. Neither the High Command nor the field officers seem to have transmitted much in the way of information to their men, who had to find their own explanations for what happened during the final days of the first phase of World War II. They did so. Here is Soro Nougbo himself:

> They said the Germans were too many for us, so we fled. It was very serious — so many dead — that's all. The Germans found us when they crossed the river. Our job was to collect the corpses — but then we

ran too. The Germans had already built a barricade—even there—
all we could do was try to escape. The officers were there too. They
were trying to get back too. The people had already run away. The
Germans were on the other side of the river and sent planes to bomb
the city, but they did not destroy it. On the retreat we were all
separated—when we found some others we joined up with them.
The captain and the other officers were with us—running with us.
They never said where we were heading for. When we would see Germans, we would hide. The Germans said they would have their
morning coffee in Paris—it was in the newspaper—the brigade commander told us. The French said that before they have coffee in Paris,
we will stop the war. So many were dead and a lot were wounded.
Most of the soldiers of the 14th were dead. We had to leave the badly
wounded for the Germans to take. I was with someone who was
badly hurt, but we were able to put him in a French ambulance. They
never told us anything about Germans, but we were afraid of them.
Why? We had been shooting at them. When the Germans said coffee in Paris, the French signed. . . . I did not know how the French
felt, but I was happy because I was not dead. I was happy. [55]

Djirigue Soro of M'Bala was nearly forty years old when he was
recalled to active duty in 1939. After spending three months in the
Somme region, his war ended. "It was about nine in the morning," he
remembered.

They sent a letter. It said the war was over—don't shoot anymore.
Then they collected our guns. The French gathered them and put
them away. They even took our shoes. We were left with only a shirt
and trousers—one uniform. They even wanted to take our helmets,
but we refused. We wouldn't let them have them. No, there were no
Germans there. I had never seen a live German, only their bodies.
Defeat? They told us the French had won. They said the English had
helped us, that's why we won. They took everything from us. They
said you won't need all those clothes in the village. We didn't know
anything. They said it is over. . . . It was all over and I hadn't seen
a live German. [56]

Tiorna Yeo of Guiembé, class of 1938, had reason to remember his fears
about being sent to war. His unit had seen furious action in the retreat.
"I don't know the name of the town—we were in the bush," he said.

They said it was Belgium, that we were at war. We didn't know. I
saw the faces of the Germans. One day I really saw Germans. There
was a pond near our camp. We were going to it when we saw the
Germans there, marching on the other side. Thank God we saw them
coming, because we were about to go into the water. It was the French

troops who saved us or we would have all been taken prisoner. One of us was. Our chief sent a message to the French to come and save us—we were being surrounded. There was nowhere to run to. A French unit was detached to save us. They made a barrier behind us. Our lieutenant got his hand broken there—Lieutenant de la Pye. Our unit was mixed in with the French, but the troop that saved us was all French. . . . We were running backward but firing all the time. The next morning the Armistice was signed. . . . They never said a thing except that France had lost the war. I knew the reason, though, nearly everyone was dead. We could only retreat. We knew we couldn't attack. I understood. We were very few and we were running. That is why they signed the Armistice. Everyone was busy—being shot at. Civilians and soldiers. Bullets make no choice between civilians and soldiers, and the Senoufo are shorter than the civilians. It was near Toulouse that they took our arms—the French, not the Germans. I saw no Germans [there]. [57]

They Died for France

That West African units suffered heavy casualties in the Battle of France is not in doubt. The magnitude of these casualties, however, is. Official sources vary widely. The most precise statistics are those from the *Centre Militaire* in Versailles. They give 4,439 *tirailleurs* killed, including 245 officers, and 11,504 missing, including 88 officers; that is a grand total of 15,943 killed or missing in action, of whom 333 were officers. [58] This should be compared with Echenberg's figure of 24,270 declared missing in June 1940, of whom he speculates that 15,000 became prisoners of war and 10,000 were killed. [59] A much higher figure, given in another document from Versailles, is that of 35,000 *tirailleurs* dead. Its anonymous compiler, however, commented, "All figures are very imprecise and must be taken more as an indication of proportional losses." [60]

The fact of the matter is that in the circumstances of the collapse of France, accurate counts of casualties were seldom made or recorded. The retreat of the Eighth RTS has been described above. It well illustrates the reigning confusion. One report had it that of the 980 men of its First Battalion, only about 600 remained at the end of the campaign. Another report on the losses of the battalion, however, lists only nine African dead and twenty-seven Africans and eleven Europeans wounded but implied that at least 169 men had deserted. According to yet another report, no less than 695 men of the 8th disappeared in those ten days of constant retreat. Yet another comments, "They seemed more or less deliberately to have left their unit and didn't rejoin it until after the danger had lessened or passed."[61] It is from such materials that the aspiring quantifier of casualty rates has to work.

In World War I some 160,000 soldiers were recruited from the AOF. The number of dead and missing was probably between 25,000 and 30,000.[62] The overall rate of loss was thus on the order of 16 to 19 percent. This led Blaise Diagne, then the deputy from Senegal in the French National Assembly, to level charges that African troops had been used as cannon fodder.[63] Whatever the case in 1914–18, in 1940 the High Command specifically denied that it had placed its colonial troops in the front lines with the object of sparing the lives of Frenchmen.[64] Surprisingly, perhaps, Ivoirien *anciens combattants* appeared to agree. They consistently maintained that they had been used in the fiercest fighting because they were the best troops available. Fonon Gano's comment was by no means atypical. "We were shock troops; that is why we were always the first ones there. We had to be there."[65] They took a strong if somewhat perverse pride in having been in the thick of the fighting and among the last to lay down their arms.

The statistics, inadequate as they are, suggest that Diagne's charges about World War I could not be made at least about the phase of World War II which ended with the collapse of 1940. If we allow that about 120,000 West Africans were deployed in France in early 1940, and if we accept Echenberg's estimate that about 10,000 were killed in action up to the time of the collapse, then we are dealing with a mortality rate of about 9 percent, considerably lower than the 16 to 19 percent for World War I. However, the two figures are not really comparable. When France capitulated in 1940, many who had faced death became, instead, prisoners of war. Their story will be taken up later.

In May and early June 1940, people in the Côte d'Ivoire (as throughout the AOF generally) were still being warned not to listen to "false" news spread by enemy radio stations. They should have full confidence in France and her ally, Britain. Notwithstanding this advice, or perhaps because of it, foreign broadcasts continued to be avidly followed. Despite the attempts of French radio stations to minimize the extent of the disaster, at least the Europeans and *évolués* were well aware of how badly things were going on the battlefield. They were thus not totally unprepared when the news came that Pétain had asked for an armistice. They were shocked but not surprised. M. Delonges, a longtime resident of the Côte d'Ivoire, recalls:

> We heard about it by radio. Like we heard about the declaration of war in 1939. I remember we were in the Tennis Club in Abidjan when the news came. . . . We knew when the Germans had entered France. The radio of course lied. They would say two or three divisions had

moved in, but there were French divisions—French troops who were closing in on them. We knew they lied, but where else could you get news from? [66]

For the remainder of the summer the AOF was almost totally cut off from news of the outside world. The last war communiqué was published in the *Journal Officiel de l'AOF* on 29 June 1940, but the paper maintained total silence on the defeat of France, and on the Armistice, until the end of July. In the villages people waited for their men to return, not knowing how many were dead, how many were prisoners behind barbed wire. They could have had little understanding of the fact that there were now three Frances, one under the Vichy government, one under the Germans, and one newly born under de Gaulle. Little could they have known that *tirailleurs* would again go to war, this time not for the defense but for the liberation of France.

NOTES TO CHAPTER FOUR

1. Interview 15.
2. Interview 30.
3. Interview 67.
4. Interview 59.
5. Interview 43.
6. Interview 24.
7. E. de Martonne, "La Vérité sur les *Tirailleurs Sénégalais*," 44.
8. SHAT, letter dd. 17 March 1936, Carton 9n720, Dossier 12.
9. Interview 42.
10. *Paris-Dakar* (6 May 1940).
11. Ibid. (12 January 1940).
12. SHAT, Carton 34n1092.
13. Ibid.
14. Interview 59.
15. Interview 95.
16. Interview 49.
17. Interview 75.
18. Interview 82.
19. Interview 35.
20. Interview 46.
21. Interview 71.
22. SHAT, Carton 7n2470.
23. Ibid.

24. SHAT, Carton 9n270, Dossier 12. This letter written on 25 December 1934 found its way into the press much to the distress of the minister of war, who demanded that the inspector general of the colonial troops investigate.

25. Interview 109.

26. SHAT, Carton 9n270, Dossier 10.

27. SHAT, Carton 9n270, Dossier 7, Pamphlet 3281 1/8.

28. Interview 5.

29. A. Duboc, *Les Sénégalais au service de la France* (Paris: E. Malfère, 1939), 47.

30. Ibid., 133.

31. Interview 103.

32. *Unités combattantes des campagnes 1939–1945; Période du 3 septembre 1939 au 8 mai 1945; Bulletin officiel du ministère de la guerre* (Paris: Charles Lavauzelle). Anthony Clayton, *France, Soldiers and Africa*, 124, gives a somewhat different order of battle. For his source see page 404, n.4. He describes his figures as slightly at variance with the ones used above.

33. Major sources for the movement of the *tirailleur* regiments are SHAT, "Participation des troupes coloniales à la campagne 1939 (Période active mai–juin 1940)," typewritten summary, n.d. Also SHAT "Copie de la liste des corps coloniaux ayant existé durant la campagne 1939–1940," 12 November 1952, Carton 9n268, Dossier 2.

34. General X, *Aux heures tragiques de l'empire*, 186. Also G. Bonnet, *Mémorial de l'empire: à la Gloire des troupes coloniales* (Toulouse: Sequana, 1941), 63.

35. SHAT, "Note de service par un sous-lieutenant de la 19ème B.T.S.," dd. 15 March 1941, Carton 3n1102, Dossier 8.

36. SHAT, Carton 34n1088, Dossier 6.

37. Interview 37.

38. Interview 32.

39. D. Barlone, *A French Officer's Diary (22 August 1939–1 October 1940)* (Cambridge: Cambridge University Press, 1942), 47. Captain Barlone served with the Second North Africa Division and later with the Free French Forces.

40. SHAT, Report of Captain Rousset, dd. 23 July 1942, Carton 34n1088, Dossier 6. It may be noted that even French officers were somewhat confused over the exact chronology of this period. Italy did not officially enter the war until 11 June, though it is true that its intentions to join the Axis had been apparent since mid-May.

41. SHAT, Carton 34n1088. Dossier 6 contains Moret's handwritten report. He wrote it in 1941 while convalescing in a Toulon hospital after the amputation of his feet. It includes a request for a combat medal based on his service in June 1940.

42. SHAT, Carton 34n1088, Dossier 6, letter from Andreucci, dd. 5 March 1942.

43. Ibid., report of Captain Rousset, dd. 23 July 1942.

44. Interview 59.

45. Interview 60.

46. Interview 59.

47. Interview 56. De Gaulle did command troops which indeed inflicted a defeat on the Germans at Laon and Abbeville in 1940. See Ben Lucien Burman, *Miracle on the Congo: Report from the Free French Front* (New York: John Day Company, 1941), 27.

48. Edward Spears, *Fulfilment of a Mission, Syria and Lebanon 1941–1944* (London: Archon Books, 1977), 91.

49. Interview 30.

50. Robert Paxton, *Parades and Politics at Vichy*, 179–82; Charles de Gaulle, *The Complete War Memoirs of Charles de Gaulle*, trans. Richard Howard (New York: Simon and Schuster, 1968), 496.

51. Interview 94.

52. SHAT, "Note de Service par un sous-lieutenant de la 19ème B.T.S.," op. cit.

53. Copy of citation in author's possession.

54. Interview 28. In 1987 Soro Nougbo remained active, farming and goat herding. Finally granted a small French army pension, he had been unable to collect it. One branch of the local Korhogo bureaucracy had refused to issue him with an identity card because another branch had not provided him with a birth certificate!

55. Ibid.

56. Interview 34.

57. Interview 44.

58. Centre Militaire d'Information et de Documentation sur l'Outre-Mer, (hereafter CMIDOM), Guerre 39–45, TI 1 P INT CI 100.

59. Myron Echenberg, "Morts pour la France," 364–65.

60. CMIDOM, Guerre 39–45.

61. For these various reports, see SHAT, Carton 34n1088, Dossier 7.

62. Marc Michel, *L'Appel à l'Afrique*, 408, 483.

63. Ibid., 337.

64. SHAT, Carton 9n268, Dossier 1.

65. Interview 39.

66. Interview 101.

5

The *Tirailleur* as Prisoner

Capitulation

ON 22 JUNE 1940, GENERALS HUNTZIGER and Keitel, respectively heads of the French and German delegations, signed the Armistice. Three-fifths of France fell under German occupation, and the French army was to be reduced to one of 100,000 men. There was to be no immediate release of prisoners of war, and the French leaders made no attempt to negotiate specific agreements even about their treatment.[1] Presumably it was thought that a full peace treaty would quickly follow the defeat of Britain, an event which seemed imminent. The French people, bewildered by the rapidity and totality of the collapse, struggled to adjust themselves to one of three new circumstances. First, there were those who found themselves in occupied France and had to serve their new Nazi rulers. Second, there were those in the truncated area called *L'Etat Français*, who had to live under the collaborationist regime in Vichy. Third, there were some—particularly in the colonies—who could at least consider the call to continue the struggle broadcast on the BBC from London on 18 June. Its author was Charles de Gaulle, an officer virtually unknown to the general public.

On 23 June, de Gaulle announced the creation of a French National Committee. *France Libre*, Free France, was born. Meanwhile in France itself, the defeated soldiers were marching into the prison camps by the hundreds of thousands. At the end of June there were over a million and a half prisoners in German hands.[2] It is difficult to determine how many *Tirailleurs Sénégalais* were among that number. As with casualties, and for much the same reasons, accurate statistics are lacking. In 1949, a tired colonel in command of the *Section d'Etudes d'Information des Troupes Coloniales*, confronted by 300,000 individual record cards, produced a figure of approximately 58,500 *tirailleurs* held in stalags in 1940.

Of these, 48,000 were from the AOF: about 12,000 each from Senegal, the Côte d'Ivoire and French Soudan, 3,000 from Togo and Dahomey, and 9,000 from Guinea. In addition, there were 9,000 from Madagascar and 1,500 from French Equatorial Africa (AEF). In circumstances explained below, many were released in 1941. Unfortunately the harassed colonel was too busy and too understaffed to compile figures for these. [3]

If these approximations are accepted, the implication is startling. Something on the order of half the 120,000 *Tirailleurs Sénégalais* in France at the time of the collapse had become captive. Another report gives 25,516 *tirailleurs* as prisoners, including 1,226 officers. The year to which this document refers is unclear, however, but it is presumed to refer to the period after 1941. [4] If so, then about half the African prisoners had been released by then. This figure is at least compatible with that in another source, also undated, which estimates that there were 16,000 *tirailleurs* among the 34,800 colonial troops in stalags in Germany itself, not counting those in occupied France. [5]

On Becoming a Prisoner

Of those *Tirailleurs Sénégalais* who surrendered, the lucky ones only lost their freedom; the unlucky ones, their lives. The lucky ones were those taken prisoner by units whose commanders respected the Geneva Convention. Among such captives was Edmund N'Guetta of Grand Bassam, whose graphic account of events merits quotation at length:

> In April 1940 I was in the Twenty-fourth RTS. There were men from Guinea, the Côte d'Ivoire and Senegal. It was the big German offensive. We were sent to the front. It was awful. So many were killed, wounded. We retreated all the time. We couldn't stop. We couldn't rest. By June we were in the Chartres region. There were refugees along the road everywhere. We marched faster than they did. Everyone — a mixture of all kinds of people — was on the road. In the region one day we were completely encircled by the Germans. We tried to make a stand — there were planes, bombardment all day. Tanks, cannons. Many were wounded. We had no more cars, no more trucks, nothing. We couldn't advance or retreat. We waited all day. Toward the evening of 6 June a great cavalry attack was made against us. Tanks and planes. They opened fire. We couldn't do anything. Our unit was separated. We were all separated. We tried to resist but we were submerged all at once. One could not resist, could not see — they were everywhere.
>
> We could see dead French soldiers everywhere. The Germans had cut the wires. There was no place to hide — just wheat fields.

We tried. The Germans said, "Come." We said, "No." The general headquarters was supposed to be in the town. In reality the generals had all left. We were jammed together. Machine guns firing on us. So many killed as they tried to escape—to hide themselves. I hid in a kiosk all night waiting for the French troops to come. I stayed there all day and all night. The next day we wanted to leave—there were three French soldiers with me. We had to leave the wounded. We had to tell them we couldn't carry them.

The town was deserted. We went to a deserted farm, took a bit of bread—fish. Then we hid in the cellar. Two days we hid in that cellar. One of the servants returned. She told us Paris had fallen. There was no more hope. We decided to surrender. It was the only thing to do. We still had our rifles. We hid them and our ammunition in the hayloft. We told no one, not even the servant. We left on the main road. Everyone was on it. Some Germans passed us and asked if we wanted to surrender. The soldier said to keep going toward Chartres. We left for Chartres with a German guard. A truck came by with other prisoners—other *tirailleurs*. [6]

Not all *tirailleurs* were as lucky as N'Guetta. Some were massacred on surrendering. The murder of Capt. Charles N'Tchoréré of Gabon, a veteran of World War I, is a notorious case. N'Tchoréré, captain of the Seventh Company of the Fifty-third RICMS, surrendered with his entire regiment. Officers were told to stand apart from their men. N'Tchoréré began to move. He was told to stay with the African rank and file. He insisted on his rights as an officer and a French citizen. He was summarily shot. His death was one of many such. [7] Léopold Senghor, the future president of Senegal, barely escaped the same fate when captured on 20 June 1940 at la Charité-sur-Loire. Only the protests of a French officer prevented the summary execution of Senghor and other captured Africans. [8]

Tirailleurs in the Fourth DIC were in full retreat from the Somme. By 8 June they had lost contact with the Tenth Army. The next night, outside Erquinvillers near Lyon, several units were obliged to surrender. On the morning of 10 June, by direct order of the German commander, between four and five hundred Africans were shot to death. Eleven officers, including Battalion Commander Bouquet of the Twenty-fourth, were marched into the woods and also executed. The following account was written in August 1940. It was corroborated later by reports from other officers and NCOs taken prisoner at the same time.

At Erquinvillers, elements of the 24th RTS and of the 16th RTS, as well as some artillerymen, having been in retreat for many long hours, had halted, exhausted. They were overtaken by a German column on 10 June. Although they fought back, weak and out of ammunition, they had to surrender. They were disarmed and a rapid division of prisoners took place; on one side, the whites, on the other the blacks. The former were left alone for the moment, but the healthy *tirailleurs* and the walking wounded were assembled along the side of the road and killed by machine guns. Those who tried to flee were left to the riflemen who fired at them as though enjoying target practice. The wounded were laid out in a group. A German officer returns, he gives a brief order and several *Sénégalais* are dragged out into the street, where they are also put to death. Then the officer pulls out his pistol, swearing at the blacks who lay on the ground, and slowly puts a bullet in the head of each of them. "Tell them about this in France!" he yells at the Europeans. Close by, Captain Babel and eleven wounded *tirailleurs* are dispatched. [9]

The German commander forbade the townspeople to tend the graves of these *tirailleurs*. He justified his action by claiming it was retaliatory. African soldiers, he (and many other Germans) believed, fought like "savages," mistreated and sometimes massacred their captives, and removed body parts from corpses as trophies of war. [10] If there is any truth in these allegations, the French military archives are silent about it. Senoufo veterans vehemently denied killing prisoners and, particularly, mutilating corpses. Yeo Mohoouo, holder of the *médaille coloniale*, spent seven years in the French army, after being "volunteered" by Gbon Coulibaly in 1938. He, along with all Senoufo veterans, was outraged by the charge:

> It is a totem of war that you cannot take anything. You could hurt the enemy while he is alive—put nails through his hand before he is dead. That I did see happen. *C'est la guerre*. The Germans took our men and killed many of them. The French didn't let us kill Germans when we captured them. We had to keep them alive. [11]

This is, however, a rather curious and somewhat ambiguous observation, for it is known that some officers did make a point of telling their *tirailleurs* not to abuse the bodies of those they killed.

Was the massacre at Erquinvillers an isolated incident ordered by a German officer, as a specific reprisal? Or was it a more general manifestation of Nazi racial ideology, or even pre-Nazi? Even the great German sociologist, the liberal Max Weber, had criticized the Allies in 1917 for having unleashed "a refuse of African and Asiatic savages" against his people on the western front. [12] In fact both oral and documentary evidence from World War II leave little doubt that many African prisoners were routinely shot, systematically executed, during their first weeks of capture, and that those who did escape such a fate were treated far more harshly than their European counterparts.

Many *anciens combattants*, most Senoufo ex-prisoners in fact, attributed their maltreatment to a legend, which some believed was spread by the French, others by the Germans, according to which the African soldier was thought to be in some sense "immortal." When he is killed, he is resurrected as twins, even triplets or quadruplets—each rising up anew to strike the enemy. Torna Sokongo, a Senoufo, gave a version of this curious story:

> They [the Germans] had liberated the French. The *Sénégalais* stayed prisoners. The French had told the Germans that we were volunteers. That if you killed a *Sénégalais*, the next time four of them would rise up. That's why they kept us. [13]

Another Senoufo prisoner, Daouda Tuo-Donatoho, alluded to the same belief.

> There was no way out. We were all taken—the French, Malagaches, Tunisians, everyone. We were the first there at the front. It was very hard. A woman from the Red Cross saved us. The Germans wanted to kill all the prisoners—the Africans. The woman said no—you cannot do this—if you capture someone you must keep him. The Germans said they had to kill us and then bury us deeply in a hole for they had heard from the French that when you kill an African soldier, he rises up again. The woman said that was not true. Then the Germans asked her why the Africans were here—why they were fighting. She said we were forced to come. She asked them if they had seen any black women? Any black children? No—they were forced to come. So we were taken prisoner. [14]

Whoever the *tirailleurs* represented as originator of the story, it seems in fact to have reflected their own traditional beliefs. Upon death, a Senoufo would normally expect to join his ancestors, a passage from one world to another ensured by the correct funeral rites being carried out by the *Poro* society. A person dying away from home, however, in a situation in which these rites could not be carried out, became a member of what Glaze calls the "wandering dead," suspended between two worlds. Those unfortunate enough to find themselves in this category were regarded by their countrymen as malevolent, a source of danger. The Senoufo soldiers appear to have seen it this way, although in the circumstances of the war, it was the Germans who had reason to fear the wandering dead. That the Senoufo also spoke of reincarnation in the form of multiple births may, furthermore, reflect the fact that, in

Senoufo country, the spirits of twins are regarded as potentially malevolent. [15]

Charges and countercharges form a common thread in the bitter memories of those who witnessed German atrocities. Fe Lia of Man had volunteered in 1937, "to earn a bit of money." He truly earned his volunteer bonus when taken in 1940. "My German prisoner number was 3322," he remembered.

> Many were being killed in the camp. Every morning they would kill some. . . . I was at many camps, Mirecourt—with the whites, then Reims, Paris, LaValle. After Mirecourt, they separated us. In the night they had us all together. We stood there surrounded by cannons, machine guns. We slept right there on the ground. Once they sent a horse out which ran over us while we were lying down. So many deaths. It cut people's feet—their heads. The Germans did that. You had nothing. No knife. No shoes. What can you do? There were escapes, but we could not. We did not know where we were. [16]

Another survivor of the camps, Tuo Lielourou, recollected the early days of his captivity:

> It took us three days to get there [the prisoner of war camp]. The Germans are not human. They gave us nothing to eat on the road. Many were dying and wounded. . . . There were many camps. We were still mixed with the whites—we slept together. They killed us in the camp. We were mistreated—all of us—white and black. We thought we would all die. . . . In 1914–18, Germans were captured by the French. Now it was the same thing. It was a debt that had to be repaid.
>
> We spent five years there. There were a lot of deaths. The Germans killed many prisoners. Why? Because in '14–18 the French had killed many Germans. They lined them up and shot them. It was the Germans who told us about that. They said they were going to settle the debt. So in camp, when morning came, they would pick a portion of the men—we were still in bed—and put them in a trench and shoot them. Others had their ears chopped off and their eyes taken out. This happened at the beginning. Of course they killed the French too, why just us?
>
> Later an old German who had fought in '14–18 stopped it. He said that no more men would be killed because they weren't the same men of '14–18. So they stopped killing us. It was terrible. They had forced the Africans—those with scarifications—to scrub their scars off with soap and not to stop until they came off. So many suffered. It was the old one who stopped it. [17]

Another Ivoirien, Ehouman Adou once again, told much the same story. "We worried about what they would do with us," he said.

Will they kill us all? We thought they would kill us and they did kill half of us. They had said if you kill a black he wakes up again. So every day for three or four days they did this. They just picked out men and shot them. What could a white say? Is there any time to tell them to stop? There was a German general who had been to Bassam before the war. He told them to stop it. The blacks are not volunteers but conscripts. It's not worth killing them. They stopped then. If they hadn't, we would have all been dead. After that we got the same treatment—we died of hunger together—blacks like the whites. [18]

The "old German" or "German general" mentioned by both Tuo Lielourou and Ehouman Adou was known to many ex-prisoners. They believed him to have visited the Côte d'Ivoire before the war, and perhaps even to have been a *colon*. For what other reason would he have stopped the massacres in the summer of 1940, they asked themselves?

Life in the Camps: Endurance

Germany had overwhelmed France so completely and so quickly that it found itself quite unprepared to house, feed, and guard the enormous number of prisoners taken. The result was chaos, cruelty, and starvation in the improvised, overcrowded enclosures rapidly thrown up to hold the men. The experience of the Twelfth RTS was typical. Its survivors were imprisoned initially at Neufchâtel, along with 7,000 French soldiers. For the first eight days their rations consisted of a quarter cup of water, two spoonfuls of rice soup, and twenty grams of lard. Corporal Pierre Va Messie of Banle, near Man, described the events of his war and capture:

We went up to the front. We were French soldiers. We weren't there to defend only our country, but theirs. The French were there. If France won—we won. At the Maginot Line, you couldn't sleep at night. The fighting was terrible. During the day, there was no fighting. We were in the front lines, mixed up with the whites. They were as good as we were. If they had a piece of bread, they shared it with us. We shared everything we had with them. The first time, we lost. We were captured. On the forty-fifth day, we were trapped. Reinforcements were supposed to come, but they didn't arrive. On the 19th of June, I was hurt by a German bullet. Someone shot at us while we were inside the wire enclosure. Commandant Grapf was the first one captured. Then the rest of the officers were taken. The commandant said, with his hands up: "You must not shoot. We are already prisoners." They gathered up all our weapons and our shoes.

Ehouman Adou

The German cavalrymen started to ride through us— grabbing our rifles. When we saw them, we thought we were already dead—it was finished for us. They killed a lot of prisoners with a small machine gun. If you even had a small knife in your pocket, they would kill you. They thought you wanted to continue the war. I had one that they didn't find. I was lucky.

When we were captured—trapped, they put us in an enclosure for eight days. There was no food, the water tap was broken. On the ninth day, they sent a truck with coffee, but no sugar or bread. When they had us in that house, they beat some of us. On the ninth day, Marshal Pétain asked that we be given food. They brought us bread and coffee. [19]

In some cases particular groups were singled out. Mossi soldiers were especially subject to persecution. They could be separated from other *tirailleurs* by their distinctive scarification marks. German guards who had encountered these fierce soldiers during hand-to-hand combat now took revenge. [20] Adding to the physical misery was the state of shock most prisoners experienced at the swift change in their fortunes. An officer reported that, "with their proverbial confidence in their commanders," the men of the Twelfth RTS "never imagined that capture was possible. It was for the majority of us, a huge surprise and a bitter deception." [21] Many officers and men, apparently, simply accepted their fate and withdrew into themselves in captivity. Hopelessness overcame the prisoners. Peleguitamnadio Yeo spoke of his capture and confinement:

We were numerous. Very, very many soldiers, French as well as *Sénégalais*. There were eleven prisoner of war camps. We saw a plane pass overhead with the French flag. It said that the war was over and we were captured prisoners. There, we had to be disarmed totally. We had to give up every weapon we had. The French said if they find even a knife or an arrow on one soldier, they would kill all of us. "Give up everything."

The Germans said that the French had told them that we eat people. So they said we're going to eat trees now. They didn't really make us eat trees, but they also told us that the French had said you can't kill an African. So there were many killed in prison because of what the French had said. They conducted experiments to see if it was true that you couldn't kill an African. They learned it was false. We, we accused the French—it was they who said that we don't die.

We walked four days and four nights before we got to the camps. At first we were just behind wire, later there were eleven houses in the camp—sixty persons in each house. They separated the French and the *Sénégalais*. We thought that meant they were going just to kill all of us. The whites were not in the same wire enclosure as we were. When we got to the houses, we saw the whites again. They were there, but in separate houses. The camp was in Mirecourt. I was there for nine months. After that we were sent to Reims. We did nothing. We had nothing to eat. We cooked leaves. When you eat nothing, you cannot work. We went in the bush to get the leaves. Many died of starvation. I was in good health at Mirecourt. At Reims I had a bad foot. Even if you cut my foot, there was no blood there. It was very cold at Reims, no snow but very cold. Blankets? Hah! The Red Cross brought us some biscuits, that's all. In prison we only thought about one thing—who would take us back to our villages? [22]

It seems to have been usual for prisoners to be sorted by color. Blacks were kept apart from whites. Panafolo Tuo described what happened in his unit.

We were going to Germany now. We marched fourteen days. They had already separated us from the whites. All of us did go to Germany, but at first we thought they were going to kill us and spare the whites. No officer protested, but one *petit blanc*, a second class like me whom I had only seen on the line, spoke up. He said to the Germans that the French had taken the Africans by force into the army to fight for them. That we were cultivators, and that we only knew how to farm. He said that the French officers were wrong when they told the Germans that we came to fight for them because they would pay us. That's what the *petit blanc* said. Then they left us. He was the only one who said anything. [23]

There was separation by rank as well as color. Kone Farnan, a veteran from Niofouin, thought it was policy to hold captured officers in Germany itself rather than in occupied France. "We raised our hands and surrendered," he said.

They locked us up—in a barbed wire enclosure—it was big, much bigger than this village. There were only Africans in the camp. We were taken with our French officers, . . . but they separated the whites, the officers, from us and sent them to Germany because they could escape too easily in France. What did we do? We cut wood. I was there for four years. Yes, it was bad, we always had to line up by fives. If you were standing alone, they killed you. It was very cold. There was so much ice—if you put your foot in it, it would freeze. We ate a small piece of vegetable chopped up and put in hot water, a little bit of potato, and some grass. We would mix it all together and eat it. I only thought about when we would get out of there— get back to my village. [24]

The majority of the African prisoners were undoubtedly too busy trying to survive to worry much about the fate of their officers.

Edmond N'Guetta did, however, recall one occasion on which the *tirailleurs* in the camp at Chartres displayed their feeling:

> One day we heard that all the officers were being sent to Germany. We were angry. We protested. We all stood in formation and hummed *La Marseillaise* while they were being loaded in the trucks. The Germans understood nothing. [25]

Tionnina Soro's attitude was more typical. "We were separated from the whites," he said. "We didn't think about them at all. We were defeated—that's all we knew." [26] In fact, the process of separating white and black soldiers gave many *tirailleurs* the idea that the French, including their own officers, had been released, and that they alone remained in captivity. The sense of being abandoned was compounded by the fact that many had seen white soldiers and officers slip out of the defeated columns on the way to the camps, or even from the makeshift camps themselves. Yeo Porio from Korhogo remembered this with bitterness:

> We were in the front line when the Germans attacked the *tirailleurs*. We were there. We didn't win. The Germans took all—they took everything. The Germans took us in one day. They took us to Berlin. Of course I was a prisoner—how else could I see Berlin? . . . We ate nothing. Something in hot water and water to drink. I can't count the number dead. They made us do forced labor—three or four times a day. I was in the camp in Berlin for three months. In prison we thought about how we could get to France and how we could then go back to our villages—the Côte d'Ivoire. Everyone had the same worries.
>
> The French are no good. When they arrived at the prison, they changed their clothes, into civilian clothes. They wore their own clothes because they were white. They were left alone by the Germans. They worked for the Germans. They were paid. They [the Germans] let them alone, but we had been abandoned. As [the French] were passing through villages—many French villages on the way to Germany—in each village at night the Germans would string up wire around them to enclose them. There French [civilians] fed their brothers—brought them clothes and the soldiers changed there. They threw away their military clothes. They took clothes from the dead. We—we had nothing. They could stay there; they weren't soldiers anymore. They escaped that way. [27]

Albert Brousse, a businessman who had lived in the Côte d'Ivoire for over thirty years, was captured in 1940, while serving with the First DIC:

My regiment was behind the Maginot Line at Sedan. . . . We were
taken at Charmes, in the Ardennes. We were taken at noon—we were
preparing food and we were suddenly encircled. My whole battalion
of 200 men. . . . [Some did escape], it was true. They would get
clothes from civilians as we passed through towns. There were no
Africans in my camp. They segregated them. You know the Germans
called them half-monkeys. [28]

But, as many Ivoiriens commented, a change of clothing could not turn
a black into a white. Because of their color they could not disappear
in the sea of refugees flooding the roads. The experience of watching
their fellow soldiers do so served to reinforce their sense of hopelessness.
Some did know that white prisoners were being held in different parts
of the same camps. This was little comfort. Indeed, the segregation seemed to contradict all they had been led to expect in the course of their
training as French soldiers. They knew, of course, that even within the
training and holding camps they had been separated from their French
comrades for meals, and they received lower pay. But in combat there
had been no barriers of race. Now, after capture, what had happened?
Were they no longer French soldiers, they asked themselves? No veteran
remembered ever being instructed, during training, on his rights should
he have the misfortune to be taken prisoner.

Conditions Improve: From Worse to Merely Bad

Many of the *tirailleurs* were initially marched into stalags in Germany.
After some months, most of them were moved to camps in Occupied
France. [29] No reliable figures have been found on these transfers. Many
of the veterans interviewed remembered being shifted from camp to camp
but had no way of knowing whether they were in Germany or in Occupied France. Their guards, after all, remained German wherever they
were. There were, one supposes, various factors in the German decision to move the African prisoners: racial distaste at having blacks in
the fatherland; fear of catching unspecified tropical diseases; a feeling,
perhaps, that Africans were unlikely to attempt escape; and a pragmatic
concern that the burden of feeding colonial troops should fall on those
who colonized them.

Gradually, the treatment of African prisoners improved as new and
permanent camps were built. [30] Robert Guerlain, a French soldier captured in the battle of the Somme, wrote of the changing attitudes toward
the Africans, who:

after a period when they had been made the object of all sorts of brutalities, had reached a point where they were almost being coddled because of the particular solicitude in which they were held by the German Colonial Office. They received frequent visits from learned professors who would measure their skulls and speak to them in their own language. [31]

As a further illustration of this "coddling," Guerlain adds that the Africans "had even been cast in a film," albeit one "designed to show the atrocities they had committed on the battlefield." This was undoubtedly the film directed in part by no less than Edwin Rommel in 1940. [32] As the Vichy government and the Red Cross were given permission to aid the prisoners, conditions improved further though no one knew how long he would be safe. Fe Lia, by now in his fourth camp, expressed the ambivalence in the situation:

> We planted potatoes, carrots. We did that until we were freed. The Red Cross brought us packages at Evreux. They would first give a package to the Germans, after that there was one for each of us. They wrote letters for us. There was never enough food. People's teeth kept breaking off. The time I was there, I worked for the Germans. They pulled out my teeth with pliers. The French didn't know what was happening to us. We were the prisoners of the Germans. We had fought them. What could you expect? [33]

The *Tirailleurs Sénégalais*, although confined in separate barracks or in designated parts of the camps, came finally to realize that they were not going to be killed and that they were not totally forgotten. Edmond N'Guetta, again, testifies vividly to the changes in their treatment:

> Before we left we knew the Germans didn't love the blacks. [34] We were very afraid [after capture]. Especially when they made us line up against a wall to search us—with our hands up against the wall. Someone talked. He was shot. We were put in a truck to Voves—21 kilometers away. They took us to an old slaughterhouse. We were locked in. No food yet. . . . We stayed there twenty days. Afterward we were sent to a Canadian's house—an ordinary house. It was better there. There were Algerians with us—everybody—an *adjutant-chef* from Upper Volta. Each morning we had to work for the Germans in town. . . . At the station we unloaded food and merchandise for the Germans. The French prisoners stole things. We did not, we were afraid. If they caught you, they beat you. We were hungry, but we were more afraid.
>   Things were all right at Chartres. After a while the Germans decided we weren't so bad because we never tried to escape. With black

skin, it would have been difficult to do it. And, besides that we were good workers. They respected us. We were easy to guard. The guards were mostly regular soldiers. There were some SS, and some of us were tortured, but there wasn't much of that. The Germans, I must say, all the same, after man to man contact, were men—just like us. Friendships developed between us. They wanted us to enjoy ourselves—to play ball. Others were afraid. I started to play and it was all right. *Les hommes sont les hommes.* Everything that was bad that they did was the fault of their leader [Hitler]. That is the lesson I learned in the camps. [35]

Conditions in the camps became even better once French civilians were allowed to provide food to supplement the diet which Pelibé Tuo described as "hot water to drink." Many prisoners died, Tuo said. "The Germans forced us to drink it. All the soldiers were forced to drink it, even the French. One piece of cabbage in the water." [36] The Red Cross began delivering parcels which are credited by many veterans as having saved their lives. The boxes did not always arrive intact, for often the German guards plundered them and left the prisoners only biscuits and a few dates and figs. Nevertheless, what did get distributed was extremely welcome. It must be remembered, however, that not all prisoners received even the limited benefit of Red Cross charity, as Torna Sekongo testified:

We didn't see anyone—not the Red Cross—no French officers—no one visited us. Then they sent us to the village to work on a *corvée,* and they guarded us. We thought things would be better in that village, but they took us to a house there and inside they took everything we had. All our money, even what we had hidden in our shoes. I had more than ten thousand francs. I had saved it—it was the most money I had ever seen—it could have been ten thousand francs. After they had taken our money, we spent three years there. The *corvée?* We just marched—walked in the village. I was lucky because I was able to steal a lot. I stole potatoes from everywhere. During a snowfall it was easy. You couldn't see far—there was a fog. I would lie down and hide. The others would leave me behind, and I went to the potato fields. I would take two sacks with me. Once someone shot at me—they didn't hit me, but I threw one of the sacks away and got away with the other. The house [prison barracks] was divided into rooms. I would share with those in my room. No, the others didn't steal. They were afraid of dying. They just waited for me to come back. [37]

Most prisoners held in French camps were to live under somewhat improved conditions. The Vichy government established a prisoners' service under the *Direction Générale de la Légion.* Donations were collected, and coffee, tapioca, soap, chocolate, and powdered sugar were sent to the camps.[38] The prisoner Tionnina Soro, who had experienced constant hunger, described the improvement.

> The prison was very far from where we had fought. They had never given us any information about what to do if we were captured. You learn that when you are taken. The camp was in Le Mans. At first they only gave us hot salted water to drink. Then Pétain called on the civilians—men and women—to bring us food and clothes. Each woman sent us a little to eat. The Red Cross sent us food, too. It was better then.[39]

Slowly the conditions in the camps became known in the Côte d'Ivoire. There was considerable soul-searching among administrators about the advisability of asking Ivoiriens to raise money and supply provisions to help feed their compatriots who were prisoners. To do so would, they felt, confirm the *métropole*'s defeat, news of which had still not reached many of the more remote parts of the colony. Finally the administration did decide to appeal for contributions. On 31 March 1941, planters, merchants, and *sociétés de prévoyance* were asked to donate kolas, corn, cornmeal, honey, and cash to the newly established *Comité pour le Ravitaillement des Prisonniers de Guerre*.[40] By July 1942, contributions in cash alone amounted to 841,095 francs. These ameliorated conditions in some camps.

Prisoners were used on work details in most camps. Initially some were employed in collecting equipment and ammunition abandoned by the French army. Others were sent to the woods to gather firewood, an irony for Senoufo prisoners, who had regarded military service as at least a way to escape forced labor in the Ivoirien forests. Later, due to the enormous labor shortages caused by having over a million and a half Frenchmen in prison camps, civilians were allowed to hire *tirailleurs* to work on their farms. Ironically, many French soldiers imprisoned in Germany were to work on German farms, where they would in time become witnesses to the fall of the Third Reich.[41] Among the Africans, to be sent on these *corvées* became a plum assignment. Virtually everyone hoped to be chosen in order to obtain the supplementary rations given by the farmers. Pierre Va Messie was one:

> I worked on the farm, taking care of the poultry. It was a French farm. The French would come to the camp and ask the Germans to give them some prisoners. The Germans said yes, but that the French must feed them. They were good to us. It wasn't forced labor—we were practically free.[42]

Lieutenant Vergez, an officer who had managed to escape from his camp, reported that the men actually fought over the right to go. [43] In addition to the food given them (or sometimes stolen in the fields), those employed were often paid small sums of money, which they were permitted to spend in the towns.

In some camps attitudes toward African prisoners softened yet further. German officers began to use *tirailleurs* as domestic servants. "The Germans took Africans as boys, cooks," Va Messie remembered. "They never made the whites do it. They would give some food to their boys, and if the boy had some bread hidden, he would share it with the rest." [44] Emile Dagba even received a commendation:

> There [Epinal] a German officer took me as his boy. There were two of us. We were on his small farm, and we served the officers. They gave us names. They called me Bibo and my friend Jambo. Names of slaves, but we were slaves. But they did give us food and a good certificate. We brought all the food we could to our comrades. All we could get. We ate well—so did our comrades. [45]

These changes were gradual and varied from camp to camp. Escaped officers and NCOs of the Twelfth RTS told of the improving treatment of Africans by the guards. Initially, they reported, the Germans had nothing but disdain for the Africans, but now they were having themselves photographed with *tirailleurs* in the yards of the camps. One junior French officer, indeed, complained that the *tirailleurs* were being treated better than the Europeans. They were given extra bread, cigarettes, and candy. [46] Another remarked that "the natives are quickly taken in friendship by the Germans, despite their initial repulsion towards them. They used to point at them and say to us: "It's that, eh, your civilization!" [47] Some suggested that the Germans were favoring the Africans as a way of bringing French culture into disrepute. *Tirailleurs* who were moved from camp to camp during their long ordeal recognized that much depended on luck. Yeo Porio, looking back on his years as a prisoner rather philosophically, observed, "There are different parts of Germany. If you are in a good part, they treat you well. If you're in a bad part, they treat you badly." [48]

Freedom—For a Fortunate Few

Under the terms of the Armistice, a French army would continue to exist. It became known as the Armistice Army. [49] It was restricted to 100,000 men, all white, and was to be based in the *Etat Français*, the

so-called Free Zone administered from Vichy. Its official and only function was the maintenance of order. It was to be dissolved by the Germans on 27 November 1942, after their occupation of the Free Zone
sixteen days earlier.

The officers of the Armistice Army were permitted to visit stalags
in Occupied France to monitor the condition of French and colonial
prisoners of war. They took the opportunity to do more. They attempted
to raise morale among the prisoners by bringing them decorations, cita-
tions, and occasionally, promotions. In speeches to the African prisoners,
they paid tribute to their heroism and in glowing terms told them how
eagerly their fathers, their women, and their children in the villages of
the AOF were awaiting their return. For the rest of their lives, the *tirailleur*
prisoners were told, the families and the village elders would sit under
trees, demanding to be told of their epic adventures. Their fighting
prowess, they were assured, had proved equal to or even greater than
that of the African and French *anciens combattants* of World War I.
This part of the rhetoric was certainly believed. "Yes," said Torno Sokongo,
who had no doubt about how good the *tirailleurs* were,

> at war we were stronger than the French. We didn't know France.
> We had black skin. The French could save themselves by changing
> into civilian clothes. They could escape. They were not good soldiers.
> We had no contacts, so we were always there. We were the best soldiers
> because we had nowhere else to go—to hide. [50]

Djirigue Soro of M'Bala combined pride in the performance of the
tirailleurs with the fatalism of a Senoufo often forced to do whatever
the French demanded. "We were between France and Germany—at the
Joux Canal," he remarked.

> In every battle it was the Africans who were in the first rank. The
> French were always behind us. If the battle got hot, they would leave
> us there. When we slept, the French soldiers would sleep next to an
> African. They said we, the Africans, had no fear. We want to sleep
> next to you to gain some of your courage. Why were we always in
> front? They led us. They had the right to put us wherever they wanted
> to. The whites thought that the first rank was the riskiest. That is
> why we were in front. They never said that, but we knew. The whites
> always put us in front. That we knew. [51]

Superiority in combat to white soldiers was a frequent subject of comment by veterans. "They were as strong as we were," said Nanga Soro
of the Fourth RTS,

> but when it was really hot, they would hide behind us. If someone
> was killed they would cry out: "Oh God! Oh Mama!" When rein-

forcements were called up to replace troops at the front, there were
some who would jump from the upper floors of buildings to try and
kill themselves. They were cured and then sent to prison. The
Sénégalais never did that. Even when you weren't being sent to replace
soldiers at the front, you wanted to go up there and see what was
happening. There was a Lobi who had done his fifteen years. They
said he had to retire, but he said no. He wanted to see war. He was
the one who took the first bullet. Dead. [52]

African prisoners appear to have disliked the overt paternalism of
these Vichy officers who could enter and leave the camps freely. No
acknowledgment of this, however, is to be found in the reports of those
carrying out the goodwill missions. One officer positively gushed with
enthusiasm and self-congratulation, noting that "these big children
quickly forgot the retreat and were encouraged to think only of their
glorious return to the AOF some day." [53] Not surprisingly, in view of their
own interest in African colonies, the Germans also engaged in a modest
campaign to win the hearts and minds of the African prisoners. They
published small magazines and newsletters, among them *Le Malinké* and
Le Bambara. These contained, for example, articles on how German
universities were training new black leaders for the colonies, once the
Nazi victory was complete. This naturally tended to make French officers still imprisoned in the camps somewhat nervous. One remarked,
with some relief, that while the *Tirailleurs Sénégalais* willingly accept
the extras they are given, they "have not yet taken up the German cause." [54]
We might comment, in turn, that the French never seemed to doubt
that the *Tirailleurs Sénégalais* had taken up the French cause!

The Vichy government made sporadic, and for the most part unsuccessful, attempts to negotiate the release and repatriation of African troops
now adding seriously to the nation's food burden. Although most African
prisoners of war were held in camps in Occupied France, the Germans
expected their Vichy collaborators to assume responsibility for their
upkeep. Additionally, some sick and injured prisoners were released to
the custody of the Vichy authorities. By late 1940, some 16,000 *tirailleurs*
had been sent to North Africa, still loyal to Vichy. Most of these were
men who had been fortunate enough to have reached the Free Zone
before the Armistice, but among them were an unknown number of
prisoners who had been invalided out of the camps. [55] Illness thus became
one of two means of obtaining freedom. Escape was the other.

Few *tirailleurs* attempted escape, even in the relatively confused conditions which prevailed during the first few months of captivity. Most
informants, as we have seen, said that they simply had no idea of where
they were or in which direction freedom lay. Somongo Soro put it well.

He had no thought of escape because, "first thing was we didn't know either Germany or France. Where would we go? There were guards everywhere. If you moved they'd shoot you."[56] Another prisoner, Tuo-Donatoho said, "We didn't know how to start—most didn't try."[57]

The disinclination of African prisoners to attempt escape was partially responsible for the relaxation of German attitudes. In much the same way that the Senoufo had come to accept, with outward docility, the system of forced labor and military recruitment at home, they now resigned themselves to their new fate in Europe. It seemed that one group of white masters had simply replaced another. Of course, for those who did escape, the reduced level of German vigilance proved of immeasurable assistance. "One day we were all ordered to leave the camp [at Mulsanne] to find wood," Edmond N'Guetta recalled.

> I decided I would escape. Five of us—Ivoiriens—decided to try it.
> . . . The Germans were very confident we wouldn't try to escape.
> They ignored us. We ran. Another prisoner—from Upper Volta—
> saw us and joined us. We asked directions from some peasants. They
> were afraid, but they gave them to us. . . . We hid for eight days.
> Then we headed for the Free Zone. We walked. The peasants helped
> us. Everyone helped us. We arrived at the bank of the Loire. There
> was one bridge left with a German sentry post on the other side.
> . . . We were afraid because many Germans were being killed by the
> Resistance. We hid, then we crossed the bridge. . . . We hid in the
> woods. Then in a village in someone's house. We were up at 4 in
> the morning and started walking toward the south. . . . We met a
> drunken peasant who said he would be our guide. His wife wouldn't
> let him. . . . We crossed the frontier two days later. We found another
> farm. The peasant warned us to be careful. We were still near the
> frontier. He told us to head for the house with the lamp. There was
> a woman there who helped many escapees. She fed us. We stayed
> there. We were very happy. We were liberated.[58]

If the treatment of those African prisoners still in the camps gradually came to approximate that of the French soldiers, this was not seen as much of an improvement. Ehouman Adou remarked, "We then got the same treatment, we died of hunger together—blacks like the whites."[59] The cumulative effect of years of hunger, cold, inadequate shelter, and disease took a heavy toll on the prisoners. Many contracted tuberculosis and other lung and chest diseases. Dysentery was endemic. Frostbite afflicted them terribly. Hélène de Gobineau has described their plight graphically.[60] Echenberg estimates that nearly half the African prisoners died in the camps.[61] Certainly the death rate during the first winter of defeat was so high that the Germans agreed to establish hospitals in all the major prison camps. These were supervised by Germans. Initially French civilian doctors had been used, but because the Germans suspected them of abetting a large number of escapes they were replaced with French military physicians, themselves prisoners.

It is to the great credit of the French medical personnel that they used their positions, at considerable personal risk, to arrange the release from Occupied to Vichy France of as many *tirailleur* prisoners as possible, on the grounds of poor health. Hélène de Gobineau was one of many who made every possible effort to relieve their suffering. One of those thus freed, Daouda Tuo-Donatoho, remembers with undimmed gratitude the French doctors and nurses who helped him:

> [At Morasse camp] we were undernourished. A small piece of bread and they'd put a little vegetable in a pot of boiling water and give it to us. Many of the men were so hungry they cut weeds and grass outside and boiled them and ate them. They got very sick—distended stomachs. I got very ill in the camp. I was sent into a village for medicine. The Germans took my *livret militaire* and never gave it back. I was then evacuated to the hospital at Reims. One woman helped me there, Mlle Regou from the Red Cross. After ten months and seventeen days there, she got me transferred to Paris. Without her help, I would have died. [62]

Some French doctors falsified diagnoses whenever possible. They often identified leprosy as the problem, hoping thereby to avoid close scrutiny by German medical overseers terrified of that disease. When release was not possible, the French staff would attempt to keep *tirailleurs* in hospital for prolonged periods so that they might rest. To assist this subterfuge, the *tirailleurs* were encouraged to cough continuously. Many needed little encouragement. The extent to which the Germans allowed themselves to be bamboozled varied. In the camp at Epinal, the German commander initially refused to hospitalize sick *tirailleurs*, restricting the beds to white inmates. However, after strong protests lodged both by French officers and by representatives of the Red Cross, he agreed that Africans could receive treatment. Even so, it was reported that releases for medical reasons, at this hospital, were made particularly difficult because of the rivalry which had existed from the prewar period between the doctors of the regular French army and those of the reserve. They disagreed on the diagnoses of their patients as a matter of principle. [63] This problem seems to have been specific to Epinal, however. In general, French medical personnel did their utmost to save as many African prisoners as they could.

Some *tirailleurs* became particularly skilled at cooperating with the hospital staff. Emile Dagba, who survived the camp in good enough

health to become eventually an Ivoirien customs official, described his
experience:

> I got out of the camp. I was liberated. They had had me working
> on a farm. Twenty-seven of us were on that farm. I wasn't sick, but
> I was tired. We had to work chopping wood, digging potatoes. I said
> to my boss—I am tired, I'm not used to this kind of work. He was
> an Alsatian. We had an argument. I said, "I'm sick." He said, "No."
> Then he sent me to the doctor. There were two of them—a French
> doctor and a German one. Also a *sergent-chef*—a Malagasy at the
> hospital. I talked to the French doctor and told him I wasn't sick,
> but tired. He said not to worry. Then they sent me to work in the
> furnace room in the hospital. I didn't know how to do that work
> either, but as a prisoner I had no choice. I did that for one month.
> Then I was x-rayed.
>
> My friend, the French doctor, came to get me. We were numer-
> ous—seventeen that day—all but me sick, really sick. When we got
> to the examination room, they listened to my heart. Five others first,
> then me. I was holding my breath. Then the German doctor came.
> Twelve were declared sick. When it was over the German general came
> to each of us to look at our photos—the x-rays. Three days later
> they came and said we were leaving the camp. He, the German
> general, said to each of the first ten, "Are you sick?" The first ten
> were passed—they were really sick. Then he came to me—looked
> at my x-ray and said, "No! No! No!" The French captain came over
> and said to the German—"He is fatigued." Then the general said,
> "All right." He signed my papers and I was out. They gave each of
> us our papers and we went into the free house. We got new clothes—
> jackets and trousers. We washed up. Then the Germans took us to
> the station. In 1941. Destination Paris![64]

The prison grapevine was well informed about the escape hatch offered by the hospitals, although the *tirailleur* might be somewhat confused about what a transfer involved. "Destination Paris," said Emile
Dagba, not realizing that Paris was still in Occupied France. Gmbale
Soro, not himself among the fortunate ones, was even more confused
about the final destination of those released. "They left to join de Gaulle,"
he said. "They never came back. After a while the Germans figured
out what was happening and they stopped it."[65] And so a few *tirailleurs*
obtained their release, but thousands were to remain prisoners until freed
by the Allies in 1944 and 1945. Some veterans insisted that, during their
years of incarceration, they knew nothing of what was happening in
the outside world. Most, however, were aware of the progress of the
war, of the invasion of the Soviet Union, of the rise of de Gaulle, of
the entry of the United States into the conflict, and of the Allied land-

ings in North Africa and Italy. News reached them in many ways. Prisoners coming back from outside work details picked up local gossip. Others, discharged from hospitals where African orderlies were mines of information, repeated what had been told them. The Red Cross and other civilians, working in or passing through the camps, brought hope. Ehouman Adou was in the camp at Nancy for three years. By the end of 1943, he remembers, "even the Germans told us when the Americans had come into the war. We had rapport with them now. They told us everything that went on."[66] Somongo Soro recalled another source of information:

> There were those who listened to the radio. . . . They told us about de Gaulle. We prayed to God. The Germans had the radios. Those who really understood French would tell us what was being said. We had hope. It would come someday. We knew that France was back in the war.[67]

The *tirailleurs* who suffered through the seemingly endless years of prison, seeing a few of their comrades being released but watching many others die of hunger and disease, wondered if they would ever return home. Some even began to take a perverse pride in the sheer length of their imprisonment. Somongo Soro was one of these.

> We saw the French. The French were together, and so were the *Sénégalais*. There was a road between them for the Germans to use. . . . At Monique we were in the same camp. We were the first ones captured, so we knew that the whites were with us—taken. Others who came later didn't know that. Those who had left to reinforce us couldn't know anything. They did a little prison, but not for long. It was we who started and spent a long time in prison—we were the *true* prisoners.[68]

NOTES TO CHAPTER FIVE

1. Robert Paxton, *Vichy France: Old Guard and New Order, 1940–1944* (New York: Knopf, 1972), 53. When Britain neither collapsed nor asked for peace, Huntziger tried to open negotiations on the release of prisoners before official peace talks began, but nothing was achieved. Paxton argues convincingly that although periodic attempts were made by Pétain to win the release of French prisoners, Hitler was quite indifferent to their fate. See 86, 360, 367–68.

2. Ibid., 360.

3. CMIDOM, Guerre 39–45, TI 1P INT CI 100, letter from the commander of la Section d'Etudes d'Information des Troupes Coloniales, dd. 7 March 1949. The file contains various reports on colonial prisoners.

4. Ibid.

5. SHAT, Centre du Documentation.

6. Interview 3.

7. Myron Echenberg, "Morts pour la France," 367, 369–70.

8. Jacques Louis Hyman, *Léopold Sédar Senghor* (Edinburgh: University of Edinburgh Press, 1971), 109.

9. CMIDOM, Guerre 39–45, Dossier T1 2P CV830. This dossier also contains other eye-witness accounts.

10. Ibid., reports by Mayor de Fouilloy, 19 August 1940. On the same matter, see Echenberg, "Morts pour la France," 369, citing Oberst Nehring, Guderian's chief of staff.

11. Interview 70.

12. From the *Frankfurter Zeitung*, no. 258 (18 September 1917). See W. J. Mommsen, *Max Weber zur Politik im Weltkrieg. Shriften und Reden 1914–1918* (Tübingen, Germany: J. C. B. Mohr, 1988), 318.

13. Interview 51.

14. Interview 5.

15. Anita Glaze. *Art and Death in a Senufo Village* (Bloomington: Indiana University Press, 1981), see especially 72–4, 149–55.

16. Interview 79.

17. Interview 37.

18. Interview 103.

19. Interview 88.

20. Hélène de Gobineau, *Noblesse d'Afrique* (Paris: Fasquelle, 1946), 11.

21. SHAT, report of Lieutenant Lagrange, Carton 34n1090, Dossier 4.

22. Interview 56.

23. Interview 30.

24. Interview 25.

25. Interview 3.

26. Interview 60.

27. Interview 18.

28. Interview 83.

29. CMIDOM, Carton Guerre 39–40, Dossier TI 1P INTCI 100. They were held principally in Stalags 1B, III A–B, IV B, VI A–C–D–F, VII A, VIII C, XX B.

30. de Gobineau, *Noblesse d'Afrique*, 12.

31. Robert Guerlain, *A Prisoner in Germany* (London: Macmillan, 1944), 32.

32. David Irving, *The Trail of the Fox* (New York: Dutton, 1977), 72. See also Echenberg, "Morts pour la France," 371–72. These scenes appeared in a Goebbels propaganda film, *Victory in the West*.

33. Interview 79.

34. French military propaganda directed at the *tirailleur* stressed that the Germans considered Africans, in Hitler's words, to be "half-monkeys." See

John Summerscales, "The War Effort in the French Colonies," *African Affairs* 39 (April 1940): 123.

35. Interview 3.

36. Interview 29.

37. Interview 51.

38. ANCI, Carton 5874, Dossier XVII–15/14.

39. Interview 60.

40. ANCI, Carton 850, Dossier XI–50/38.

41. A fascinating view of wartime Germany through the eyes of French prisoners can be found in Jean-Marie d'Houp's "Prisonniers de la guerre française témoins du défaut allemand," *Guerres mondiales et conflits contemporains*, no. 150 (1988): 77–98.

42. Interview 88.

43. SHAT, report on escape from prisoner of war camp by Lieutenant Vergez, 12th RTS, Carton 34n1090, Dossier 4.

44. Interview 88.

45. Interview 104.

46. SHAT, various reports of escaped officers of the 12th RTS, Lieutenants Philippe, Vergez, and Dutel, and Adjutant Benetry, Carton 34n1090, Dossier 4.

47. Ibid., report of Lieutenant Dutel.

48. Interview 18.

49. Paxton, *Parades and Politics*, 9–10.

50. Interview 52.

51. Interview 34.

52. Interview 74.

53. General X, *Aux heures tragiques de l'empire*, 232.

54. SHAT, report of Lieutenant Philippe, 12th RTS, Carton 34n1090, Dossier 4.

55. General X, *Aux heures tragiques de l'empire*, 221.

56. Interview 69.

57. Interview 14.

58. Interview 3.

59. Interview 103.

60. de Gobineau, *Noblesse d'Afrique*, 12–15.

61. Echenberg, "Morts pour la France," 365.

62. Interview 5.

63. SHAT, report of Lieutenant Vergez, Carton 34n1090, Dossier 4.

64. Interview 104.

65. Interview 71.

66. Interview 103.

67. Interview 69.

68. Ibid.

6

African against African; Frenchman against Frenchman July 1940–December 1942

The Lines Are Drawn

UNDER THE TERMS OF THE Armistice of 22 June 1940, France was allowed an army of 100,000 men. As Paxton has shown, this should not be regarded as a concession won from the Germans. On the one hand, it suited the victors to have the French assume responsibility for the preservation of order in the Free Zone while preparations were made for the invasion of Britain.[1] On the other hand, it suited the French military caste in at least affording the officers an illusion of honor. In principle, the Armistice Army was to be one of volunteers only, to be drawn from men of European descent. The matter of France was thus disposed of. There remained the matter of the empire. If Germany's immediate concerns were with Europe, it certainly had long-range interests in France's overseas possessions, not least in those parts of Africa which had once been German colonies.[2]

By Article 10 of the Armistice, Pétain had virtually guaranteed that the empire would accept the authority of the government of the Free Zone. Vichy France was, in other words, to remain an imperial power. This the Germans did regard as a concession. It was one viewed with some unease in high circles.[3] At the beginning of July, however, British naval operations against French ships at anchor in the Oran base, and the heavy casualties which resulted, did much to rally the empire to the Vichy government. Many officers in the colonies, originally responsive to de Gaulle's call for continued resistance, now closed ranks behind

Pétain. "In French Africa," Paxton wrote, "a wave of animosity to London swept over circles which only recently had longed for a way to keep up the war alongside Britain."[4] By September 1940, the Germans had become convinced that Vichy authority in the Africa colonies was effective. While the size of the Armistice Army in France was held constant, the army in Africa was allowed to expand to a ceiling of 115,000 men.[5]

Pétain was under intense German pressure to remove all colonial troops from European soil. The problem of their repatriation became one of his most immediate concerns. The magnitude of the task is illustrated by the case of the *Tirailleurs Sénégalais*. Virtually all the *tirailleur* units which had seen action in the Battle of France had either disintegrated or been disbanded during June and July 1940 (Table 3). Of the approximately 120,000 *tirailleurs* in those units, perhaps about half of the survivors were in prisoner of war camps in Occupied France or in Germany. The other half, however, were in Vichy territory. They needed to be fed and housed. To preserve a semblance of being soldiers, they needed officers at the very time when officers were being discharged or in some cases reassigned to the Armistice Army.

The case of the Nineteenth BATS is illustrative though not necessarily typical of the experience of the *tirailleurs*. Over half of the battalion's men had been captured, killed or posted missing during the retreat. Nevertheless, 251 survived. They spent the summer months recuperating at Belabre. They drilled. They marched in the Bastille Day parade, receiving accolades from the population. They laid a wreath at the war memorial and listened to a rousing patriotic speech by the local priest.[6] Such attempts at normalcy, however, could surely not conceal from them the immensity of the defeat, though they had been given little information about the overall situation and the implications of the Armistice for them. What, then, was to be done with such men?

A number of the West African soldiers were transferred to the Levant, where two *tirailleur* regiments and two detached battalions were stationed, and others were posted to North Africa, to augment the eight *tirailleur* regiments already there. They were to become, for a time, *tirailleurs* in the service of Vichy. There was, however, no alternative but to repatriate the great majority of the *tirailleurs* to the AOF, either to be incorporated into units there or to be dispatched to their homelands for discharge. Insufficient shipping made any such program an impossible one to accomplish immediately. Thousands of *tirailleurs* remained in army camps in southern and southwestern France, inactive and bewildered, awaiting repatriation.

Confusion Confounded

Yeo Yehoua, a Senoufo from Guiembé, was recruited from the class of 1938. He had been taken for forced labor four times, but he was one of the few who disliked the army more. As he said, "You never knew if a war would find you. . . . You did not know if you would ever come back." He did know, however, that an uncle of his had been killed in Europe in World War I. He left camp at Bouna and was moved, via Abidjan, Dakar, and Casablanca, to Algeria. He arrived there just when war was declared. He was in Tunis, with the First Battalion of the Fifth RTS, when the Armistice was signed. All guns were collected, and Yeo Yehoua began the long journey home. He was one of the fortunate ones. A Lieutenant Ferride, he remembered, accompanied them as far as Casablanca. They marched,

> but he [Ferride] rode in a car. He said *au revoir*. He shook everyone's hand. He said to be ready to come back. Perhaps we will start again. The war wasn't over yet. Be ready to come back. He also told us that the Germans were coming to attack Port Bouët [the port of Abidjan] and that was why we were being liberated—to defend our home. Then he left us.

This was in September 1940. Yeo Yehoua spoke of the journey home:

> There were many French people on the ship. Civilians, even women. No, we did not talk about what had happened. I just stayed with the three or four people near me. We talked about it among ourselves. We were very tired, but all the same we were beaten. We thought the Germans would be waiting for us at home. When we arrived in Dakar, they stopped us and said that a boat had been bombed. That's when we thought we would be attacked here [in the Côte d'Ivoire]. They said that a ship had been bombed and that we had to get off. So we took the train after one week in Dakar. We took the train to Bobo[-Dioulasso]. At Bobo we started to worry less. We didn't forget about it, but we were already close to home. It was there that they told us that the Americans had come in and that they were now in charge of the war. It was in Korhogo, in Korhogo that we found out that the Americans had entered the war. Yes, I heard about de Gaulle. Thanks to de Gaulle, we are free. De Gaulle asked pardon of the Germans, and that is why we were liberated. Many people [in my village] had said we would not come back. When they saw us coming, everyone came out to greet us. One had died over there, but nine of us came back. [7]

Table Three
Status of African Units, June 1940

FRANCE

Regiment	Division	Date of Creation or Location at Mobilization	Date Disbanded or Disappeared	Circumstances of Unit on June 25, 1940
INFANTRY:				
4th RTS*	2nd DIC†	Toulon	July 1940	Not in combat, region of Menton.
8th RTS	2nd DIC	Toulon	July 1940	2,000 men survived; disbanded.
12th RTS	1st DIC	November 1940; became 12th RIC‡; reformed March 1940.	June 1940	Surrendered at Dubuisson.
14th RTS	1st DIC	Mont-de-Marsan	June 1940	Prisoners at Mirecourt.
16th RTS	1st DIC	Mont-de-Marsan	July 1940	Dispersed, disappeared between the Somme and the Oise on 9 June 1940.
24th RTS	4th DIC	Perpignan	July 1940	Dispersed, disappeared between the Somme and the Oise on 9 June 1940.
25th RTS	8th DIC	April 1940	June 1940	In Free Zone; disbanded.
26th RTS	8th DIC	5 April 1940	July 1940	Survivors: 18 officers, 590 men; disbanded.
5th RICMS	6th DIC	May 1940 became 5th RTS.	July 1940	Surrendered at Dubuisson.
6th RICMS	6th DIC	May 1940 became 6th RTS.	July 1940	51 officers, 2,400 men lost; 150 French, 500 Sénégalais surrendered at Dubuisson.
27th RICMS	9th DIC	5 June 1940	June 1940	Captured at Cherbourg; disbanded in the Dordogne.
28th RICMS	9th DIC	5 June 1940	June 1940	Disbanded.
33rd RICMS	7th DIC	April 1940	July 1940	In region of Miallet; disbanded.
45th RICMS	5th DIC	April 1940	July 1940	Practically annihilated at the Battle of the Somme.
53rd RICMS	5th DIC	April 1940	July 1940	Practically annihilated at the Battle of the Somme.
57th RICMS	7th DIC	16 May 1940	July 1940	In region of Miallet; disbanded.
Pionniers	General Reserve			Disbanded.
Sénégalais				
55th BMIC//	—	5 June 1940	—	In combat from 14 June to Armistice in region south of Evreux.
17th BATS#	7th DIC	25 May 1940	June 1940	In combat region of Miallet; disbanded.
19th BATS	—	25 May 1940	6 August 1940	36 Europeans, 251 Africans survived; disbanded.

ARTILLERY:

1st RACMS**	1st DIC	June 1940	Captured in Crepey region.
2nd RACMS	2nd DIC (2nd DICL)††	July 1940	Disbanded.
201st RACLMS‡‡	1st DIC	September 1939	Captured in Crepey region.
202nd RACLMS	2nd DIC (2nd DICL)	September 1939	Disbanded.
	(2nd DICL)		
208th RACLMS	8th DIC	April 1940	Disbanded.

NORTH AFRICA AND THE LEVANT

Regiment	Stationed	Regiment	Stationed
INFANTRY:			
24th RIC	Levant	13th RTS	Algeria
3rd RTS	Morocco	15th RTS	Algeria
5th RTS	Tunisia	17th RTS	Levant
6th RTS	Morocco	18th RTS	Tunisia
10th RTS	Tunisia	1st BMTS///	Levant
11th RTS	Algeria	2nd BMTS	Levant

SOURCES: (France) SHAT, Carton 9n 268; (North Africa), SHAT Commission d'Enquête 1939–1940, "Corps Coloniaux Ayant Existe Durant Les Hostilités 1939–1940."

*RTS=Régiment des Tirailleurs Sénégalais
‡RIC=Régiment d'Infanterie Coloniale
//BMIC=Bataillon de Marche d'Infanterie Coloniale
**RACMS=Régiment d'Artillerie Coloniale Mixtes Sénégalais
‡‡RACLMS=Régiment d'Artillerie Coloniale Légère Mixtes Sénégalais

†DIC=Division d'Infanterie Coloniale
§RICMS=Régiment d'Infanterie Coloniale Mixtes Sénégalais
#BATS=Bataillon Autonome des Tirailleurs Sénégalais
††DICL=Division d'Infanterie Coloniale Légère
///BMTS=Bataillon de Marche des Tirailleurs Sénégalais

Yeo Yehoua had a decidedly shaky grasp of the situation in the AOF to which he was returning. It could scarcely have been otherwise. The situation was both extraordinarily complicated and rapidly changing. [8] On 25 June 1940, the High Commission of French Africa was created. Governor-General Pierre Boisson of the AEF, *grand mutilé* of World War I, was appointed High Commissioner of what was to be a federation of the AOF and the AEF, France's west and equatorial African colonies. Before leaving for Dakar, Boisson assured the AEF colonists that their interests would not be ignored: "Economic life is suspended. We must look for new ways, to the greatest extent possible, of managing. You will lack for many of life's conveniences. The essentials you will not lack. This I will promise you." [9] Once in Dakar, still without having committed himself to either Pétain or de Gaulle, Boisson attempted to calm Europeans. "We still retain the integrity of our territory," he reminded them. "The task is to conserve and to defend that which has been entrusted to us." [10]

The new High Commission of West Africa notwithstanding, the AEF heeded de Gaulle's call for the continuation of the war from the colonies. The governor of Chad, Felix Eboué, born in French Guiana, took decisive action on 26 August, despite having two sons who were now German prisoners of war. He declared that he and his administration no longer recognized the Vichy regime. In this he had the support of René Leclerc (alias de Hautecloque), who would lead French Forces on to the beaches of Normandy in 1944; René Pleven, future colonial minister; and Hettier de Boislambert of the Colonial Army, who had arrived from London two days earlier. French Cameroun rallied to the Free French on 27 August. The next day French Congo followed suit after a successful coup led by Col. Edgard de Larminat, who had entered the colony from Leopoldville to receive the support of the small local garrison. Oubangui-Chari (modern Central African Republic) rallied the next day. Only in Gabon was it necessary to mount an actual military campaign. Its governor, Georges Pierre Masson, had initially accepted the authority of de Larminat but, conscience-stricken and under heavy pressure from the Catholic church in the person of Monsignor Louis Tardy, Bishop of Gabon, first wavered and then refused adherence to the new regime in Brazzaville. Ground and air attacks began on 17 October. Lambaréné, home to Albert Schweitzer, was bombed on the twenty-second; and Libreville was taken on 10 November. Gabon joined the rest of the AEF in the Gaullist camp. During the night of 16 November, Governor Masson, in custody aboard the *Savorgnan de Brazza,* committed suicide. [11]

By the middle of November 1940, the entire AEF had repudiated Pétain and his government, and the Free French forces had acquired a territorial base within the African Empire — indeed, the only one they had other than the Pacific islands of Tahiti and New Caledonia. It was a different story in the AOF. Boisson hesitated for several weeks, testing the prevailing winds. The almost total lack of communication from France, and the refusal of the AEF to accept the Armistice, initially tempted many in the AOF to swing to support of de Gaulle, now broadcasting almost nightly on the BBC. There were public demonstrations in Dakar, St. Louis, Ouagadougou, and Abidjan. Letters to Boisson and his colonial governors, and to the French government still sitting paralyzed in Bordeaux, urged resistance and protested the Armistice, but telegrams to the same effect sent to France never arrived, for the authorities had blocked the cable system. [12] By autumn, however, Boisson had decided that the best means of preserving the empire was to acknowledge the authority of Vichy. The vast majority of the AOF administration apparently concurred. They expected that Britain would fall within weeks. The Gaullist option seemed, therefore, doomed to failure. That France had been allowed to keep her empire under the terms of the Armistice, without physical interference by the Nazis, became the preeminent rationalization for the policy of active collaboration with Germany.

Resistance Grows

Boisson brought the AOF within the Vichy camp apparently without any major opposition from his subordinates. This was true of the Côte d'Ivoire in particular as of the AOF in general. There were, nevertheless, indications that all was not as it seemed. Reports reached Abidjan that merchant ships, leaving France for the AOF, were sailing instead to British ports to unload and take refuge. [13] Conversely, a ship carrying 1,000 "colored sharpshooters"—including, presumably, recruits from the class of 1940—left the Côte d'Ivoire for France but was diverted to the Gold Coast, where the *tiraillleurs* were incorporated immediately into the British West African Frontier Force. [14] Soon after news of the Armistice had reached the Côte d'Ivoire, a few young army officers and civilians left for British territory to offer their services to either de Gaulle or the British. In some cases whole units were involved. In July, Captains Bouillon and Laurent-Champrosay led twenty-four men of the Thirty-sixth Battery of the Sixth RAC from Bobo-Dioulasso into the Gold Coast. From Ouagadougou, Lieutenants Chevillot and Grandperrin took a platoon of corporals under training, carrying four cannons with them, across the same frontier. From the military district of Batié, the entire garrison decamped on 11 July under the command of Lt. Bonnard. [15] The young Baba Camara of Bouna was there:

I was in Batié that day with my parents. I remember well one morning when the commandant sent me to look for the European at Tehini, Jean Jacques. At one o'clock in the morning they had cut the wires and crossed over. . . . They all went—the agent, the doctor—all the Europeans in Batié left with practically all the soldiers—more than two platoons. It was during the time of the great rain.

The next morning someone telephoned Bouna to inform the commandant that the wires had been cut. The commandant at Bouna, Captain Margou, went to Batié right away. They had left and taken all the equipment with them. A few young soldiers were left behind to guard the town. Margou continued right on to the Volta River—twenty-five kilometers from Batié. He left and then he returned. The captain cried. He had lost faith. They were his best friends. We thought that they crossed over into Ghana [Gold Coast] because de Gaulle was there at the moment.

That day Batié was practically in mourning. Also in Bouna—so many of the men were from here. The Captain gave orders and advice to the few who remained. Told them to be calm—that they would be reinforced. Not to move. The sergeant, an African, was left there to maintain order. They [the *tirailleurs* who had left] all stayed with de Gaulle. They came back after the war if they were still alive. [16]

The records of such defections are, for obvious reasons, fragmentary. According to one report, in July 1940 three detachments of troops, comprising 40 Europeans and 300 *tirailleurs*, mainly NCOs, had crossed into the Gold Coast. [17] From the *Centre d'Instruction des Indigènes* in Ouagadougou came 620 students, arriving in the British colony with 20 automatic rifles and 20 cases of ammunition. [18] That these early recruits to the Free French cause were all from Upper Volta was not a coincidence. Its lieutenant governor, Edmond Louveau, was one of the few senior administrators in AOF to support de Gaulle. He had cabled the general on 22 June to this effect and had spoken publicly in favor of continued resistance by the empire. In July, he was denounced by a European merchant living in Banfora and, as a result, summoned to Dakar in August. Tried and convicted of treason, he was sent to a concentration camp in France. [19]

By the summer of 1940, the Free French had established a skeletal presence in the Gold Coast. Those who were decamping from the Côte d'Ivoire immediately made contact with them. It is doubtful whether many of the African "recruits" shared the ardor of their officers for de Gaulle, even had they heard of him. When they realized that they were now expected to serve in a new army, virtually a phantom one, a revolt broke out. No less than 1,700 African soldiers, along with a few Europeans, demanded to be returned to French territory. The British military authorities stepped in. They offered substantial bonuses to those who chose to enlist instead in the Gold Coast forces. Twelve hundred accepted. The rest returned to the AOF. When it was all over, only 105 privates, 30 NCOs, and 12 of their officers remained with the Free French. They were sent to Cameroun, where they formed the nucleus of the Fourth *Bataillon de Marche*.[20] It was not exactly an impressive beginning for Free French recruitment from Vichy West Africa.

A trickle of French Africans continued to cross the border to join the Free French, but most of de Gaulle's African troops would come from the AEF. There, by the winter of 1940–41, three infantry battalions were ready for combat, and three more were in training.[21] In general, however, few Africans volunteered for service in the Free French ranks. They lacked the knowledge of the situation to enable them to make any such decision. It was usually made for them. Henri Boileau had escaped France through Spain to join de Gaulle in London and was later to command *tirailleurs* in North Africa. He summarized the attitude of most Africans. "Very few joined him as volunteers," he said. "If they fought for de Gaulle, it was because they found themselves *chez* de Gaulle like those Africans in the AEF. They joined him, but it wasn't heroism or patriotism."[22]

These early defections from the Côte d'Ivoire to the British and the Free French should scarcely have caused Boisson great concern. Yet Boisson, while still officially uncommitted, clearly feared revolts among the AOF population and particularly in the event of a British invasion. He proclaimed a state of siege throughout the AOF on 9 July 1940. No more than ten people were permitted to assemble, alcohol sales were forbidden after ten at night, and all residents of urban areas were ordered to turn in their firearms.[23] Recognizing, perhaps, that he had overreacted, Boisson then cancelled the decree on 29 July. The governor-general, as we have seen, shortly thereafter decided that Pétain was a safer bet than an unknown junior general speaking from London. England, despite its recent status as an ally, was after all France's ancient enemy and primary rival for colonial supremacy. Even among those who did join de Gaulle, Boisson's attitude was deemed not unreasonable. The French *tiraillleur*, Gerard Faivre, expressed it in this way:

> Ah—the English. All the same they were our allies. Everyone liked them well enough until the debacle. When the disaster came, the English realized they couldn't stop the Germans, so they managed their departure. Evacuated for England. Look at our history books— on all the pages—the English. There were others, Austria, Spain, but always the English. I think Lafayette went to the American War of Independence for the pleasure of beating the English.[24]

Only five administrators in French West Africa decamped to either British territory or Liberia. Another four openly supported de Gaulle. Boisson, however, eventually dismissed 31 of the AOF's 400 administrators for "political" reasons, but these included being Jewish, Communist, foreign-born or (in ten cases) Freemason. The rest stayed on. Conversely, all but forty administrators remained in office in the now Gaullist French Equatorial Africa.[25] In short, then, the vast majority of French functionaries, military and civilian, simply played Follow the Leader, whatever their private feelings may have been.

As the Vichy era dragged on in the AOF, those who stayed came to justify their position by accepting the wisdom and necessity of the Pétain personality cult and the new "ideals" of his National Revolution. Its motto, Work, Family, Country, seemed infinitely better suited to the colonial situation than Liberty, Fraternity, Equality. But in the AOF, during those first months after the Armistice but before the propaganda machine was assembled, inertia and a sense of hopelessness were the overriding factors determining the stance of the French. The Anglo-French raid on Dakar in September 1940 changed all of this despite its failure. There was outrage that Frenchmen should fire on Frenchmen.[26] The majority of AOF administrators became convinced that the National Revolution was more than an excuse for the Armistice. Henceforth they began to see it as a crusade against the decadence which had seeped into France and caused her defeat. This, then, was the atmosphere the repatriated soldiers of the 1939–40 army encountered upon their return to the Côte d'Ivoire.

The Forgotten Men

In 1940, no less than 35,000 AOF *tirailleurs* were transported from North Africa as least as far as Dakar. Another 27,000 awaited transportation.[27] Unfortunately, yet again the statistics fail us. We do not know how many of these men had actually begun their long journey in France. Whatever the case, in 1941, the ongoing repatriation of African soldiers was severely hampered by the British, who now considered the AOF enemy territory and who controlled the sea south of Senegal. From their base in Sierra Leone, the Royal Navy blockaded the shipping lanes, making it virtually impossible for troopships to proceed any further than Dakar. Truck and fuel shortages, moreover, sharply reduced the number of men who could be moved out of Dakar by overland routes. The result was a massive bottleneck in the Senegalese capital.

Facilities at Dakar were inadequate for such a large number of soldiers awaiting transport to their homes. A voyage of about 1,500 miles still separated the Ivoiriens, for example, from their home ports. Severe disciplinary problems arose. The men could not understand why they were being delayed. Disoriented, angry, having lost respect for a defeated France, living in cramped quarters with strangers, having had frequent changes in their officers, and awaiting demobilization bonuses which rarely seem to have materialized, the men were near mutiny. The problems were recognized by the AOF High Command. On the one hand it was hoped that "when the demobilization is complete, the [remaining] AOF troops then will rediscover the stability and homogeneity desirable to renew the military." On the other, however, it was acknowledged that the *tirailleurs* were "morally shocked by the defeat, depressed by the disorder of their embarkation." In a frank assessment of the disorder, blame was squarely placed on the officer corps, which had, it was reported, "shown itself unequal to its task"[28]

Even when transportation from Dakar was available, problems arose. Many *tirailleurs* had no papers. Thus officials had no way of verifying the repatriate's colony, or whether or not he was at the time a reservist or was still on active duty. The authorities had to accept soldiers' words for where they wished to be taken. Some new recruits, scheduled for posting, are known to have claimed to be reservists and demanded to be sent home. Others clamored for the medals and decorations promised them in France and North Africa. The worst problem encountered in Dakar arose from demands for money. Not only did most of the repatriated men insist they had been promised bonuses on their arrival in Dakar but many presented unreadable bank books and stamped receipts for savings deposits they had opened in France. They wanted cash, not promises. Even when the army accepted these claims, there were no funds to give them. Consequently, officers temporized, giving assurances that the money was waiting for them in their own colonies, in their own *cercles*. Serious disturbances broke out. In Guinea, demobilized *Tirailleurs Sénégalais* rioted in Kindia and Kankan, and in the Côte d'Ivoire, in Dédougou. The most violent incident was that in Kindia. Having been told first that their money awaited them in Dakar, there they were told they would receive it in Conakry. In Conakry, they learned it would be paid by their *cercle* commandants. Arriving finally at Kindia, it was evident that they would receive nothing there either. Furious, 31 men attacked the commandant and the stationmaster. [29]

The experience of these men was repeated throughout the AOF, even though the reactions were not always so violent. Somongo Yeo speaks of the bitterness he felt on arriving in Korhogo and being abruptly dispatched to his village, Natiokabadara:

> We didn't talk about our experiences, the war, on the ship. We were very angry. We had suffered and we got no money. That was the first reason we did not talk much on the boat. The second reason was because the boat was full of the wounded—many of them with arms and legs cut off. The boat smelled of sickness. Some even died on the ship. There were doctors, but they still died. . . . I thanked God that I was coming home in good shape. We arrived in Korhogo, group by group. There were even men from Bobo. Once there everyone had to find his own way home. We were given a reception by the commandant. He gave us drinks and food. Then we went home. That's all—no money. He never mentioned money to us.[30]

Actually, Somongo Yeo received a comparatively warm welcome. Commandants had been alerted to the tenseness of the situation throughout the AOF and were strongly advised to disperse the returning soldiers as quickly as possible. Few were even fed before being hustled off to their villages.

Certain categories of discharged soldiers, however, were given some assistance. In the Côte d'Ivoire, help centers were set up to aid demobilized Frenchmen and those Africans who were citizens. Those who were unemployed were provided with housing, food allowances, and job counseling.[31] About 200 Africans qualified. Such treatment contrasted sharply with that given the ordinary *tirailleurs*. No longer regarded as devoted soldiers of France, they were now seen as a possible threat to the fragile Vichy regime which had authority over them. There was a marked lack of sympathy and understanding for what they had undergone in the war. As one officer in the Côte d'Ivoire remarked of them, they "came back with bad attitudes, undisciplined and are trying to pose as victims."[32]

The annual report on the military forces of the AOF attributed the "bad attitudes" of the repatriates to the loss of French prestige as a result of the collapse, to extremist (but unspecified) propaganda to which the *tirailleurs* had been exposed while abroad, and to the insufficient surveillance which had been exercised over them in the camps in France and North Africa. The army, aware of the problems, undertook to reinvigorate its internal security network. Commanders were invited to assign a specialist to the position of intelligence officer to gather information on the soldiers. They should, it was urged, "take this man seriously." A fund of 48,000 francs was set aside for the payment of informants and to meet the "small expenses" of the intelligence officers—presumably to buy the drinks necessary to loosen the tongues of African NCOs willing to cooperate.[33]

The governor of the Côte d'Ivoire, Hubert Deschamps, former socialist turned Vichy apologist, was in compliance. He required his commandants regularly to "evaluate the morale" of the newly returned soldiers. The reports are replete with complaints about the men's arrogance and their tendency to regard themselves as a privileged class, above the law. In the Man and Mossi areas, repatriated combat soldiers were said to look down upon those who had got no nearer to the front than Dakar, while throughout the colony, ex-soldiers were refusing to accept the authority of either their village or canton chiefs. [34] A report of the commandant of Korhogo, however, was more sanguine. It will come as no surprise that he was able to assure Governor Deschamps that there were no problems in the district, despite the fact that the men had been left to walk home from Bouaké. "His" veterans were very happy, if rather surprised, to be home. The main difficulty was domestic rather than political. Several wives had deserted their absent husbands, and he was having to help locate them. [35]

For the Vichy regime, the matter of respect for chiefs was a serious one. The new *politique coloniale* placed great symbolic importance upon the hierarchy, from *chef de province* down to *chef du village*, as the custodian of what they imagined to be traditional African culture. The same colonial administrators who had formerly been told to destroy chiefly power were now charged with rebuilding it. Under Vichy, *évolués* and *citoyens indigènes* were "out," tribal values were "in"! The *colons* in the Côte d'Ivoire, never known for their political liberalism, had been delighted to see the abandonment of plans to reform the colonial system projected by the Popular Front government of Leon Blum. Under Vichy, all African associations and labor unions, save officially sponsored clubs, were now banned, as were all public meetings. [36] The small measure of representative local government granted Abidjan in the immediate prewar period was removed. Laws had been passed in 1939 which extended the right to French justice to Africans throughout the AOF who had satisfied their military obligations, were holders of the Legion of Honor, or had been elected to municipal assemblies. [37] These were repealed by Pétain on 5 January 1941 and replaced by law 838 of 8 March 1941. All Africans, subjects and citizens alike, were again brought under the jurisdiction of the *Indigénat.* A new "native" penal code was introduced by the same Vichy legislation. This gave commandants the right to impose, without trial or hearing, prison terms, fines, and confiscation of property for a wide range of minor offenses. Collective punishment, taxes in kind, and additional forced labor became increasingly common. As a result, the number of convictions under the *Indigénat* rose sharply between 1940 and 1942. [38]

The social ramifications of the new decrees paralleled the legal. The old policy of assimilation, whereby the acquisition of French language and culture would turn Africans into Frenchmen, was officially abandoned. A color bar was established in hotels, restaurants, and the cinema. The *citoyen* and *évolué* alike were virtually forced to return to a traditional way of life. Many were fired from their jobs to make room for Frenchmen. Even Boisson admitted that returning to their villages might prove difficult for them but nonetheless felt that "they can be readapted to the rural African milieu under the control and with the help of local authorities."[39] If the administration could dispense so casually with the services of the Ivoirien educated elite, what chance had the returning soldier to find advancement within the same system?

Not surprisingly, in these circumstances the level of tension rose. There were small acts of defiance, even violence. Ex-soldiers in Man stripped travelers of their clothes, especially khakis, in order to replace uniforms routinely confiscated by Ivoirien military authorities upon their return.[40] The chiefs were expected to avert such incidents. When they failed to do so, malcontents received harsh punishment. In Boromo, a *tirailleur* was jailed for six months for urging people to ignore their canton chief. When he declared that before he would accept the chief's authority, he would join the English, he was awarded two extra years of prison.[41] Even in the Korhogo region, whatever the commandant had reported, some Senoufo were infected by the discontent. There, many veterans also began to ignore, even threaten, their chiefs. "We have the monopoly to beat people," Nanlougo Soro said,

> no matter who. Even the village chief. We were soldiers, afraid of no one. We could beat him [the chief] and he would beg our pardon. We could have killed him if we wanted to. We were no longer afraid of the chief. Before he had the power to send anybody anywhere, now we were not afraid of him.[42]

It was in an attempt to stem the rising discontent that commandants encouraged *anciens combattants* to join Pétain's *Légion des Combattants et Volontaires,* founded in 1941. This new organization demanded complete obedience to its founder. Legionnaires were charged with seeking out those who opposed Pétain. Interestingly enough, membership was open to all European and African *anciens combattants*, except of course Freemasons, Communists, and Jews, and was compulsory for European officials. By October 1942, 1,703 Europeans and 4,685 Africans were members of sections in the Côte d'Ivoire. The ethos of the Legion may be judged by this characteristic piece of purple Pétainist prose.

Have confidence and faith in *"Patrie, Pétain, Légion."* This is our
awakening; to those who cry that we have fallen, we say France will
band together again—with Pétain, venerable chief, who will regain
for our flag its splendor. [43]

Rallies and parades figured prominently in the activities of the Legion.
A large fete was held in Abidjan on 30–31 August 1941, for example.
More than a thousand Ivoirien *anciens combattants* were trucked in from
all over the colony. [44] The Europeans seemed to take particular comfort
in watching "their" Africans march for France. "Enthusiasm abounds,"
one observer reported.

> The breadth of the ceremony, the order and the discipline of the
> Legionnaires, these aged natives covered with medals, coming from
> the north of the colony with their old 1914 uniforms—sometimes
> in tatters. It is the united empire which passes and continues. [45]

What were these legionnaires truly thinking? Intelligence reaching the
United States led U.S. analysts to believe, wishfully perhaps, that the
veterans had by no means forgotten their war. According to one State
Department report,

> It is especially the natives who fought against the Germans in France
> who have retained intact a spirit of revenge against the latter. It is
> difficult for them to accept this *imposed* neutrality when they think
> of their prisoners in Germany and of the large number of wounded
> who have come back to the Côte d'Ivoire and who are kept at the
> Abidjan hospital out of the reasonable fear that if they returned to
> their villages the spectacle which they would offer and the story of
> their suffering and martyrdom would stir up a movement of revolt
> against Germany. [46]

This report accurately reflects the discontent of many of the returned
veterans, though the desire for their promised benefits may have been
at least as important a cause as hatred of the Germans. Djirigue Soro
of Sirasso made the point quite explicitly:

> We revolted in France because we hadn't got our money—our pay.
> They told us that we would get it in Korhogo. We didn't believe them
> and we revolted. After that the French didn't tell us anything anymore.
> That is why they didn't tell us what de Gaulle was doing. They took
> our guns. The war was over. They said, "Get on the boat." But before
> boarding the ship, we said, "No. You may be too strong for us, but
> we want our money." But we didn't riot for too long—they might
> have left us there. That would have been more serious.

We got to Korhogo. We spent three days there. They gave us nothing. The commandant—we asked him for our money. He said it hadn't come yet. Five times we went back to him. Now, I am mad. I'll just stay in my village. He never told us that France had been beaten. He said that the French didn't have any CFA [money], but they would send money orders in French francs and they would be exchanged for our money. That's what he *said*. [47]

However widespread was the anger and discontent of the veterans of the Battle of France, the public posture of the Ivoirien authorities gave little hint of it. The Church hierarchy counseled its missionaries, priests, and lay members to give total support to the Pétainist movement, then in the process of repealing the "immoral" legislation passed during the Blum era and emphasizing the importance of traditional family values. One clergyman, taking as his text the heroic struggle of Joan of Arc, reminded his parishioners that she was burned at the stake by the English, "the Gaullists of that Epoch." Monsignor Kirmann, legionnaire and head of the Sassandra Catholic Mission, told his flock of the depths to which the Third Republic had fallen by "placing a Jew [Leon Blum] on the throne of Louis XIV." [48]

The Battle of Dakar, as it was to be known during the Vichy years, combined with the sinking of the French fleet at Mers-el-Kebir, convinced most of those in the AOF, who probably did not need a great deal of persuasion anyway, of the perfidy of the English and their puppet, de Gaulle. They gave their support to the Pétain government in the person of Pierre Boisson. Remarkably, the governor-general convinced himself that, with the exception of the repatriated *tirailleurs*, the mass of the people would remain unaffected by the events of 1940. "I have only one concern," he announced,

that of maintaining French prestige in the eyes of the natives. Certainly they know that France has been beaten, but if, for them, nothing will change in the AOF, it is possible that this defeat, which I see as temporary, will be softened. This defeat took place far from them. Had the German presence materialized here, it would have made them more aware of it. And, let it be clearly understood, that the German presence would have been accompanied by German propaganda which would, as it has done everywhere, find adherents. I want France to find her natives exactly the same as she has always known them. [49]

From the rhetoric to the reality: back in the real world of the villages, the most veterans could hope for was a sympathetic commandant. He might give *anciens combattants* small administrative tasks such as interpreting or supervising road gangs. No matter the technique, it is clear that all commandants experienced problems with the process of reintegrating the veterans into their traditional (by which they meant subservient) roles. [50] In these years of defeat, the administration forgot its lofty image of the *tirailleur* as a messenger imparting the grandeur of French civilization to his fellow villagers. They worried only about his anger being transformed into an instrument capable of destroying French colonialism.

Those veterans of 1939–40 had known only bloody combat, headlong flight, imprisonment or close escapes, confusion, and deprivation. They returned to the Côte d'Ivoire with little or no money and with most of their personal possessions left behind in French army camps. They came back to a colony under the increasingly repressive control of an insecure administration. They were usually greeted with indifference, if not outright hostility and suspicion. There had been no glory in their combat, and none awaited them in their homes. These men had few ways of expressing their disappointment or their rage. For the most part they were left alone. In the villages of the Senoufo, beset with increased labor quotas and taxes in kind, they never attempted to act as intermediaries with either the canton chiefs or the administration in attempts to relieve conditions. They talked to no one of their experiences but other *anciens combattants*. Later, a few emerged as local leaders in the nationalist struggle, but for the most part, these former *Tirailleurs Sénégalais* became, and remain to this day, a forgotten generation.

The Military in the AOF

The Armistice Commission had originally envisaged a gradual reduction of military forces in the AOF to 25,000 men. No such massive reduction occurred, although recruitment was temporarily suspended. By September 1940, as we have seen, the Germans had decided to allow the army in Africa to expand. This had repercussions in the AOF. Its High Command argued that, since the AEF had declared for de Gaulle, French West Africa could not be adequately defended by 25,000 soldiers. Authority was sought to increase the force to 32,000. From the Côte d'Ivoire, Governor Deschamps argued vehemently for the increase. He could not, he argued, withstand an invasion from the Gold Coast without more men. [51] Ultimately, by 1942, the forces in the AOF had swollen to no less than 125,000, a fifth of whom were Europeans legally or illegally transferred from the Armistice Army. This extraordinary increase reflected the fears of the French High Command, under General

Weygand, that Anglo-American operations against the empire were likely. However, despite these increases, between 1940 and 1942 the army in West Africa fell on hard times.

An initial reduction in strength to approximately 40,000 men did in fact occur. According to Boisson's analysis at the end of 1940, only twenty men in a thousand were adequately trained—those recruited from the class of 1940 who had not been shipped to France.[52] The policy of rapidly discharging the returned veterans, who were feared to be politically unreliable, had the effect of depriving the army of its best pool of trained men. There were great shortages of both officers and NCOs.[53] Moreover, weapons, especially machine guns, were scarce.[54] Most of the 30,000 rifles in the AOF arsenal were of World War I vintage or older. There were few opportunities for target practice since ammunition was scarce, and field maneuvers were infrequent due to gasoline shortages.[55]

These unpromising conditions did not discourage the army from planning a series of ambitious actions against the British and the Free French. Among the proposals was an attack on Freetown, capital of Sierra Leone, first scheduled for 8 July 1940, called off because of bad weather, rescheduled for 21 October, and finally left on the drawing board for an unspecified later date. Bathurst, capital of Gambia, was targeted for an October raid. A November attack on the northern Nigerian town of Kano was also projected. Proposed military actions against Chad came to nothing.[56] None of these grandiose plans ever got off the ground in part because of Vichy reluctance to test the loyalty of their African soldiers in a confrontation with those serving in the Allied armies. In fact, only four military operations were carried out by AOF forces in 1940: the bloodless occupation of the oil wells of Toumno in Libya; the repression of the Hamallist Islamic brotherhood in Nioro, French Soudan; the defense of Dakar; and the unsuccessful attempt to keep Gabon out of Gaullist hands.[57] No units based in the AOF were to see action again until 1944.

In the course of 1941, recruitment was slowly revived. The class of that year was registered in May, but physical examinations in each *cercle* did not begin until 20 December. The Free French estimated that about 3,000 men were called up from the Côte d'Ivoire. It was the only year during the war in which recruitment fell below 10,000. Despite this, considerable resistance arose locally. For example, when the recruitment commission arrived in Ouagadougou, the commandant of the *cercle* reported that most of the young men had fled to the Gold Coast. The Mossi ruler, Moro Naba Kom II, demanded a great reduction in the number of men taken and did little to prevent wholesale draft evasion.[58]

Many Ivoirien recruits from the class of 1941, enlisted in 1942, found themselves in labor battalions used on public works projects under conditions nearly indistinguishable from those of forced labor. [59] This was hardly conducive to an improvement in morale. The repatriated *tirailleurs* who had remained in the army were unlikely to have an inspirational effect on the new recruits. They were, as we have seen, regarded as potentially dangerous, even subversive. [60] Due to shortages in matériel, many of the class received sketchy training and were discharged after only a few months. Some Korhogo recruits never left the *cercle*. Their basic training involved innumerable assaults on 300-meter-high Mount Korhogo. Gnoumagai Soro of Sinematiali was one of them.

> I spent one year in Korhogo, then two years in Bouaké. In Korhogo we learned how to fight wars. The camp was on the road to M'Bengue. We also built a camp on Mount Korhogo. After I came to Korhogo, I didn't see my village again, but my family did come to see me. I didn't know when I started my military service that I would spend a year in Korhogo. When we found that out, we were happy—thought we would come home right after we finished there, but we were sent to Bouaké. I didn't know there was a war on. We were all Senoufo in the camp except for the NCOs from Bouaké. They taught us some French. There were French officers, but I don't remember their names. There were just a few of them. They did no harm to Africans. They were good men. [61]

Life in Bouaké was to prove less pleasant. *Tirailleurs* in the camp there appeared to have suffered more than just forced marches. Even NCOs taking a special training course were brutally whipped, a minimum of fifty strokes being awarded for even the smallest mistake. Ordinary recruits were punished by being made to run in full field kit, carrying three sacks of sand, for up to four hours a day. [62] Others found themselves planting vegetable gardens to make up for cuts in rations. They were not even issued with new uniforms. Some received lice-infested clothes appropriated from discharged veterans of the Battle of France. [63] Many of the camps had neither bedding nor mosquito nets, a matter of particular hardship for European soldiers but not exactly pleasant for the Africans. Weavers' villages were assessed much higher quotas of taxation in kind to make up the shortfall. Soma Koné spoke of these hard times:

> Before the war there were many imports—manufactured goods— but when the ships were blockaded during the war, there was a rupture of imports. They stopped. There was no cloth. During the war they made our weavers send the cloth to Europe for uniforms. There

was a tailor here who was forced to sew uniforms for them, but he
was never paid. During this time we worked for the glory of Gbon
Coulibaly. He took a part of the harvest. We took the rest of the
harvest to eat. We lived. [64]

The fact was that to run an army on a shoestring, even a colonial one
with no definite raison d'être, proved no easy task.

By 1941, it was impossible to speak of the *Tirailleurs Sénégalais* as
an entity of any sort. Some of them languished in the stalags of Germany and Occupied France. Others, in North Africa, awaited reassign-
ment or repatriation. Yet others were defending French imperial interests
in the mandated territories of the Levant. A few had found their way
into the Free French or British forces. And finally, there were those, new
recruits for the most part, who were in limbo in West Africa, knowing
neither why they were in uniform nor what the future held for them.
These men, drafted in 1941, like their peers in 1939 and 1940,
remembered how little information about events in Europe they had
been given by their officers and NCOs. Ditiemba Silué, who was later
to fight in Italy and France, was one such:

> When we were recruited, they told us if we were lucky we wouldn't
> have to go to war. In the village we knew nothing about the war.
> There was no 1939, 1940 class. I was the first to go. My father had
> fought the '14–18 war before I was born. When I was young he told
> me about the war against the Germans. It was very tough. [65]

Unlike Ditiemba, Zie Soro of Koloko—although of the class of 1940—
never got further than Abidjan. "I did my military service," he explained,

> but I never fought. I left here and went first to Bouaké. I did one
> year at Bouaké. From Bouaké we left for Abidjan. There I guarded
> the lagoons. I never left Abidjan. . . . When the army took me they
> said we were going to war, but I never fired a shot against the enemy
> the way you are supposed to during a war. They taught us every-
> thing—how to fire guns. The year that the French and English were
> at war, an English plane was downed and after that we waited at
> the barricades. We waited a week—on the bank of the lagoon—one
> week. We dug a trench—and hid in it all day. The English planes
> came—they passed over us, but they didn't fire. There was one plane
> which came down over Abidjan, but no one was killed. No, they
> never told us why we were now fighting the English. When I started
> in the army we were fighting against the Germans. [66]

In the event, it was to be the *tirailleurs* in the Levant who were to be
the next to see battle.

NOTES TO CHAPTER SIX

1. Robert Paxton, *Parades and Politics,* 3–10.
2. For a detailed examination of Nazi Germany's African objectives, see Kumia N'Dumbe III, *Hitler Voulait l'Afrique* (Paris: Editions d'Harmattan, 1980).
3. Paxton, *Parades and Politics,* 29.
4. Ibid., 37.
5. Ibid., 47–48.
6. SHAT, *Journal de marche,* 19th BTS.
7. Interview 54.
8. Paxton, *Parades and Politics,* 77–93.
9. Maurice Martin du Gard, *La Carte impériale* (Paris: Editions André Bonne, 1949), 102.
10. Daniel Chénet, *Qui a sauvé l'Afrique?* (Paris: L'Elan, 1949), 3.
11. Archives Nationales du Républic Gabonaise, "Le Point de la situation générale au Gabon en 1940," Carton 1557, Dossier A.
12. Charles de Gaulle, *The Complete War Memoirs,* 107; Chenet, *Qui a sauvé l'Afrique*; Robert Bourgi, *Le Général de Gaulle et l'Afrique Noire* (Abidjan: Nouvelles Editions Africaines, 1980), 52.
13. ACCCI, note on stocks of goods awaiting shipment at the port of Abidjan, dd. 13 July 1940, Carton 20, Dossier 9.
14. de Gaulle, *The Complete War Memoirs,* 111.
15. Bourgi, *Le Général de Gaulle,* 53.
16. Interview 93.
17. Bourgi, *Le Général de Gaulle,* 53.
18. Edmond Louveau, *"Au Bagne": entre les griffes de Vichy et de la milice,* 17.
19. Ibid., 21–31.
20. Jean-Noel Vincent, *Les Forces français libres en Afrique: 1940–1943* (Paris: Ministère de l'Armée de Terre, Service Historique, 1983), 47–48.
21. SHAT, Centre de Documentation.
22. Interview 40.
23. *La Côte d'Ivoire Française* 12 July 1940.
24. Interview 108.
25. William B. Cohen, *Rulers of Empire: The French Colonial Service in Africa* (Stanford, Calif.: Hoover Institution Press, 1971), 158–59.
26. For the best account of the Dakar fiasco, see John Watson's 1940 report, *Echec à Dakar, septembre 1940,* trans. Daniel Martin (Paris: Laffont, 1968).
27. SHAT, "Rapport annuel de l'Etat Major, 3ème Bureau, Troupes du groupe de l'AOF, 1940," op. cit.
28. Ibid.
29. Myron Echenberg, "Tragedy at Thiaroye," 113.
30. Interview 38.
31. ACCCI, law on assistance to insolvent European and native citizens, Carton 55.

32. SHAT, "Rapport annuel de l'Etat Major, 3ème Bureau, Troupes du groupe de l'AOF, 1940," op. cit.

33. Ibid.

34. ANCI, annual report of the governor, 1941, Carton 6954, Dossier XXIX–3–5.

35. ANCI, Carton 2858, Dossier IV–44/11.

36. ANCI, Carton 6956, Dossier XXIX–3–7. Also Jean-Noël Loucou, "La deuxième guerre mondiale et ses effets en Côte d'Ivoire," *Annales d'historie de l'université d'Abidjan* 8, ser, 1, 182.

37. *Journal officiel de l'Afrique Occidentale Française*, 1939, 1941. Refer to law of 19 April 1939, published 27 May 1939 and law of 22 August 1939, published 23 September 1939.

38. Jacques Richard-Molard, *Afrique Occidentale Française*, 166. Similarly, Michel Devéze, *La France d'outre-mer: De l'empire colonial à l'union française, 1938–1947* (Paris: Librairie Hachette, 1948), 22.

39. ANCI, Carton 850, Dossier XI–50–38.

40. ANCI, Carton 425, Dossier XII–49/8, monthly political report, Man, September 1942.

41. ANCI, Carton 3204, Dossier XVIII–18/8.

42. Interview 35.

43. ANCI, Carton 5355, Dossier XV–4/12.

44. ANCI, Carton 5874, Dossier XVII–15–14.

45. ANCI, Carton 2871, Dossier IV–48–7.

46. National Archives, Washington D.C., 851t.00/47, "Economic Situation on the Ivory Coast," undated but the text suggests it was written in the spring of 1942.

47. Interview 34.

48. *La Côte d'Ivoire Chrétienne* (October 1942).

49. Du Gard, *La Carte impériale*, 105.

50. ANCI, Carton 9235, Dossier VI–28/19.

51. Hubert Deschamps, *Roi de la brousse; mémoires d'autres mondes* (Paris: Berger–Levrault, 1975), 238.

52. Du Gard, *La Carte impériale*, 137.

53. SHAT, "Rapport annuel de l'Etat Major, 3ème Bureau, Troupes du groupe de l'AOF, 1940," op. cit.

54. Général Nyo, "Le problème de nos cadres africains," *Tropiques*, 54, no. 385 (June 1956), 33–40.

55. Du Gard, *La Carte impériale*, 137.

56. SHAT, "Rapport annuel de l'Etat Major, 3ème Bureau, Troupes du groupe de l'AOF, 1940," op. cit.

57. Ibid.

58. ANCI, Carton 426, Dossier XII–49/22.

59. Chénet, *Qui a sauvé l'Afrique*, 130.

60. SHAT, "Rapport annuel de l'Etat Major, 3ème Bureau, Troupes du groupe de l'AOF, 1940," op. cit.

61. Interview 57.

62. Joachim Bony, "La Côte d'Ivoire sous la colonisation française et le prélude à l'émancipation, 1920–1947: Genèse d'une nation," Ph.D. diss. Université de Paris I (1980), 747.

63. ANCI, copy of letter from Philippe Yacé, Dossier 2234.

64. Interview 9.

65. Interview 15.

66. Interview 26.

7

Changing Partners:
From Pétain to de Gaulle

A Little War in the Levant

AS A RESULT OF THE COLLAPSE of the Ottoman Empire in 1918, France was awarded a mandate over Syria and Lebanon. The status of these territories notwithstanding, France came swiftly to regard them as inviolate parts of its empire. The fall of France in 1940 only served to harden its resolve to maintain authority in the Middle East. Indeed, in the spring of 1940, despite the disastrous campaign in Belgium, units of the *Tirailleurs Sénégalais* were transferred to the Army of the Levant. It consisted of approximately 20,000 soldiers, 14,000 of whom were North African *tirailleurs* and 4,000 *Tirailleurs Sénégalais*.[1] In 1941 the Allies faced a problem of great complexity. Which France was the legitimate "protector" of Syria and Lebanon? The empire was in disarray. Indochina was occupied by Japan. French Equatorial Africa had opted for the Free French. The Vichy regime retained control of North Africa, the West Indian possessions, the AOF, and, under the watchful eye of the British navy, Madagascar, Eritrea, Somalia, and the Levant. The point was that, for the Allies, Vichy France remained technically neutral.

Immediately after the collapse of France, Admiral Andrew Cunningham on behalf of the British and his counterpart Admiral Godefroy on behalf of the French agreed that vessels of the French Mediterranean Fleet should be given sanctuary in the Egyptian port of Alexandria. It soon became clear, however, that the French Naval High Command had decided to follow Pétain. One of the more bizarre gentlemen's agreements of the war was reached: Since Vichy France was "neutral," the French ships would be allowed to remain docked in Alexandria. They were, such was the fiction, merely immobilized there by a lack of fuel, and their "neutral" officers and crews would have their salaries paid by the British government and their movements, accordingly, supervised by the British navy. [2] With this pattern of accommodation established, French administrators in Syria and Lebanon, also firmly in the Vichy camp, nonetheless agreed to be "neutral," or in other words to give no support, moral or material, to Germany. The volatility of the situation, and the dangers inherent in it, were later described by Edward Spears, Winston Churchill's hand-picked liaison officer with de Gaulle and the Free French:

> That the French ships, which he [Cunningham] allowed to use Vichy codes, transmitted information from the Levant States was anything but helpful to our cause, but this Cunningham refused to recognize. He also allowed sailors on leave from the Vichy ships to spend their leave periods in the Levant. This was taken advantage of to use the white-hot hostility of naval officers to stoke up anti-British feeling in the Lebanon and Syria, and was besides a considerable security risk, as information concerning our fleet and troop movements certainly reached Vichy from Alexandria. [3]

If the situation was an extremely complex one for the British, it was an intolerable one for de Gaulle. The general saw Africa as the next battle to be fought and won. He reflected upon the importance of the empire and, as a true son of France, saw England as well as Germany as a threat:

> To take part in the Battle of Africa with French forces and territories was to bring back, as it were, a fragment of France into the war. It was to defend her possessions directly against the enemy. It was, as far as possible, to deflect England—and perhaps one day America—from the temptation to make sure of them on their own account, for their fighting needs and for their advantage. It was, lastly, to wrench Free France free from exile and install her in full sovereignty on national territory. [4]

De Gaulle did not speak from a position of strength. Other than the AEF, Tahiti, and New Caledonia, the overseas territories had failed to rally to his cause. His one success had been the conquest of Eritrea. The campaign began in late March 1941. On April 7, Massawa was taken and 4,000 men captured in the attack. Another 10,000 surrendered. Among his troops were elements of the Foreign Legion who had rallied to him, and *tirailleurs* from the camps in AEF. The latter included, in fact, two artillery batteries which had originated in the AOF. Their commander was the same Laurent-Champrosay, now a lieutenant-colonel, who had led *tirailleurs* from Upper Volta to the Gold Coast in July 1940. [5]

More action, military action, was needed to reestablish the early momentum of de Gaulle's Free French. They had to justify their other name, the Fighting French. The Levant was the obvious arena. In the belief that the Vichy forces there, commanded by General Dentz, would rally to his cause, de Gaulle worked feverishly to convince the war cabinet in London to launch an Anglo-French invasion. This is not the place to attempt to untangle the complicated web of personal animosities, diverse military and political strategies, misinformation, and general inertia which characterized the months of intrigue and indecision leading up to the events of June 1941. The Nazi-backed, but unsuccessful, Rashid Ali revolt in Iraq in May was perhaps the decisive factor in Churchill's decision to act. On 8 June, British, Australian, and Free French units entered Syria and Lebanon. That same day, General Georges Catroux, de Gaulle's representative in Cairo, declared Syria and Lebanon "sovereign and independent," their new status to be guaranteed by the British. [6]

The Free French contingent in the invasion of the Levant included, again, *tirailleurs* from the AEF and Laurent-Champrosay's AOF artillery batteries. [7] They found themselves confronting fellow *Tirailleurs Sénégalais*, soldiers in regiments under Vichy command. Many of these had been transferred to the Levant from North Africa without ever having seen combat in France. They drilled and they guarded installations, finding little difference in their daily routines from those they had known in training in the AOF. Few of them had a clear understanding of the nature and depth of the rift between Pétainists and Gaullists. When the Allies invaded, they obeyed their officers and fired their first shots for Vichy France. Frenchmen found themselves fighting Frenchmen, Africans fighting Africans. To this day, many ex-*tirailleurs* are still confused about who was who and what was what. One Senoufo combatant, Namble Silué, recalls his surprise:

> I was in the 2nd *bataillon de marche*, from 1939 to 1941. . . . There was war—against de Gaulle. They said to us, "Tomorrow we go to Damascus for maneuvers." De Gaulle's men attacked us. The Camerounians attacked us. We were amazed because they weren't Germans. They were black. Why were they attacking us? They had never told us we were fighting against the French. De Gaulle? I had never heard his name before. [8]

The invasion of the Levant did, however, make the name of de Gaulle one familiar to many of the *tirailleurs*.

A countryman of Namble Silué, a blacksmith from near Korhogo, had fought in Belgium. He was transferred to the Levant in late 1940.

He had a firm, if totally incorrect, idea about the leader of the Free French:

> We won in Belgium, but there was no parade, no fête for that. There they said we'd won but the war wasn't over completely. Then they told us that the Germans were to be found on the other side—in Lebanon. My regiment left. We boarded the boat in Bordeaux for Lebanon. We arrived and got off in Beirut. I spent one year in Beirut. Pétain was the French leader. After Pétain had said that the men were tired and he would lower the flag, de Gaulle said that he didn't want that—to stop the war. So he went to the English for help against the Germans. For de Gaulle was a nephew of the English. His mother was English and his father was French. So he went to his family to get them to help France. Thus the English troops came to help de Gaulle chase the Germans out of France. The English were good boys, stronger than we were—they fired more than we did. [9]

Tuo Mahon's interpretation of the nature of Gaullism was clearly shared by many of his comrades as they tried to unravel the mystery of de Gaulle. Who was he? Why was he fighting the French? The Senoufo *tirailleur*, like others of peasant background, sought an answer in traditional terms. That de Gaulle embraced the Allied cause could only be explained with reference to descent, to lineage, to family. One Senoufo chief, Navaga Ouattara, arrived at an all-encompassing interpretation from what he had learned from veterans returning to his village, Siliekaha. "After the defeat of Marshal Pétain," he said, "the Germans took Paris. De Gaulle's mother was English and his maternal uncle was American. That's why the English and the Americans helped the French." [10] To appreciate the full force of this comment, the reader is reminded of the prevalence of matrifiliation among the Senoufo.

Ouattama Soro of the Ninth DIC describes the action he saw. It will be noted that he was led to believe that resistance to the Allied invasion was ordered by the Germans rather than the Vichy French.

> We left for the Levant. We did exercises to teach us how to fight a war. The Germans had already taken France by then and de Gaulle had formed the 8th Regiment. That regiment wanted to cross the Levant. The general of the Germans didn't want them to do that. That's where the war started. Our Colonel Barreau who commanded us told us this. The Germans had occupied all of France except for the Levant. They telephoned that the English wanted to come through. The German general said not to let them pass. From the moment of his birth [the General said], de Gaulle has never seen the evil things he will see today. . . .

> Our colonel told us that when the English come—don't shoot. They came on foot. . . . There was a young Yacouba called De Robert. He saw an English plane overhead. He fired first. All of us knew that he had done wrong. He fired, but he didn't get it. Then the battle started. It was Marshal Pétain who commanded the French. We fought the English for thirteen days. . . . We saw Africans, but the English had captured them the first day. There was even one from Korhogo. They were mixed up with the whites. We fired on each other. [11]

The Allied invasion had been launched on 8 June 1941. On the eighteenth, Damascus was encircled and the Allies advised Dentz to evacuate his forces. Three days later, after heavy fighting, Free French forces took the city. Word had already reached Cairo on 19 June that the Vichy authorities in the Levant were ready to discuss an armistice. [12] Negotiations opened, and on 9 July, Dentz asked for the terms. Two days later, he accepted them. On 14 July, the armistice was approved by Vichy and signed by a British commission. It had been a little war. No great battles had been fought. Less than one thousand men had been killed in action on both sides. Nonetheless, it was an important victory for the Allies, who achieved their objective of denying Syrian air bases to the Germans.

Which Side Are You On, Brother?

The British armistice commission had included only one representative of the Free French. De Gaulle himself was in Brazzaville during the negotiations. He returned to Cairo on 20 July. Spears, who was present at the time, vividly described the general's reaction.

> He was very pleasant with me personally, but on the question of the Armistice terms and his relationship with us, his attitude could scarcely have been worse. . . . He gave his fury with Catroux full rein. He accused him of being prepared to accept anything at our hands, hypnotized as he was by his longing to become High Commissioner of the Levant. [13]

Accusing Great Britain of usurping France's authority over the territories of the Levant, de Gaulle's anger appears to have been generated by one article of the armistice in particular. Vichy troops would be given the free choice of whether to rally to de Gaulle or to be repatriated. [14] Apparently, General Sir Henry Wilson had agreed virtually to deny Free French officers access to the Vichy forces. Spears thought that Wilson had been

Alphonse Dionkla

convinced, based on the general failure of French troops stationed in England at the time of the fall of France to rally to de Gaulle, that the appeal would in any event have little effect and result only in pitched battles between the two factions which Wilson's men would have the unpleasant duty to suppress. [15]

The fact of the matter was that de Gaulle had hoped to gain large numbers of new recruits to his cause from among the defeated Vichy Army of the Levant. Massive defections to the Free French did not, however, occur. Only one-third changed sides. [16] De Gaulle, moreover, wanted to establish Free French control over the Levant, for it could provide him with a more convenient base for continuing the struggle than could French Equatorial Africa. For once, de Gaulle found considerable support for his views among the British civil authorities in the Middle East. After some tense days of direct negotiations with Oliver Lyttelton, minister of state at Cairo, a new interpretation of the armistice convention was arrived at. Free French forces were, after all, to be given access to the interned Vichy troops. It was agreed that,

> the choice—Repatriation or Rally!—must be the free choice of each individual. This liberty of choice can only mean that the Free French authorities will be permitted to explain their point of view to the personnel concerned with the same completeness and the same liberty accorded to the Vichy authorities by the fact of the presence of Vichy officers and noncomissioned officers now with their troops. [17]

Six weeks were allotted for the two sides to present their respective cases to the men. The British army was to serve as the referee, in principle to ensure an atmosphere of fair play wherein the rules would be scrupulously observed. The desired procedure was elaborately detailed. Only one senior Vichy officer and a noncommissioned officer would be allowed to enter a camp while the Free French delegation was present. British officers would be stationed in each camp to ensure that all Vichy soldiers had ample opportunity and time to study the documents presented by the Free French. Choices were to be signaled to a British officer only and never while the men were at assembly in the presence of their own officers or that of the commanding officer. The scenario was an improbable one. It is small wonder that the Ivoirien soldiers, like most *tirailleurs*, found the situation virtually incomprehensible. Namble Silué was one of those who "joined" de Gaulle. He saw the event as yet another *rite du passage*:

> We fought for 15 days. They captured us. They were stronger than we were. Let us not speak of the dead—too many. De Gaulle came

to take us out of prison. He said he had need of blacks. He said we were now his soldiers. We changed our uniforms. Put on his uniforms. No, no one asked the question why we had been fighting each other. We asked ourselves: Who are we with now? The old ones or the new? We didn't even know who we were with at that moment. We went to Djibouti then. It was better with de Gaulle than with the old regiment because in this second war we got a bit of money and new uniforms. Our old leaders were prisoners of war—the others had run away. The French officers had fled—the African ranks were there. Where could they escape to? The behavior and the words of the first officers were not the same as the new ones. The second told us all the secrets. Be careful! Prepare yourselves! If there was a lot of the enemy in a town, they would tell us. The first weren't like that at all—everything came as a surprise. [18]

In their attempt to attract men to the Free French cause, de Gaulle's officers were at a disadvantage. Time was short, and their Vichy counterparts had ample opportunity to explain to the *tirailleurs* that if they stayed loyal to Pétain they would be sent home. In most cases the choice, when presented at all, was offered as one between personalities rather than philosophies, between fighting on or going home. The *tirailleur* Alphonse Dionkla of Man was among the half of his unit to remain loyal to Vichy.

They gathered us in a town and asked those *Sénégalais* who were volunteers to continue the fight. They placed two tables in front. One for de Gaulle—one for Pétain. Then they asked those who were for Pétain to go to his table, and those who were for de Gaulle to go to the other. I chose Pétain because I wanted to go home. . . . There were small meetings just with our officers and NCOs, who told us if we chose Pétain we could go home. . . . Most of the Africans wanted to go to France and then home, and they chose Pétain. Most of us were for de Gaulle, but because we were so far from home, we were obliged to choose Pétain. Others chose de Gaulle because the Germans, most of them, wanted to continue the war, and they were very bad, especially with Africans. I learned this from my brother who was at the front. . . . They killed them. All that hurt me. Most of the NCOs stayed with de Gaulle and about one-half of the regiment. [19]

Other *tirailleurs* in the Levant were never offered a choice. Their officers made the decision for them. Nanga Soro was one of these:

The Germans had occupied all of France except the Levant. The radio told us that. We understood. . . . I was with the French when de Gaulle came into camp. I didn't know who he was. He took us by force and dressed us. He fired on us first—some were hurt and some were dead. He took us like prisoners. We all changed uniforms—all the French changed too. We said nothing. We changed. [20]

Ouattama Soro was another *tirailleur* who opted for Pétain in the hope— unfulfilled in his case—of returning home.

> We had refused to be with de Gaulle because we were with Pétain. When de Gaulle formed his troops to cross the Levant, he wanted to take us all to fight with him in Djibouti against the Germans. We didn't want to be with de Gaulle, and it was for that reason that we fought de Gaulle. I was on Pétain's side, and I stayed in camp, because the French told us that those who went to de Gaulle would continue the war and those who stayed with Pétain would have leave and then go home. After our leave, de Gaulle won in the Levant. We all became men of de Gaulle and continued the war. Pétain and de Gaulle were really the same thing. It was the *Tirailleurs Sénégalais* who just did not understand that. [21]

Life with Charles

Only some 6,000 officers and men of the Levant forces were won over by de Gaulle. Among them were 1,500 *tirailleurs* from the AOF who, by choice or happenstance, ended up in the Free French army. Many in time became part of the famous First *Division Française Libre* (1st DFL). [22] The relatively small number of converts does not appear to have been a spectacular success for the cause of Free France. Yet, for the Ivoirien soldier, whether he "rallied" or chose repatriation, the name of de Gaulle assumed epic proportions. Many of them actually saw him when he made what was described by an unsympathetic British observer as a "royal progress" through the Levant in late July of 1941. [23] His great height and enormous presence deeply affected the men in the camps. Here at least was a victorious Frenchman and one who certainly looked the part. Tuo Mahan, just before he was repatriated to the Côte d'Ivoire, remembered seeing the general:

> De Gaulle was there [Beirut]. There we paraded. Then they said we could go home to our villages. De Gaulle was the pivot of the war. *Un grand garçon, un beau gars.* He walked everywhere to see—to meet his soldiers. *Vraiment un garçon!* It was de Gaulle himself who said we could go home to our villages. "Africans have suffered enough—and you are very tired, thus you can go home. But those who wish to may stay with me." No palaver. We were very tired so

we came back. All of our regiment returned. The next day de Gaulle
came to our regiment—it was there and then that he said we were
very fatigued. That whoever wanted to leave could do so and those
who wanted to stay could also do so. It was there I got the combatant's medal. I thanked de Gaulle. Our commander interpreted
directly what de Gaulle was saying. We decided among ourselves to
return home.[24]

De Gaulle seemed to have a profound effect on men who saw him
for the first time. Henri Boileau recounted how he escaped to England.
"In 1939 I joined the air force," he said.

After June 1940, like many of my colleagues, I was put in the *Jeunesse
de la Montagne.* Three times I tried to escape from the *Jeunesse.* The
third time I was caught, they took me to court. I was given the choice
of joining the Armistice Army or going to jail. My lawyer told me
not to be so stupid and sign the paper "enlisting" in the army. He
said you can't do anything in jail. So I joined the army. After the German occupation of the free zone [November 1942], my colonel called
three of us in. He said that with our records and backgrounds, the
Germans would either shoot us or send us to concentration camps.
He burnt our dossiers right there and told us to get out—to escape.

Boileau, after escaping to Spain, somehow got to England, where he
met de Gaulle. "I was put into an interrogation center for fifteen days,"
he continued.

I didn't think I'd ever get out but one time an officer whom I knew
came by to look us over. He was from de Gaulle's office. He told
me not to worry, he would get me out. Next day I was taken to see
de Gaulle. He was so tall, and I was the same size I am today [5
feet 2 inches]. He looked at me. You see, they weren't sure how much
of a communist I was. They weren't sure if I was all communist, part
communist, or what I was. De Gaulle said, "Here there are no Jews,
no Freemasons, no communists. There are only Frenchmen." He
shook my hand, and I became a member of the BCR, the *Bureau
Central des Renseignements.* I was parachuted several times into
France. Oh yes, then he said, "We are all Jews. We are all Freemasons.
We are all Communists. But we are all French."[25]

For West African *tirailleurs* the legend of de Gaulle was born in the
Levant. In time it would spread even among those who remained in
the Vichy forces. Soma Kone, who served in Algeria, reflected on
the matter.

I knew de Gaulle, but I was not in his army. I was in the other French army. . . . Every once in a while we would be given news about Pétain, not de Gaulle. Later I knew he was a man—a good soldier. Later they said about him that he killed many Germans. Germans who had killed Frenchmen. Without de Gaulle, there would be no France. [26]

The *Tirailleurs Sénégalais* of the AEF, who had found themselves *chez de Gaulle* in 1940, had their own version of his origins. A correspondent for *La France Libre,* the monthly publication of the Free French in London, reported that one *tirailleur* sergeant told him the "black legend of de Gaulle":

De Gaulle was a corporal and had been dead for five years. He was a corporal, in an African village, with much seniority in rank: being a *tirailleur* gives one considerable power. Being dead is also an advantage: one who is dead can do things which a living man cannot. Thus, Corporal de Gaulle from the depths of his grave, sleeping for five years, heard talk that a German corporal, whose name was unknown, had taken Paris. Filled with indignation, Corporal de Gaulle rose from his tomb and said, "Now, I am a general. *Attention!* The war is going to begin." [27]

It is important to note that the correspondent, Denis Saurat, commented that the *tirailleur* sergeant had not only an intelligent face but a great sense of humor!

De Gaulle's fame continued to spread among African soldiers. For West Africans it started in the Levant and North Africa but soon reached the AOF itself. Veteran Zie Soro spent his war in the Côte d'Ivoire, but his vision of de Gaulle reads like a fragment of an ancient saga.

They told us that the French had been beaten by the Germans and that de Gaulle had run off to the English. De Gaulle asked the English to help him regain the land of his father, and the English said, "Wait. We will tell the Americans, and the Americans who are with the English will fight." We heard this through talk—rumor. No, we never talked about why de Gaulle went to England. At first everything came by letter. Then the Americans and the English started to help de Gaulle in the war. Then de Gaulle himself came to Abidjan. He came to tell us that we were going to fight, and after this war is over, there will never be another war in this world. After the war ended, he sent us a letter telling us that the war had ended. Our colonel had the paper. After he read it he called us all together and told us. [28]

Following the departure of those soldiers who had taken the repatriation option, the approximately 1,500 *Tirailleurs Sénégalais* who remained with the Free French were regrouped into *bataillons de marche*. Initially, they were used mainly on guard and police duties, to remind the Syrians and Lebanese that the change of regime had not weakened France's resolve to maintain her presence in the Levant. The *tirailleurs* appeared not to have appreciated their new role. Serious disciplinary problems arose. The French blamed this on two factors, first the supposed effect of an incessant barrage of German radio propaganda warning the African troops that de Gaulle was preparing to turn them over to the Germans, and second and more probably, the insufficient numbers of European officers and NCOs.

There were at least two incidents of near mutiny, the result of Berlin Radio's report that General de Larminat had handed over an African battalion to the Germans. Despite the total implausibility of the broadcast, it is a measure of the *tirailleurs'* lack of confidence in their new officers that they took it most seriously. The First Battalion in Damascus balked at being loaded into trucks, although assured this was for a training exercise. They said they preferred to remain on foot. A company of the Second Battalion, comprising mainly men from the AOF, ignored their officers and set off to join their comrades of the First. Their officers had no choice but to follow. "We don't want to be delivered," their men told them. [29] In the summer of 1942, the Free French generals, Catroux, de Larminat, and Koenig, preparing to move all but six battalions of the *tirailleurs* from the Levant to North Africa, expressed reservations about their reliability. De Larminat was particularly troubled about the unrest:

> This is happening because these troops are no longer in a colonial war. They are armed and trained to the teeth. Paternalism is no more. We have in fact created gladiators with a powerful armament. If we want them to keep their heads, we must have quality leadership as well as arms. [30]

The generals, in fact, had little to fear. The West African soldiers showed considerable zeal whenever anything like action was called for. Spears, who in February 1942 became the first British ambassador to Syria and Lebanon, swiftly developed a strong distaste for the African troops. He considered them trigger-happy, ever ready to oblige their French commanders by putting down civilian disturbances and not averse to carrying out executions of Frenchmen condemned as traitors. He catalogued what he described as an "avalanche of horror." He cited British military reports that French armored cars, manned by *Sénégalais*, had charged and fired into an unarmed crowd in Tripoli, killing at least eleven people. "English and Lebanese kept coming into the Legation," he added, "reporting the presence of Senegalese soldiers, some in armoured cars, some in lorries, some patrolling the streets, apparently intent on dispersing any crowd or gathering."[31] By mid-1942, then, the Africans seemed to have once more identified totally with the French army. Even among Muslim soldiers, there was little sympathy for their Arab co-religionists.

Few of the Ivoirien veterans interviewed in 1985–86 spoke of this period. For those who had been in the Levant, the events of 1942 were completely overshadowed by those of 1945. On 5 May of that year, the *Tirailleurs Sénégalais* ruthlessly put down a Syrian revolt occasioned by French proposals for a new Franco-Syrian treaty. Donipoho Sekongo of the 17th BM fought in Damascus. "We got on the tank," he remembered.

> Four Africans and one white. The three other Africans were killed. There was only me and the white left. I wasn't calm. They said we had to go on, but you couldn't think about anything then. We were in a line—*Sénégalais*—all in a line. The white drove. I was alone. The others were dead in the tank. We couldn't stop to take their bodies off. Two people have to fire a cannon. One loads and the other fires. So we couldn't use the cannon—just the rifle and the machine gun. We kept going just to the village. We fired until about 4 o'clock. Then we stopped at Damascus. Then we took our bayonets at night and starting slashing. They had subterranean houses. In the night you don't shoot. We entered the houses and killed everyone found there. You cut their heads off. These underground houses—they were afraid, they had hidden in them group by group. There they had no defense. We killed them all. Killed them like ants. Everyone—all the men. Not the women or the very small ones.[32]

Namongo Ouattara, who was in the same action, was somewhat more introspective:

> In 1945, the Lebanese wanted their independence, but the French didn't want to give it to them. So the war began again. We started shooting in Damascus. The firing was crazy. Then we really bombed Damascus—destroying so many things. Yes, there were problems about being a Muslim. There was no time to pray, but I shot. The houses there were leveled. Anyway the rebels were all mixed up—they weren't just Muslims. It did bother me, but it was an obligation. Anyway, I didn't know what it was to be independent—to be free. In those days I didn't know. But when I came home and listened to Houphouët, then I realized that they had been right.[33]

In 1945, it is clear that no sense of what is now known as Third World solidarity existed among the *tirailleurs* in the Levant. It would take the subsequent mistreatment afforded them by French authorities, upon their return to West Africa, to politicize them. Yet no matter how bitter the Ivoirien *anciens combattants* became, the name of de Gaulle continues to evoke pride in them. Tenuous though the connection might be, they had all somehow been soldiers of de Gaulle.

North Africa: December 1941–June 1943

A few *Tirailleurs Sénégalais* saw their first action in the ranks of the Free French in the little war in the Levant. Many more would be involved in the great campaigns in North Africa, where they faced the seasoned Panzer divisions of General Erwin Rommel. As 1942 opened, soldiers from both the AEF and AOF constituted, as elsewhere, the largest element in de Gaulle's forces in North Africa. [34]

The First *Brigade Française Libre* (BFL), commanded by General de Larminat, was moved from Syria to Egypt on Christmas Day 1941. From there, they were deployed in the Western Desert under command of the British Eighth Army. They first saw action on 17 January at Halfaya, when the Germans and Italians in Cyrenaica were forced back on the El-Agheila Line. The story of the subsequent attacks and counterattacks for the control of Cyrenaica are beyond the scope of this study. They are treated in detail by, for example, Michael Carver. [35] On 1 February, the British were forced to pull back to the Gazala Line. The First BFL, 3,600 strong, took up positions at Bir Hakeim, the southernmost point in that line. It was the same day that Rommel launched an attack that brought the advance troops of the *Afrika Korps* to within 60 miles of Bir Hakeim.

The approximately 1,000 AOF *tirailleurs* in that brigade, of the 2nd and 7th battalions, found themselves part of probably the most diverse group of Francophone soldiers ever gathered together in one unit. The First included men who arrived in England to join de Gaulle during the summer of 1940, foreign legionnaires who had participated in the Norwegian campaign, a marine battalion who had joined the Free French in Cyprus, another battalion composed of men from Tahiti and New Caledonia, the Second *Bataillon de marche* from Chad, an artillery group widely recruited from the colonies and the *métropole*, engineers, and finally, a special battalion of marine sharpshooters. The men of the brigade were equipped with French arms commandeered in Syria, including the outmoded 75mm heavy gun. The brigade's own story has been excellently chronicled in the official history of the First *Division Française Libre*, of which it became part. [36]

The First Brigade dug in at Bir Hakeim. On 26 May, Rommel launched the third and greatest of his counteroffensives in the Western Desert. The Gazala Line disintegrated. Cut off from British lines, inadequately supplied by airdrops, pitted against vastly superior enemy ground and aerial forces, the First BFL fought off attacks by the Italian Ariete Division. On 2 June, Rommel replaced the Italians with Germans. The First continued to hold out, and on 6 June, Rommel was obliged to send the Fifteenth Panzer Division to reinforce the troops assaulting Koenig's positions. Against such odds, on 8 June, Koenig's forces finally had to give ground. The British attempt, on 9 June, to send reinforcements failed. On 10 June, *Afrika Korps* assault troops overran the French positions. That night, under cover of darkness, Koenig led the survivors of the First through German lines to rejoin the Allies, leaving behind less than 100 men too badly wounded to travel. During these months of battle, he had lost more than 800 men, but the defense of Bir Hakeim had played a major part in holding up the German offensive and allowing the British to reinforce El Alamein. [37] No figures have been found for the number of *tirailleur* dead. It was one of their finest hours, and it is a matter of considerable regret that all attempts to locate veterans of Bir Hakeim in the Côte d'Ivoire proved unsuccessful.

While the First Brigade was under siege at Bir Hakeim, a second Free French brigade, under General Cazaud, had been formed in the Levant and moved to the Western Desert. It arrived at Gambut, near Tobruk, where the Eighth Army was bracing itself for Rommel's attack. Koenig and the survivors of the First BFL joined their sister brigade. [38] On 18 June, Gambut fell to Rommel and the Free French joined the British in the withdrawal to the Egyptian frontier. On 21 June, Tobruk fell. On 24 June, Rommel attacked Egypt. For the events of the next four months, the reader is again referred to Carver's study, as Axis and Allied forces attacked and counterattacked in the Egyptian desert between Mersa Matruh and El Alamein. Finally, on the night of 22 October, the British Eighth Army moved into position for the assault, which opened the next day. By the beginning of November, the Axis forces were in full retreat. Though numerically insignificant in the Allied forces, the two Free French brigades, which included three *tirailleur* battalions, nevertheless participated in some of the fiercest fighting and acquitted themselves honorably.

A share in the victories of the Western Desert belongs to this hodgepodge collection of French escapees and colonial conscripts and volunteers. Their participation gained much needed respectability and respect for the cause of what was now called Fighting France, and helped to some degree to eradicate the memories of the collapse in 1940.[39] The stage was set for Operation Torch. The triumph in the Western Desert had opened the way for the Allied landings in North Africa.

Operation Torch

While *Tirailleurs Sénégalais* were fighting with the Free French in the Western Desert, there were thousands of them in units stationed in the Maghreb who still remained loyal to Vichy. Operation Torch, the Allied invasion of North Africa, was launched in the early hours of 8 November 1942. American and British forces landed in Algiers, Oran, and Casablanca. Simultaneously, President Franklin Roosevelt sent a communiqué to Marshal Pétain informing him of the landings and appealing for his cooperation. "I need not tell you," wrote the President, "that the ultimate and greater aim is the liberation of France and its Empire from the Axis yoke. In so doing we provide automatically for the security of the Americas."

That the message emanated from Washington rather than London is significant. Churchill and Roosevelt had agreed, granted the chronic suspicions of British designs upon French imperial possessions, that it would be politic to keep the British as much in the background as possible. In any case, the gambit was unsuccessful. Pétain replied the same day:

> I have always declared that we would defend our Empire if it were attacked; you should have known that we would defend it against any aggressor, whoever he might be. You should have known that I would keep my word. We are attacked, and we defend ourselves. This is the order that I give.[40]

It remains a matter of great controversy whether Pétain did secretly give the Vichy High Commissioner in Algiers, Admiral François Darlan, discretion to negotiate with the invaders.[41] In any case, the hope that French troops would welcome the Allies as liberators was quickly dispelled. Most French officers ordered their men to defend Algeria and Morocco. It was the turn of the Vichy-led *Tirailleurs Sénégalais* regiments to find themselves in action. Among the French forces in Algiers who engaged the invaders on the morning of 8 November were several companies of *Sénégalais*. They had a singular triumph in capturing an American battalion led by Lt. Col. Edwin Swenson and holding it for several hours until the order to cease fire was issued.[42] This "victory," indeed the entire operation, only accentuated the singular confusion about what was going on in North Africa. One *tirailleur*, Ditiemba Silué, believed that de Gaulle himself was with the assault forces:

> At Casablanca there were the American ships offshore. Yes, there still were only the men from the Côte d'Ivoire. We were at Casablanca eighteen days before the Americans landed. There were many American planes. De Gaulle and the American officers arrived. We built fortifications and started to fire. When the American boats landed, we fired on them. Then the Americans fired back. Many, many Africans died. When de Gaulle descended from the airplane, he unfurled the flag and waved the flag in front of us—the Africans. We stopped shooting. No, the French were not there. When the shooting had started they ran away. De Gaulle descended from the plane and said: Cease firing. We stopped shooting. The officers had fired too. When de Gaulle was in the plane, he had called our captain to tell him that it was not the Germans landing, but these are the Americans who are going to help us. Our officer was Colonel Chretien, the commandant. Of course we were happy when the shooting stopped. There were so many dead. [43]

De Gaulle was, of course, not present during the invasion. The United States government had ruled out his participation for a series of complex political and strategic reasons which will not be discussed in any detail here. Suffice it to say that Roosevelt and his advisers felt de Gaulle was so unpopular with the North African military command—the Armistice Army of Africa, which continued to view him as a traitor and an English puppet—that his presence would greatly increase French resistance. Washington chose instead to support General Henri Giraud, recently escaped from a German prisoner of war camp. It was intended that Giraud accompany the first landing parties, but he did not arrive until 10 November. By that time, the Americans had been forced to deal with Darlan, who, with or without the authority of Pétain, ordered the end to all resistance on that same day. All resistance ceased as early as 7 A.M. on the 11th, the same day that German troops occupied Vichy France. On 13 November, Darlan met with General Eisenhower in Algiers. Henceforth, the French forces in Morocco and Algeria were to align themselves with the Allies. Fighting France now had a sizable army which was to be completely reequipped by the United States and Great Britain. Whatever the newly attached French officers thought about the transition, it proved to be an extremely popular change with the African troops. Senoufo Fonon Ganon had been impressed by the amphibious landing craft:

> We saw them come in a truck that walked on the water. *Formidable!* They were the second God. Those great *pirogues* on the water. They

were with us. Yes, I know at the beginning we were against them, but then we became like this [holding up two fingers tightly pressed together]! [44]

Guy Ahizi-Eliam had arrived in Casablanca the day before the landings. "The next morning," he recollected,

the American bombardment began. Lasted three or four days. We stayed in camp. We liked the Americans. They came and visited us and brought candy and cigarettes. Hard things to get. Most of our visitors were American blacks. [45]

Clearly the Americans made a great impression on the Ivoiriens. Tuo Nahon, whom we have already met, compared the Americans with the French, to the disadvantage of the latter:

No Frenchman ever invited us to join his family at home. Only the Americans. They had taken all our French uniforms away and given us American ones. They even gave us American food [that is, K rations]. They told us we were special now—and the same as they were. They—all of them—invited us to drink with them, go into town with them, to do everything with them. [46]

A group of Senoufo veterans interviewed in Guiembé recollected particularly the improvement in their small arms.

The war we fought—without the Americans, all of us would be dead. They gave us their guns—everything. The French guns only had five shots, then you'd have to reload. There were ten bullets in the American rifles. When the Americans saw our French rifles, they would look at it—tap it on something and it would break. They'd say, See that? It's no good. [47]

Gastronomic affairs, were by contrast, uppermost in the memory of Gnoumagai Soro, who arrived in Algeria in early 1943:

We continued to train. We got prepared along with the English and the Americans. We did have some contact with them—we would go in bars with them—have a drink together. The Americans were very nice. You would go to town with them—they bought food and we all ate it. Bread, sardines—those things that Arabs eat. We had contact with both black and white Americans. The blacks were the same as we were—they behaved the same as we did. [48]

Some of the many veterans of Guiembé

The Axis response to the successful invasion of Algeria and Morocco was swift. A rapid buildup of first German, then Italian troops in Tunisia occurred in mid-November. By 16 November, all Tunisia was occupied by Axis forces. The country became a bloody battleground as American, British, and Free French troops began the long, drawn-out campaign to clear North Africa of Axis forces. [49] By the spring of 1943, there were 60,000 French troops engaged in the Tunisian sector. [50] Given the rapid reorganization of French forces as units switched sides, it is not surprising that it is virtually impossible to identify West African *tirailleur* units with precision. [51] Table 4, however, lists two regiments of *Tirailleurs Sénégalais*, one colonial infantry division, and five *bataillons de marche* in which *tirailleurs* must also have been strongly represented. These units were in combat at various times during the next seven months. Fifteen thousand soldiers of the French were killed in the fighting. [52]

Namongo Silué of the Second Battalion was lucky to escape with his life. "In Tunisia," he remembered,

> we were against the Germans and the Italians. It was there that I got shot. I was shot in the knee. I also lost one finger, and I have a scar on my chest from when I fell. Yes, the Americans were there. We were all together. The war was harder there. The Germans had

Table 4
North African and Levant Campaigns of Free French Units
1941–1943*

Eritrea	Ethiopia	Syria	Libya	Tunisia
BM† 3	BM 4	BM 1	Bir Hacheim	BM 1
	BM 5	BM 2		BM 2
	with British	BM 3	BM 2	BM 4
	9th Army		BM 7 with the	BM 5
			1st BFL‡	BM 7
			Tobruk	13 RTS§
				15 RTS
			BM 6 with the	
			2nd BFL	43 RIC//
			With British 8th Army	
			BM 3	
			BM 4	
			El Alamein	
			BM 5	
			BM 6	
			BM 7	
			BM 8	

SOURCE: Bulletin Officiel du Ministère de la Guerre, Unités Combattantes des Campagnes

*In February 1943, all French units, including the African *bataillons de marche* in the region between Bardia and Tobruk, were regrouped into the First Division Français Libre (DFL) commanded by General de Larminat.

†BM=*Bataillon de Marche*
‡BFL=*Bataillon Française Libre*
§RTS=*Régiment des Tirailleurs Sénégalais*
//RIC=*Régiment d'Infanterie Coloniale*

seven generals and one other commanding the war. Finally he, the commander, escaped by plane. There were many tanks, not even the cannon balls could penetrate them. Bombs only penetrated a little. It was only mines that would turn them over. The mines were small, just lightly covered by sand. When a tank went over one of them, just slightly touching it, it would blow up. It was the first time we'd done that. There were French tanks too, but they were taken away by the Americans. It was in the desert. The first line were our tanks, the second line was the infantry. [53]

Namongo Silué's memory is accurate. Three days after the fighting in Medenine on 6 March, Hitler ordered Rommel home, not wishing to risk further his favorite general on the disintegrating Tunisian front.

Nanga Soro, who had fought as a Vichy *tirailleur* in the Levant, was now with the Free French in Tunisia. He reminisced about both campaigns. In the Levant, he recalled,

we had done no fighting, but the day the Germans were going to attack us, de Gaulle landed to push them back. Then he captured us because we had not been with him. They captured us and took off our French uniforms. They gave us English ones. We had an English rifle and cannon and American war vehicles. Then we all pushed the Germans back. . . . [In Tunisia] de Gaulle made us move a lot. . . . We attacked the Germans. We left in a group—at night— we spent three days without eating or drinking in a trench. We beat the Germans, but they were well hidden. After the battle, I was the one who guided the French so we could find our camp. I led them back to it. When we got back to camp, the captain said we could have some rest. He told us to go back to the third line. He was wrong. It was worse there than where we had been. We wanted to go back to the front line. . . . What I will never forget is the infinity of corpses—*Sénégalais* and French. I found some whose souls had not yet left them, but I knew they were going to die. You could not eat because of the smell of the bodies. The blood.

Nanga Soro was proud of the part he had played in saving lives. "There was a young man at Karok who was injured," he remembered.

I wanted to carry him, but the captain said no. I took him anyway and placed him in a trench until the nurses could get to him. After that, the captain was shot and I carried him, too. Then the lieutenant, who was a priest, was also wounded. We took them all to the hospital. They were all cured. That same day, the captain decorated me. This was in Tunis—against the Germans. We were there together with the French and the Americans. While we were fighting in Tunis, the

enemy had put barbed wire in front of us. Then they chased you
toward it and put another line of barbed wire behind. To escape from
them, you had to try to jump over it.

That he suffered nothing worse than an encounter with barbed wire
he attributed to the advice of his brother and the beneficence of God:

> I was not a volunteer—I was forced to go. No. There were no
> volunteers. I was working in the fields when they called me—they
> told me I had to go right away. I walked to Korhogo. . . . My elder
> brother died after his military service and then they called me [in
> 1939]. He had told me how to fight a war. He said to me that if
> you kill someone, you must never take money from his pocket or
> you will die there. I was not ready when I left. I did not have a fetish.
> But God is my fetish. I did not need a fetish. I counted on God. I
> left and nothing hurt me. My only wound came when I tried to jump
> over some barbed wire and one of the strands stuck in my knee. [54]

The last German forces in Tunisia surrendered on 13 May 1943. About
a quarter of a million Germans and Italians were taken prisoner. While
heavy fighting had led finally to the surrender of Tunisia, two relatively
minor operations had been carried out in other parts of Africa. Between
May 1942 and January 1943, British forces slowly established control
of Madagascar with the aid of a successful naval blockade and with
only token resistance from the Vichy authorities. On 8 January, the British
commander, Gen. Sir W. Platt, handed the island over to the Free French
High Commissioner, General Paul-Louis Le Gentilhomme. Meanwhile,
in French Somalia, forces loyal to Vichy still held out in November 1942.
The garrison consisted of six battalions of *Tirailleurs Sénégalais*, with
some artillery and aircraft support. On 28 November, Lieutenant-Colonel
Raynal and a third of the garrison crossed British lines and declared
themselves for de Gaulle. A month later, these men, with elements of
the British Kings Africa Rifles, reentered the colony. By the end of the
year, French Somalia was in the Free French camp. Yeo Mohoouo was
with the Free French forces, having been "taken by de Gaulle in the
Levant." He saw no action in Somalia but seems to have enjoyed the
experience:

> We liberated Somalia. We were mixed in with the French troops. My
> roommate was Sergeant Plevin. We were given American uniforms,
> everything, even guns—machine guns. We [first] went to Djibouti.
> Everyone was mixed up—British, Americans, Africans. It was better
> than the camp. We were free—we rode in cars mostly. The Americans
> were very good. They gave us a lot to drink. They were very con-

siderate to us. I was very happy with the Americans. In Somalia, we were the only African troops. . . . In Somalia, I was guarding the frontier. I did not fight. It was after we left that the war started. Thanks to us, Tunisia was freed. We were front line troops. [55]

Meanwhile, alone among France's African possessions, the AOF had quietly switched its allegiance without a shot being fired.

From its humble beginnings in the AEF in August 1940 to the final surrender of Axis forces in Tunisia in May 1943, the Free French movement had succeeded in winning the political and military struggle for the soul of France. By June 1943, Charles de Gaulle was the unquestioned leader of Free France and the French Empire. "Everyone knew France would reappear," he wrote. "Everyone wondered what France she would be." [56] Far from the action, the colonies of French West Africa would soon discover what the France of Charles de Gaulle had in store for them.

The Home Front

In the AOF, news of the Allied landings in North Africa took Boisson by surprise. Throughout the summer of 1942, both military and civilian authorities in the AOF had assumed that the first Allied invasion of Africa would occur at Dakar. [57] Boisson was obliged to make a statement: "American forces," he announced on the radio on 9 November 1942,

> have attacked North Africa. Our turn will not be long in coming.
> I have carried out the Marshal's orders. For two years we have assisted
> France in the defeat; now we will defend her with arms. [58]

In the Côte d'Ivoire, Governor Hubert Deschamps quickly followed Boisson's lead. He urged continued fidelity to Pétain: "We must preserve the AOF for France." [59]

Despite these declarations of continued loyalty to Vichy, events overtook Boisson and his subordinates. Four days after the cessation of resistance in the Maghreb on 10 November, Darlan sent a confidential mission to Boisson to inform him that Pétain himself had telegraphed approval of the cease-fire. Boisson dispatched three of his staff to Algiers seeking confirmation. They verified the existence of the telegram from Pétain. Boisson hesitated a few more days. Adding to the confusion, Pétain broadcast a message on 19 November, in which the Free French officers, among whom Darlan was now included, were branded as traitors and rebels. The Marshal ordered the army to ignore all commands but his own. Despite this, by 23 November, the AOF had been shifted, almost imperceptibly, into the Free French camp. [60] Thirty months after the collapse of France and the signing of the Armistice, French West Africa went back to war.

In the Côte d'Ivoire, Deschamps and his subordinates continued to follow what seems best described as Boisson's drift rather than lead. Henceforth, all efforts were officially to be directed toward the liberation of France. The colony, however, was far from united behind this goal. Many of the *colons* remained staunchly loyal to Pétain. They regarded the political change as a capitulation to traitors rather than an opportunity to liberate the homeland. That the best-organized portion of the French resistance movementwas Communist did little to inspire confidence among the fiercely capitalistic merchants, planters, and timber contractors of the Côte d'Ivoire. Nowhere else in the AOF was the *Légion des Combattants* as strong as in the Côte d'Ivoire. Led by a small group of fascist fanatics, the Legion would not readily embrace the Gaullist leadership. The Catholic church hierarchy was also openly hostile toward the prospect of rejoining the war on the Allied side, fearing the renewal of the pernicious influence of Freemasonry and Communism. It did, however, lend limited support to the newly launched bond issue, *Pour la France,* "the land of Mary," and succeeded in not mentioning the name of Charles de Gaulle in its appeal. [61]

For the mass of the Ivoirien population, the struggle between Vichy and the Free French had impinged little upon their lives. Other than among the *évolués,* few Ivoiriens had means of learning of the new developments. Enlightenment came only when the commandant arrived to give them news—always of course "glorious"—and at the same time to announce increased quotas for the renewed war effort. In areas where administrative propaganda had successfully nurtured a Pétain cult among Africans, particularly *anciens combattants* of World War I, authorities stressed the need to rescue the old Marshal, now depicted as being in the clutches of the Nazis. Tuo Nahon, a Senoufo of the class of 1941, made the point succinctly:

> Marshal Pétain was arrested by the Germans and General de Gaulle, with his army, said he didn't want to submit to Germany. So he left for America to tell the Americans, the English, the Italians, and the Russians that they must help liberate France. We left and landed in the middle of that business. It was only at Bouaké that I had heard Pétain's name. I was ready to go because the Germans had taken my brother. I was ready to go to liberate France. [62]

Sometimes the new economic war effort was presented as a means of freeing thousands of Ivoirien prisoners of war. Generally, however,

Ouanlo Silué

the villager was offered little explanation to justify yet another strain on his already overstretched resources. Ouanlo Silué was in his home near Sinématiali at this time. "I knew something about the war," he remembered,

> but I was not really informed. I knew the Germans had taken France and immobilized our soldiers. That I knew from the soldiers who had returned. Some of them were injured there. We asked them about it — how they got hurt — but I was young. Here it is the elders who ask questions. We were never told that France had got back in the war. [63]

Despite the general apathy and ignorance which prevailed throughout most of rural Côte d'Ivoire, there were two districts, those of the Abron and the Mossi, where the changeover from Vichy to de Gaulle was particularly welcome. Kouadio Adjoumani, ruler of the Abron, had delighted the French in 1939 when he made a widely publicized speech proclaiming that "German despotism has forced France to take up arms again," and declaring that all the resources of the colonies must be mobilized to defeat the Nazis and preserve the liberties enjoyed under French rule. [64] Seven months after the fall of France, he decided that life under the Vichy regime had become intolerable and he left the Côte d'Ivoire for the Gold Coast with a number of his people. The moving spirit behind the exodus was his son, Kouamé Adingra, who was immediately made a lieutenant in the Free French forces. Adingra began broadcasting and declared that he and his people had joined the Allies for the liberation of Europe. One Ivoirien historian claimed, improbably, that 10,000 Abron followed their leaders. [65] Equally improbably, Deschamps maintained, in his biographical apologia, that at most only a few hundred left. [66] Kouadio Adjoumani and Kouamé Adingra were tried *in absentia* by a military tribunal, charged with having "left French territory to place themselves at the service of the Anglo-Gaullists in the Gold Coast, leading several frontier villages with them." [67] Found guilty of treason, they were condemned to death and their property confiscated. Punitive action was taken against their home villages, some of which were burnt. Their cocoa and coffee plantations were destroyed. Notables suspected of sympathizing or aiding the flight were arrested. Many were tortured to secure information. Several died in prison. [68]

In early 1943, the Abron welcomed the news that the colony was again in the Allied camp. They expected that the border with the Gold Coast would be immediately reopened and the prewar abundance of consumer goods would be restored. [69] The border was reopened in May 1943. De Gaulle sandals and de Gaulle clothes appeared in the marketplaces, where they were purchased by some Ivoiriens sporting de Gaulle hair styles. [70]

In Ouagadougou, Moro Naba Kom II had remained a less than enthusiastic supporter of the Vichy regime. We have seen that, in September 1941, he offered Boisson his support in return for the reestablishment of Upper Volta as a separate colony. When Dakar categorically denied his demand, he opened discreet contacts with the Free French in Accra. He was reportedly furious with Boisson for aligning the AOF with Vichy. [71] What support other than moral the Moro Naba actually gave to the Free French movement is unclear. His death on 12 March 1942 gave rise to rumors that he had committed suicide rather than continue to serve under Vichy tyranny. The administrators insisted that his death was due to natural causes. He had suffered, they said, for many years from heart trouble. He had suffered, the Mossi rejoined, forever from the whites. His successor, Saga II, continued a formal cooperation with Abidjan and Dakar but maintained the contacts with the Free French. [72] This was to serve him well when the regime changed. General Giraud, taking time off from his bitter feud with de Gaulle, visited Ouagadougou in January 1943 and personally decorated the Moro Naba with the *Croix de la Légion d'Honneur.* [73]

On 7 December 1942, Boisson signed an accord with Eisenhower and Darlan setting out the position of the AOF vis-à-vis the Allies. France's West African Empire was to remain intact in that no occupation force was to be stationed on its soil. Its ports, however, would be open to Allied shipping. The over 100,000 *Tirailleurs Sénégalais* in the AOF were to be placed at the disposal of the Allied Supreme Command. [74] This new spirit of cooperation, however, did not save Boisson his job. Darlan placed him on the Council of the Empire headquartered in Algiers and Giraud confirmed his appointment. Nonetheless, one of de Gaulle's first actions when he assumed undisputed political control of Fighting France in June 1943 was to fire Boisson. He was arrested but died before his trial for treason opened. [75] Pierre Cournarie, a resistant of the *première heure,* and former governor of Cameroun, was appointed governor-general. In the Côte d'Ivoire, Hubert Deschamps had already gone. He and Georges Pierre Rey, governor of Senegal, had exchanged positions on 24 January 1943. Deschamps's transfer was most likely due to his inability to work with *colons*, for although he had dutifully collaborated with the Vichy regime, he was also known to them as being of a socialist persuasion. [76]

The new man, Georges Pierre Rey, was certainly no Gaullist, having loyally served under Boisson and conducted a vigorous campaign against suspected dissidents. Jean François Toby replaced Rey on 3 August 1943 and holds the record for shortest tenure. During the three days he spent in Abidjan, Toby managed to do what no other governor had ever achieved—he created total unity among the *colons*. They were unanimous in their hostility toward him. The 200 or so European settlers retained powerful connections even among the supposedly new administration in Algiers. Toby was replaced on 26 August by André Latrille and sent to the presumably more tranquil surroundings of Niger. In the years to come, the *colons* may have regretted their hasty judgment on Toby, for the Latrille era changed the face of French colonialism in the Côte d'Ivoire forever.

At lower levels in the Ivoirien administration, there were few personnel changes. There simply were no qualified replacements for commandants and assistant commandants. If many of them remained Pétainist at heart, there were few opportunities to manifest these sentiments, other than to keep their Pétain posters on their walls and take advantage of any occasion to obstruct the more liberal policies which would be forthcoming under Cournarie and Latrille. The economic and political transformation of the Côte d'Ivoire under the Free French administration has been discussed by the writer elsewhere.[77]

The focus of the struggle turned, finally, to the liberation of Europe. The families of the *Tirailleurs Sénégalais* would once again be mobilized to provide labor, crops, and soldiers for the renewed crusade against Germany. Some thousands of *tirailleurs* remained, of course, prisoners in Europe. Others recuperated in hospitals in France. Four battalions continued to protect French interests in the Levant. There were *tirailleurs* being demobilized from the AOF army of 100,000, while others, the class of 1943, were in the process of being recruited. The first to see action once again, however, were to be the approximately 10,000 West African soldiers already in North Africa.

Notes to Chapter Seven

1. SHAT, Centre de Documentation.
2. Edward Spears, *Fulfilment of a Mission*, 21–25.
3. Ibid., 22.
4. Charles de Gaulle, *The Complete War Memoirs*, 106.
5. *La Première Division Française Libre, Epopée d'une reconquête* (1946), 23.
6. Spears, *Fulfilment of a Mission*, 97–8.
7. de Gaulle, *The Complete War Memoirs*, 612. Laurent Champrosay's war ended in 1944 when he was killed in Italy while commanding the artillery of the First DFL.
8. Interview 64.
9. Interview 43.
10. Interview 12.
11. Interview 95.
12. Spears, *Fulfilment of a Mission*, 119.
13. Ibid., 132.
14. SHAT, "Convention d'armistice 14 Juillet 1941," accord to end the fighting in Syria and Lebanon, agreed upon on 11 July 1941. Carton 4h357, Dossier 2.
15. Spears, *Fulfilment of a Mission*, 124–25.
16. de Gaulle, *The Complete War Memoirs*, 201. Also, see Anthony Clayton, *France, Soldiers and Africa*, 136, who states that 1,500 AOF *tirailleurs* opted for de Gaulle.
17. SHAT, Carton 4h357, Dossier 2; also, Spears, *Fulfilment of a Mission*, 143–44.
18. Interview 64.
19. Interview 81.
20. Interview 74.

21. Interview 95. Most young men of draft age were obliged to join the *Jeunesse de la Montagne,* Mountain Youth, and to spend time in forest camps working and to be "inspired" by the goals of Pétain's National Revolution.

22. de Gaulle, *The Complete War Memoirs*; Clayton, *France, Soldiers and Africa,* 136.

23. Spears, *Fulfilment of a Mission,* 216.

24. Interview 43.

25. Interview 40.

26. Interview 9.

27. Denis Saurat, "Attention au Tchad," *La France Libre,* 2, no. 8 (20 June 1941).

28. Interview 26.

29. SHAT, Carton 4h406, Dossier 4.

30. Ibid.

31. Spears, *Fulfilment of a Mission,* 239–41.

32. Interview 67.

33. Interview 45.

34. Myron Echenberg, "Morts pour la France," 364.

35. Michael Carver, *Dilemmas of the Desert War* (Bloomington: Indiana University Press, 1986).

36. *La Première Division Française Libre,* 43.

37. Ibid., 47–53.

38. Ibid., 53.

39. In the spring of 1942, de Gaulle changed the name of his movement to *France Combattante,* Fighting France, "just as one unfurls the banner at the edge of battle" (de Gaulle, *The Complete War Memoirs,* 251). Others feel the reason was to defuse French colonial antagonism against the name "Free French" implying that they were not in fact free.

40. For this exchange, see William Langer, *Our Vichy Gamble* (New York: Knopf, 1947), 365–67.

41. See various sources including Langer, 348–68 and Robert Murphy, *Diplomat among Warriors* (New York: Doubleday, 1964).

42. William Breuer, *Operation Torch: The Allied Gamble to Invade North Africa* (New York: St. Martin's Press, 1986), 168–71.

43. Interview 15.

44. Interview 39.

45. Interview 1.

46. Interview 46.

47. Interview 52.

48. Interview 57.

49. For a detailed look at the action in Tunisia, see Charles Messenger, *The Tunisian Campaign* (Shepperton, Surrey: Ian Allen, 1982).

50. Clayton, *France, Soldiers and Africa,* 140.

51. Ibid., 137–45, for the best attempt to deal with the tortuous series of reorganizations.

52. Marcel Gallienne, *De Psichari à de Gaulle* (Paris: La Pensée Universelle, 1978), 179.

53. Interview 64.

54. Interview 74.

55. Interview 17.

56. de Gaulle, *The Complete War Memoirs*, 741.

57. Louis Berteil, *L'Armée de Weygand* (Paris: Editions Albatros, 1975), 151.

58. *La Côte d'Ivoire Chrétienne* (9 November 1942).

59. Ibid.

60. Jean-Noël Loucou, "La Deuxième Guerre Mondiale et ses effets en Côte d'Ivoire," 190–91.

61. *La Côte d'Ivoire Chrétienne* (May 1943).

62. Interview 46.

63. Interview 55.

64. ANCI, "Discours pronouncé par Kouadio Adjoumani, roi des Abron," Carton 4018, Dossier VI 13/13.

65. F. J. Amon d'Aby, *La Côte d'Ivoire dans la cité africaine*, 41.

66. Hubert Deschamps, *Roi de la brousse*, 254–55.

67. National Archives, Washington D.C., 851T.20/30, memo no. 166 from the American consulate in Dakar, 11 September 1942.

68. Loucou, "La Deuxième guerre mondiale et ses effets en Côte d'Ivoire," 189. The main source of Loucou's article appears to be Governor André Latrille's 1944 annual report.

69. ANCI, monthly political report, Bondoukou, dd. January 1943, Carton 426, Dossier XII–49/25.

70. Jean Rouch, "Contribution à l'histoire des Songhay," *Mémoires de l'Institut français d'afrique noire*, 29 (1953): 238.

71. Edward Mortimer, *France and the Africans, 1944–1960, A Political History* (London: Faber and Faber, 1969), 175.

72. Albert Balima, *Genèse de la Haute–Volta*, 80–82.

73. ANCI, monthly political report, *cercle* of Koudougou, January 1943. Carton 426, Dossier XII–49/22.

74. Marcel Chailley, *Histoire de l'Afrique occidentale 1638–1959* (Paris: Berger–Levrault, 1968), 440.

75. Georges Chaffard, *Les Carnets Secrets de la Decolonisation*, vol. 1 (Paris: Calmann-Levy, 1965), 30.

76. Loucou, "La Deuxième Guerre mondiale et ses effets en Côte d'Ivoire," 191.

77. Nancy Lawler, "Reform and Repression under the Free French: Economic and Political Transformation in the Côte d'Ivoire, 1942–45," *Africa*, 60, no. 1 (1990), 88–110.

8

The Liberation of France

Able in Elba: *Tirailleurs* at War Again

ON 9 JULY 1943, ALLIED forces launched the invasion of Sicily. Thirty-nine days later, General George Patton's troops took Messina. All German resistance ended. On 3 September, General Bernard Montgomery and the Eighth Army invaded the Italian peninsula, beginning the long, drawn-out Allied drive northward which was to culminate on 4 June 1944, when Rome passed into American hands. A French expeditionary corps, composed mainly of Moroccan and Algerian infantry, had joined the British and the American invaders in November 1943. No *Tirailleurs Sénégalais* units as such were in the corps, although a small contingent of Central and West African troops, serving with the Colonial Artillery, did participate in the campaign. [1]

For the most part the *tirailleur* regiments being prepared for combat remained in camps in North Africa, where they were almost entirely reequipped and uniformed by the United States. A few of them were among the French units which invaded Corsica on 21 September. That is was the birthplace of Napoleon made it an appropriate beginning to the liberation of France. The fall of the island on 4 October was much hastened by the fact that significant parts of the Italian garrison went over to the French. It was not, however, until June 1944 that the *Tirailleurs Sénégalais* were to be used in strength. This was to be in the invasion of another island, Elba, which had been Napoleon's first prison.

On 17 and 18 June 1944, 12,000 troops of the mainly West African Ninth DIC, which included the 4th, 6th, and 13th regiments of *Tirailleurs Sénégalais*, landed on Elba. [2] The battle was brief. By 19 June, the German garrison was destroyed. The victors took 2,300 prisoners and sixty field pieces. [3] The *tirailleurs* of this reconstituted army displayed as much courage and fighting spirit in their first battle for the liberation of Europe as those who had lost in 1940, the Battle of France. In the action, the gallantry of the Second Battalion of the 13th RTS earned a special citation from de Gaulle:

> Ardent and magnificent, this unit covered itself in glory on the 17th of June, 1944, during the course of the operations and landings on the isle of Elba. Under Battalion Chief Gilles, a renowned leader who had formed the unit in his image, the battalion, with great spirit, attacked fortified positions on the beach of Marina di Campo, protected by an extensive minefield and dense barricades. Attacking with grenades and flamethrowers, they destroyed the blockhouses and captured the enemy's artillery positions. [4]

Among the many who received individual decorations was the Senoufo sharpshooter, Ditiemba Silué of the Thirteenth. Ditiemba, who had fired on Allied landing craft at Casablanca, now found himself going to a new war on the side of the Allies. His recollections of the Elba landings under fire are vivid:

> From Casablanca, we were sent to Elba, in Italy, on an American boat. We arrived in Italy with French, African, and American troops. But it was us—our boat, in the front. There as well was a war. The guns destroyed 17 ships. Many were dead. Everyone on those boats. They were firing on us when we were 20 kilometers out. A terrible bombardment. When we landed, the Italians were firing on us. The American ship was smart—it circled around—used a telescope and spotted the gun. The American cannons hit them just as they were about to fire. . . . Our sergeant, a Frenchman, Sergeant Soleil, landed first to look around. It was four in the morning. Then he was shot at. We all disembarked now. The war was heating up. Many were dead—on the ground. To get off the boat, there was a long rope. The water was waist-high, we had to hold on to the rope or drown. We were being bombarded. Captain Mory[?] commanded. The Italians had killed many of us, but we killed the maximum possible. The battle was very heated. One week [sic] of fire—fire—fire. Twenty-four hours a day. I fired my machine gun. My finger got burned, the gun was red it was so hot. It recoiled and hit me in the mouth— see the teeth I lost? The French? They were afraid. If they were shot at, they cried: Oh Mama! and dropped to the ground. It was the Americans and the Africans who were the true *tirailleurs*. [5]

Ditiemba Silué is still revered by the *anciens combattants* as the best hunter in the Korhogo region, although he is now over seventy. Tuo Nahon fought alongside him and retains equally vivid memories of the landings:

Ditiemba Silué, the sharpshooter

We went to Elba by boat. We left France [North Africa] at 5 in the evening and arrived at 5 in the morning. The Germans started firing at us while we were still in the water. All the same, we captured them. The landings were difficult. When you left the boat—to get on the sand—they were shooting at you. Six were killed on the shore of the sea. We were lucky. Where our boat landed, we found a small house, near the sea. There was a telephone there. We found four men inside. We took them, then cut the lines, and that is what won the battle—it was thanks to that. . . . We were fighting alongside the French, not the Americans. But the French were afraid. One asked me if I had a gris-gris [talisman] that I could give him. How could I give you mine? We are not from the same land. You are from France and I am from the Côte d'Ivoire. If I give it to you, then I will die. [6]

Gnoumagai Soro, he who had marched up and down Mount Korhogo during his training, also saw action in Elba. He was with the 4th RTS.

I fought with de Gaulle, on Elba. We were in the boat, we landed, and the Germans started shooting at us. There were American and French troops with us. We left from Casablanca. Yes, it was my first battle. The French and the Americans had fought before, but it was the first time for us, the Africans. They had told us that we were going to attack. In the boat, we just thought about the boat. We were ready. I was well trained. We had had exercises showing us how to fight a war. Some of us would be on the one side, and some on the other. We fired at each other, not with bullets, just with powder. We'd move forward—kneel down, and shoot. It was a 36 rifle, French. Why was I there? The French said it was because I was defending France and the Côte d'Ivoire. I knew I was leaving for war. . . .

[In Elba] it was hard. Everyone was getting killed. French and *Sénégalais*. We were not together with the Americans—they had been bombarding the city before we got there. The Germans were in foxholes. We fired at them. You just shot—you could not see what or who you were firing at. There was shooting for two days. We captured all of them in that city—I don't know its name. [7]

In the battle for Elba, 250 men of the Ninth DIC were killed in action. Another 600 were wounded. The Germans lost approximately 500 men. On 28 June, the division was transferred to Corsica, leaving the 6th RTS behind to guard the 2,300 German prisoners taken in the operation. [8] The stage was set for the invasion of southern France.

The Battle for Toulon

Two months after the liberation of Elba, Operation Anvil was launched. Ultimately to involve a force of half a million men, the objectives were to seal the Italian frontier with France and to join up with the Allied forces moving on Paris from the Normandy beachheads. [9] On 15 August, the American Seventh Army under General Patch and the First French Army under General de Lattre de Tassigny carried out landings on the coast of Provence between Toulon and Cannes. [10] Under heavy naval cover, 94,000 men landed that first day, and only 183 were lost. The next day, de Lattre's First French Army—consisting of two artillery and five infantry divisions—began the advance along the coast westwards with the object of taking Toulon and Marseille before beginning the drive up the Rhone Valley. The divisions thrown into the battle for Toulon were the West African Ninth DIC, fresh from its triumph on Elba, and the French Third DIA and First DMI. [11]

The advancing troops met heavy resistance from General Weise's Nineteenth Army. [12] Kiwalte Kambou of Bouna remembered the fierceness of the fighting near the coast, though it is unclear precisely where this particular encounter with the Germans occurred:

We started to fight. We had to cross a bridge. They started firing
their 75s at us. Mortars. Ten were killed by the first round. Next
day, the commander said, "We can't advance." At five in the evening the Germans radioed that they are going to kill 100 Africans.
The French said, "You kill 100 Africans and we will kill 200 of your
prisoners." At 5 in the morning they started firing their machine
guns. To make us afraid. At five in the evening, the captain said,
"We will attack." And we attacked. The Germans pushed us back
into a village. We were hidden all over in that village. In the morning, around 7, we were in the same place. There were anti-tank and
anti-personnel mines all over. A captain, a colonel, and General
Leclerc gave us our orders. We must not retreat but advance. Then,
at 8 we started to do it. By 10 A.M. we captured all the Germans,
an entire division.

De Gaulle and Leclerc gave orders that there would be no more
retreating. "The French and the Africans are stronger than the
enemy. Why are we in retreat?" We were all informed of these words,
company by company. Mine was the 15th BIMA. That's what gave
us the power. . . . The next morning, after we had eaten, we started.
We kept advancing. Firing a little. At 7 A.M. we attacked again. The
Germans were in retreat. We took one post, then rested. We only
had those sardines to eat. After we rested, we started again at 2 P.M.
At 4 P.M. it was combat with bayonets—man to man. I myself was
leading the way. I saw them first. We were all in a line—someone
would wave his hand and we would crouch down. We started forward when the cannon fired. The Germans were falling—so were
we. There were wires—to hold up the grapes—in the vineyards. They
told me to throw a grenade. I did and it took me right into the wire.
I was caught with my head in French territory and my feet in German. I had thrown the grenade 75 meters—it should be 100. If you
can throw it that far you can take it easy. It's far enough away. Anyway
the captain and others kept firing and got me free. The cannon kept
on firing—ten, twenty times. Finally all the Germans dropped their
guns and came out with their hands up—waving a white cloth—the
flag. We thought that the war was getting smaller—over—even the
commander thought that, but there was a whole war ahead of us. [13]

It was not until 23 August, the very day that Paris was liberated, that
French forces including men of the Ninth DIC entered Toulon. Fighting
street by street, the *bataillons de marche* continued their advance. On
25 August, Weise withdrew the bulk of the Nineteenth Army into the
Rhone Valley but left garrisons behind to defend both Marseille and
Toulon. The Germans in Toulon barricaded themselves in the fort of
Sainte-Marguerite, perched upon a sheer cliff overlooking the port.
Gnoumagai Soro of the 4th RTS was there. He described the action
graphically:

We started for Toulon, war. We took Toulon. The Americans bombed it first. There was a big mountain there and the Germans had built a city inside of it. They were practically all inside. The Americans bombed. The Germans resisted. They wouldn't surrender. Then the German commander said they would surrender the next morning at nine. The Americans continued to fire on the mountain until it caught fire. The next morning, their captain came out and surrendered. "We are beaten." We took them all prisoners. I saw him come out with his hands up. Then everyone else came out, in a line with their hands up. We had already surrounded the mountain. We were happy. We had beaten them. We, the *Sénégalais*, took them prisoner and sent them to the back of the lines. [14]

The German garrison surrendered to the Ninth DIC on 28 August, the same day that Marseille fell to Algerian and Moroccan regiments. Gnoumagai Soro, along with his entire battalion, received the *croix de guerre avec palme* by virtue of an order of Charles de Gaulle.

An elite unit, inspired by its commander, Lieutenant-Colonel Gufflet, a superior officer of the highest caliber and indomitable energy. He had already distinguished himself in the conquest of the isle of Elba.

Once again, he gave proof of his extraordinary ability in combat and tactics. On 24 August 1944, penetrating Toulon from the north, after fierce combat, led with speed and great mastery, he relieved the Fort of La Tour Blanche on the Faron, the Jaureguibery Stadium, and forced entry to the arsenal, taking a total of 400 prisoners. On 25 August, by sheer force of arms, he took the entrance to the arsenal and due to the energetic action of the 1st company seized, without firing a shot, the forward positions of the fort of Malbousquet. And, with the same élan, he attacked the fort itself, forcing the surrender of the garrison of 1,400 soldiers and 400 German civilians. This, with one fifth of his troops out of action. [15]

The Sixth RTS was likewise cited for the role it played in the advance on Toulon. [16]

Operation Anvil was an unqualified success. By the end of August, the entire coast from the mouth of the Rhone to Nice was under Allied control. Although the bulk of Weise's army escaped inland, 48,000 prisoners had been taken. [17] There was little time for victory parades, but some of the *Tirailleurs Sénégalais*, like Gnoumagai Soro and Tuo Nahon, were granted a few days in which to savor their accomplishments.

We celebrated for ten days. There was no parade, but we went in town and ate a great deal and drank a lot. The civilians put barrels of wine out in front of their houses, and you just drank, filling up your canteens as you went along. They were everywhere. You just drank and drank. We ate in camp, but alcohol we drank in town. The people there were very kind. [18]

Tuo Nahon remembered the flowers and the flag:

When we captured prisoners near a town, the people were very happy. In towns, they would send us flowers. If we were alone in town, they would give us gifts. After we liberated a town, we raised the French flag. There was only one—the one we raised. [19]

From Provence to Alsace

From Toulon and Marseille, the First French Army moved up the Rhone Valley to the west of the river in conjunction with forces of the U.S. Thirty-Sixth Division to the east. Their immediate target was Lyon. The Americans reached its outskirts on 2 September, but having determined that the Germans had abandoned the city, halted. This was done to permit the French forces, which had been slowed down by gasoline shortages, to have the honor of liberating the city. Twenty-four hours later, de Lattre entered Lyon. General Weise had offered strong resistance to the French and American advance but had to fall back continuously rather than risk encirclement. He succeeded in extricating about half of the Nineteenth Army. On 4 September, the American and French armies resumed the advance north. On 6 September, French forces entered Chalon-sur-Saône. The Americans took Besançon the next day, and the French entered Beaune and Autun on the eighth, Dijon on the tenth. Many *Tirailleurs Sénégalais* remembered the liberation of French towns and villages, rather than fighting the Germans, as the most satisfying aspect of the advance. "The Air Force," Yeo Kouhona explained,

dropped bombs ahead of us. Then we would go forward and liberate—save a village. There were French and American troops with us, too. When we liberated a village they would gather all the children together—get a soldier to guard them and then feed them. Then we would move on. The people—did they give us presents? There was no time. They didn't have quiet hearts. It was us who opened up the shops—you took what you wanted—you did not pay for it— and went on. [20]

General Jacob Devers took operational control of both armies on 15 September. In the advance to the Rhine, American forces took the left flank directed toward Strasbourg, the French the right flank toward Belfort, near the Swiss border. [21] The end of the dash through southern France had brought the First Army to the Vosges by 16 October, but losses were so heavy that de Lattre was forced to slow his offensive the next day. The advance was stalled as de Lattre once again faced Weise and the Nineteenth Army. On 24 October de Lattre drew up plans for Operation Independence, the objective of which was the capture of Belfort. These were approved by Devers on 27 October, within the plans for the general Allied offensive on the Rhine. Alsace and part of Lorraine were now the only regions of France awaiting liberation. The French advance was resumed on 14 November, and by the eighteenth, Belfort was virtually encircled. Two days later, troops of the First French Army entered its suburbs.

Operation Independence marked the end of military action for virtually all black Africans. In their camps in the Jura Mountains, the *tirailleurs* were experiencing the first phases of what was to be a particularly severe winter. Huddled around their fires and wood stoves, they dreamed of their villages and sang, somewhat cynically, of France:

La France est notre mère,	France is our mother
C'est elle qui nous nourrit	It is she who feeds us
Avec les pommes de terre	With potatoes
Et des fayots pourris!	And rotten beans. [22]

Tafolotien Soro, a Senoufo serving in the 13th RTS, remembers the time:

It was very cold. It broke our feet. We were in the forest. Too many blacks were killed there. The Germans were hidden in that forest. [The battle] was heated. You couldn't see the enemy—they were hidden. Our officers were still the same. They were very good officers. Captain Penco[?]—he was from St. Louis in Senegal. He told me he was from there. We did one month at Belfort—fighting every day. It was cold. They told us that the Russians were going to replace us. Everyone was happy—everyone. [23]

However likely it might have seemed at the time, Tafolotien was wrong in thinking that the Russians were to move in. De Gaulle had, in fact, decided to withdraw the *tirailleurs* to the south and replace them with Frenchmen from the interior, drawn mainly from irregular units and guerrilla bands of the Resistance. As de Gaulle wrote,

Since winter in the Vosges threatened the health of our Negro troops, we sent the 20,000 soldiers from Central and Western Africa serving in the First Free French Division and the Ninth Colonial Division to the Midi. They were replaced by a similar number of *maqui-sards* who were immediately equipped.[24]

Not surprisingly the news that they were being withdrawn was greeted enthusiastically by most *tirailleurs*. It was truly a welcome release. Yeo Kouhona voiced the sentiments felt by many:

> We did not go into Germany. . . . They came to tell us to stop—it is over. Then they led us away and we followed them. We were over-joyed. We were sure we would return to our villages to see our fathers. One was truly happy. To see our *Sénégalais* brothers arrive. We danced—we sang—it was more than the word *happy* can express. First they telephoned to tell us, then they took us to Marseille. It was the telephone which told us everything. That was when we danced.[25]

Ditiemba Silué shared the joy but knew some of his comrades in the Thirteenth RTS felt differently.

> At Belfort, winter was coming in a few weeks. It was the first cold for me. They gave us winter clothes. We were well dressed but it was so cold—ice everywhere. Afterward de Gaulle decided that Africans were not used to the cold—the snow—and he asked for a change—for replacement of African troops with the French. . . .
>
> We were sent south to the French. We were happy—very happy. It was so cold you could not walk. Some were furious when we left though, because we had started the war and it was almost over now and we were being replaced by French troops who had been afraid. We wanted the Africans to win the war. But after we left, we were happy. We had escaped the cold.[26]

Tuo Nahon was one of those who saw things in a different light. He had come to war with a particular goal—to liberate his brother, a prisoner since 1940. "The snow had started to fall," he remembered:

> I got terrible pain and cold in my feet. They were terrible. They had to send me to the hospital in Metz. Thanks to the snow, they sent all the *tirailleurs* back—all of them—because of the cold. . . . There was the snow. I don't know if the men were unhappy about not finishing the war. I was in foxholes with my gun, wet to my knees. If my feet had been dry, I would have gone on shooting to free my brother. I was furious at being sick. Thank God, we won the war and my older brother was liberated and died at home—in the village.[27]

Some battle-weary men, long accustomed to the vagaries of the military authorities and the dubious truth of the army rumor mill, were more skeptical than angry in their reactions. Nahoua Silué spoke for them:

They told us that the *Sénégalais* would not return to the war in France. If the war does go on, it will be among those who are there. The *Sénégalais* will no longer join in. They didn't say that the war was over. It was General Amblow[?], an American, who told us this. Yes, in French. Some of the *Sénégalais* asked why we were not to return to the war. The General said, "The Africans will have their presidents, and they will have their freedom." The *Sénégalais* who asked the question asked it because they were all tired and we wanted peace, tranquility. They wanted confirmation that we were finished with the war. They wanted to be sure it was true. Our officers held a meeting with us and read the report to us. "They, the *Sénégalais*, will go home and have their repose." In my mind, liberty means repose. That is what I thought it was then. [28]

Whitening the Army

Philippe Yacé was an Ivoirien *citoyen*. He responded to the withdrawal of the Africans from the front in 1944 in a way quite different from that of the *tirailleurs*. "I was with the First French Army," he said.

When we arrived, we headed for Besançon. In the winter, a general order was received saying that all men of color should be evacuated to the south, where it was relatively warm. If the war didn't end during the winter, they could be brought back in the spring. I was among those who refused to leave the front, so I now signed up as a volunteer.

Remember, we were among the Africans who were citizens, and that the order was for the *tirailleurs*. I was not a *tirailleur* but in the regular French army. But when the officers saw the words—men of color—they tried to send us back, too. When we said we would not go, they asked us if we agreed to volunteer, and we signed up. You understand, it was a question of our status, not love for war. We were French, not subjects. [29]

Yacé knew that whatever the compassionate reasons involved in withdrawing the Africans from combat, complex political considerations were also involved. The decision to replace the Africans was de Gaulle's. It was to be policy to "whiten" the Free French Forces (*blanchissement*). [30]

The future shape of the French nation itself, and its restoration to international prominence, was de Gaulle's paramount consideration. Unity of purpose had to be achieved, for the nation remained torn by the years of defeat and occupation. Despite the great military successes of 1944, the wounds of the Vichy years remained largely unhealed. There were bitter divisions between those who had rallied to the Free French and those who had fought in the Resistance on the one hand, and those in the Armistice Army who had actively supported Pétain or had at least

passively accepted his authority on the other. De Gaulle sought to amal-
gamate all the fighting men into a unified army, which would achieve
victory with the final defeat of Germany.

Military considerations aside, de Gaulle was also greatly disturbed
by the attitudes and expectations he had encountered among civilians
when making a tour of liberated France in September 1944. He wrote:

> Many Frenchmen tended to identify the liberation with the end of
> the war. There was a temptation to regard the battles still to be waged,
> the losses to be sustained, the restrictions to be endured until the
> enemy's defeat, as empty—and therefore all the more burdensome—
> formalities. Misapprehending the extent of our debacle, the terrible
> penury we were confronting, and the servitude the pursuit of the con-
> flict imposed upon us, our citizens supposed that production would
> resume rapidly and on a large scale, that provisioning would be im-
> mediately improved, that all the elements of a quick renewal would
> soon be co-ordinated. The Allies were imagined, like storybook
> heroes, to possess inexhaustible resources and to be eager to lavish
> them upon a France they had fondly delivered and now desired to
> restore to all her former glory at their sides. . . .
>
> As for myself, having reached this poverty-stricken Paris at the end
> of a dramatic summer, I labored under no such illusion. . . . I in-
> tended to apply the entire credit France had accorded me to lead her
> to salvation. [31]

Initially, it seems, de Gaulle had no desire to dispense with the services
of his African troops, the nucleus of his original Free French forces. In
order to integrate the irregulars who had been operating in Occupied
France into his new unified army, he first requested the Allies to provide equipment for 100,000 additional soldiers who would take part
in the final drive into Germany. The Allies, however, refused the request
despite the highly creditable performance of France's First Army in the
advance from Provence to the Rhine. It was in these circumstances that
de Gaulle took the decision to replace Africans with *maquisards* and
other young Frenchmen eager to take part in the last stages of the war.
Even the 4th, 6th, and 13th *tirailleur* regiments, which had seen fierce
combat in Italy and France, were "whitened" by the end of 1944. They
lost not only their African soldiers, but their very designations. They
became, for the remainder of the war, *régiments d'infanterie coloniale.* [32]

It had, we have seen, been French military practice since World War
I to withdraw the *Tirailleurs Sénégalais* from northern stations during
the winter. De Gaulle was thus fortunate in being able to present his
whitening policy as a case of the established wintering policy. Many
of the *tirailleurs* were indeed fortunate to find themselves spending the
winter of 1944–45 in the south of France. Others, however, were not.

They remained in their mountain camps, joined in their misery by the newly incorporated white soldiers. Among the newcomers was Gerard Faivre. A native of Belfort, in 1943 he was one of the half million Frenchmen required to do forced labor in Germany.[33] He chose instead to take to the mountains and join the Resistance. In September 1944 he became a second-class *tirailleur* in the 8th RTS and took part in Operation Independence. He became much attached to his African comrades and felt great sympathy for them:

> They were taken off the front, but they stayed in the rear lines for months. They truly suffered from the cold. Lots of ice and snow. There were many who caught bronchitis that winter. For us it is nothing, but they died of it.[34]

The whitening policy will long remain a matter of controversy among historians. What is absolutely clear, however, is that the withdrawal of the *tirailleurs* from combat had nothing whatsoever to do with their performance in the field. From de Gaulle downward, no one doubted this. "God," said Faivre,

> they were brave. And so many were killed—so many. They were all forced into the army, but they were still motivated because there was such a good ambiance in the military. They were motivated—France is your mother. The Germans were terrified of them—they took few prisoners.[35]

The Release of the Prisoners

If those *tirailleurs* who were withdrawn from the Rhine front to the south regarded themselves as more fortunate than those who remained in the frozen camps of the Jura Mountains, it was a relative matter. *Les misérables* were truly those who had been taken in the Battle of France in the summer of 1940 and awaited liberation from their prison camps.

By August 1944, news of the success of the Normandy invasion, and of the rapid advance of American and French armies through the south, spread quickly to the camps. Hospital workers, members of the *maquis*, Red Cross officials, and occasionally even the German guards themselves, brought news to the *tirailleurs* behind barbed wire. Ehouman Adou of the Ivoirien class of 1938, whom we have met several times before, spent 18 months in a stalag in Germany before being transferred to a camp in Occupied France. He remembered his release:

The second camp was at Nancy. Three years. . . . It was the
Americans who delivered us. One day, the Germans said that today
you will be delivered. I was in the hospital. I asked the cook what
was happening. They [Americans] came in trucks, cars, and stopped
before our camp—and they took us. They asked if we had eaten.
We said no. They gave us packages of food. Every morning after that
they gave us the same packages. We got into the trucks. We were
sent to Paris by truck. [36]

Gmbale Soro, of the Korhogo class of 1937, had to wait much longer
for his liberation, for his camp was in Germany. He too went to Paris.
He talked about his capture on the Maginot Line, and about his release
five years later:

We were all taken to a courtyard. We stayed under the sun for a least
one week. They gave us one spoonful of potato—that's all. While
we were in that courtyard, if you stood up you would get dizzy, so
to talk was a problem. Everyone was there—the French and the
Sénégalais—we were in separate houses. I was taken on the 17th of
June [1940] and liberated the 1st of May 1945. . . . When the war
was spoiling, we were prisoners. We worked for the Germans in their
fields—everywhere. The white prisoners did the same work but in
other fields. When de Gaulle came with the Americans, we had to
hide bullets everywhere—even when the Americans were close—we
had to keep moving things, carrying things. . . . The Americans
liberated us. In the forest all night, we heard firing all night. We could
not sleep. In the morning there were no guards. The Americans were
in front of the camp. They did not speak French, so that is how we
knew they were Americans. I was very happy. We left the camp right
away and went to a small village. There were many who did not have
shoes, so we could not go far. We went into houses and took what
we needed. This was in Germany. When we got to France, the people
really applauded us. We arrived in Paris. Women came and carried
our little bags for us. The women! Our old shirts were in them,
nothing of importance. We stayed there, ate well, and then we came
home. Whenever we arrived in a train station, people would say: "The
prisoners are here in that train!" And they applauded us. Every time
they saw us. They knew us by our clothing. They even wrote on the
rail cars: Attention! Prisonniers. [37]

The tirailleur Tionnina Soro, also from the Korhogo class of 1937,
was another to be liberated in the spring of 1945. "I was in Le Mans
for five years," he said.

Five years in the same camp. The Red Cross came. We were there.
In the town, after bombings, they would send us into town to fix

the broken things. If there was a bomb that had not exploded, they sent us to gather it up. . . . Yes, the Red Cross told us what was happening. They said—secretly, they whispered it to us—be calm. We are going to capture all the Germans one day. [One day] the Red Cross came by to say that the people, the Americans, were near. Not farther away than Korhogo [from Kakologo, 25 kilometers]. You will be free—they are close. In the morning, around 6 A.M., we saw the Americans passing by. They stopped and asked us, "What are you doing here?" [We answered] "We are prisoners." They replied, "What? We don't see any Germans. Get out of there." The Americans are good guys. Thanks to them we didn't see any Germans. They'd all run away.

When we got out of that camp, we went to a small village and the Americans came to get us. We were at least a regiment. The camp was bigger even than this village [Kakologo]. They sent trucks for us to take us into the interior of France. When the Red Cross had told us the news, we were already happy, but when we got out of that camp, that was joy! We danced! We rested! [38]

Somongo Soro still keeps his prisoner of war identification tag to remind him of his deliverance. POW No. 1781 of *Front Stalag* 150, Somongo too remembers every detail of that day:

It was the soldiers who came, not de Gaulle himself, and the American whites and blacks and the French. And they came. That morning we had seen no guards, we had already opened the gates. We were outside. We saw them coming. We cheered. We applauded. They put the [German] prisoners in the camp and gave rifles to some of us so we could guard them. They asked us where the Germans had gone. Because we had searched the forest before, we went with them to look for the Germans. We found many of them in holes in the forest. We captured them and put them in the camp. The same day that we took the Germans, trucks came for us and took us into the interior of France. They took us to the train station at Nancy. They put us on a train. At the station, the French cheered us. At that moment, we knew we had not been forgotten. But really, while we were in the camp, we did not think much about the French, we only thought about returning home. [39]

Not all prisoners experienced so smooth a transition from captivity to freedom. In some cases, as the Nazi defeat seemed imminent, camp commanders tried to evacuate prisoners held in French camps by train to Germany, presumably to hold them as hostages. French civilians took extraordinary risks to prevent this happening. Near Orleans, *maquisards* and French railway workers combined to thwart one such attempt to load a train with 900 African prisoners from the camp in the city's Dunois quarter, and 200 sick and wounded soldiers, both black and white, from the St. Aignan Hospital. Knowing how close the Americans were, railway employees staged mechanical breakdowns to delay departure of the train for thirty-six hours. But the local *maquis* had lacked the time and the ammunition to blow up a vital bridge and thus shut down the line. Further delay was secured through a dangerous ruse. A Commandant Remion, hospitalized himself, ordered *his* officers to tell the Germans that all *their* officers had been captured by the approaching Americans. Remion promised the guards—by now mostly older noncombatants— that he would let them escape. They, however, refused, but only on the grounds that they had no civilian clothes. Remion made them another offer. He would personally guarantee their lives if they put themselves under his protection. Ten Germans accepted, were disarmed, and together all waited for the Americans. The Germans never discovered the lie, and the *maquisards* were able to destroy the bridge. All 1,100 were saved from deportation. [40]

In another incident at Salbris, on 17 August 1944, 375 African prisoners were on board a departing train. The *maquis* successfully attacked it, and the freed men were incorporated into the Resistance until the Allies liberated the area. [41] Panafolo Tuo, a Senoufo reservist of the class of 1934 it will be remembered, narrated the drama of his close escape from transportation to Germany:

> We heard that de Gaulle and the Americans were fighting the war. A plane dropped leaflets on the camp. Then the Germans ran when de Gaulle was engaged in the war. They took us all out of the camp to go to Versailles where we would get a train to Germany. But the *maquis* had cut the rails. At Versailles, they created a diversion—the *maquis*—to try to arrange for our escape. The German captain had paid for some wine for himself. A white woman came to us and told us we would soon be free, that French troops had surrounded the town. When we saw a truck, we were to come, not run, and get in. We were well instructed. There were seven trucks. The *maquis* was there. They said, "Climb in." Then we were taken to the interior of France. I do not know how many we were. We hid in the forest until the trucks came. We didn't just go over to the trucks like we were going to our offices. We used to call to each other in Dyula, to stay well hidden. While we were waiting, the citizens of Versailles took care of us. In the camp we had thought ourselves forgotten. In Versailles, we realized that they still thought about us. [42]

For those *tirailleurs* who were involved in liberating their fellow Africans, it was a time of supreme satisfaction. For the first time in all the action they had seen, they were fighting not merely for France but

Tuo Nanzegue

for their own people. Ditiemba Silué described his reaction when his regiment, the Thirteenth RTS, freed a camp holding mainly African prisoners:

> The Germans found out that many Africans were coming to save their brothers. When they heard we were coming, they were afraid that the Africans would kill them. So they let our brothers go. We found these prisoners. We greeted each other and asked, "What news?" They said to us, "You have liberated us."[43]

For obvious logistical reasons, the French had initially decided to use freed *tirailleurs* as prison guards in camps now to hold Germans. Tuo Nanzegue, a reservist of the Korhogo class of 1934, liberated in February 1945, quite liked the idea. "It was a strange affair," he laughed.

We worked for the Germans in the camp. One day we saw the
Germans fleeing, throwing their weapons away. Then we thought,
"Hah! We can leave too." Thus we were liberated in a strange way.
We were coming back after work to the camp when this happened.
When we got to the camp, we found that now the Germans were
inside it. The men of de Gaulle were there. We knew nothing about
the French army being so close. It was a surprise. We were content,
that's all. It was the first time we had seen whites in prison. The
French troops said to us that these men had guarded you in prison,
so now if you want to be their guards, go ahead. It was at that moment
we knew the war was over. Then they [the French] decided they could
not leave us there to guard them, because after all the evil they had
done to us, we might want to do the same [to them]. It would be
very serious for them [the Germans] if we leave you to guard them.
So it was the men of de Gaulle who guarded them. What did we
do? We were happy, that's all. We ate well. Then right away, the same
day, they took us to Paris. [44]

The order forbidding the use of the *tirailleurs* came from above. No
opportunity should be given to former prisoners to seek revenge against
their captors who, although German, were white. Doubtless such fears
were justified, but there were soldiers like Tuo Nahon who had quite
different feelings. He spent several weeks guarding German prisoners
after the victory at Toulon:

When I used to escort the German prisoners to work, I had pity
because I thought of my brother who was being submitted to the
same kind of thing. You know some of the *tirailleurs* killed the
Germans [POWs] because they had killed many of us and other
tirailleurs were still prisoners—so they killed them. But I used to give
old uniforms, and extra food, to the prisoners. The commandant
found out about it and was going to put me in prison. I explained
to him and he understood. I did not go to prison. [45]

Politicians and Prisoners

In deciding not to use the *tirailleurs* as camp guards, concern for the
welfare of German prisoners may well not have been the most immediate
concern of the French authorities. Even in those first euphoric days of
liberation, politicians looked to the imperial future and began to express
fears about the long-term effects of the prison years upon liberated
Africans. In October 1944, René Pleven, colonial minister in de Gaulle's

provisional government, wrote to Governor-General Cournarie of the AOF. He drew attention to the potential dangers present in the imminent repatriation of the released prisoners.

> Thousands of men had been separated for several years from Africa. They have acquired European habits and a different mentality. When liberated by the Allied armies all at once, some immediately joined the Free French Army of the Interior. Others joined the partisans and were involved in commando and hand-to-hand raids. Others were taken in by French families and the rest by *marraines*. This confused situation has been bad for morale. [46]

The *tirailleurs* knew nothing about such suspicions. Following their release, they were sent to base camps throughout France to await repatriation. They took at face value such flowery sentiments as those expressed by Paul Giacobbi, who had succeeded Pleven. Addressing one group of *tirailleurs* on 26 April 1945, Giacobbi spoke of their "gift of blood and soul" for the liberation of France. "You have returned!" he told them.

> Today is the first step in your return and you must feel, in your hearts, how your great country has received you. We bring to you the feelings of an entire people who recognize what you have done. Let us assure you of the solicitude which all of France has toward you in these glorious hours of liberation. [47]

African soldiers retain joyful memories of those first days of freedom. The ordinary Frenchman was full of warmth and appreciation for them. *Tirailleurs* were welcomed everywhere. Ehouman Adou spoke for many. According to his own testimony, he was freed on 24 June 1944, and after the liberation of Paris, was among a group of prisoners sent there by truck:

> What didn't we do! We got to Paris and everyone asked us what they could bring us. They sent us drink, sheep, everything. At the station in Paris, they gave us food. There was a kitchen that was always open for us. Four months I was in Paris and it never stopped. There was always a pot on the fire. I was happy to be free. All the people were so glad to see us. You couldn't return to camp. [48]

Ex-prisoners like Adou might find themselves in Paris, and so might those still on active service. Ditiemba Silué of the 13th RTS recollected his visit there:

> The day that Paris was liberated, we were on the way there. I did participate in the celebration of the liberation of Paris with de Gaulle.

"The tower in Korhogo? The one in Paris is twice as high."

It was a grand fête. The whites and the Africans marched in a long parade—you could have walked from Paris to Korhogo—the distance we walked that day. All along the route people gave us flowers, wine, beer, lemonade. Everyone was very happy. After that we were given one month's leave in Paris. We walked around. We ate well. We saw everything. All the monuments. You know the tower on the Post Office in Korhogo? The one in Paris [the Eiffel Tower!] is twice as high. We climbed it to see the size of Paris, but even there we couldn't see all of Paris. [49]

Panafolo Tuo of the 16th RTS, after his liberation by the *maquis* near Versailles, was sent to a holding camp near Bordeaux. "Everyone was happy," he reminisced.

We drank all night. *Vive* de Gaulle! *Vive* de Gaulle! I saw him in Bordeaux. He was a tall guy wearing a decoration on his left shoulder. It was de Gaulle who assembled us all—there was a grand parade—we were mixed in with the French troops—shoulder to shoulder. It was a fine parade. He made a speech there. "Forgive us. What happened was God's doing. Evil comes as does good. Those who were in prison are now free. Come to the camp for one month and eat and do no work." [50]

All, however, was not wine and roses. As France began to deal with
the reality of healing its wounds, of reconstructing its economy, of trying to paper over the rifts between former collaborators and *résistants
de la première heure*, African *tirailleurs* became increasingly irrelevant
to the main themes dominating society. Whether it was the result of
the rising level of frustration among those awaiting repatriation in their
camps, or whether the newly liberated people of France thought it time
for the *tirailleurs* to go home, there were unpleasant incidents. Aoussi
Eba, the conscripted teacher forced to walk from Bondoukou to Bouaké
camp in 1941, was a sergeant in 1945. He witnessed bloody clashes
in the camp among soldiers awaiting repatriation.

> While we were at Nantes there were soldiers from the West Indies
> who really spoke French. Generally the men from here didn't speak
> French. They called us *nègres*. They set up an ambush for our men.
> The *tirailleurs* came out of their barracks to go to town. When they
> came back, the West Indians surrounded us. They killed three of our
> men. The others returned and told the story. They said that the West
> Indians were armed while we were not. That night our men found
> the killers and they were dead the next morning. There was a
> captain—a West Indian—a teacher. I went to see him—to try to stop
> all this. He said, "But you are an African." I replied, "But you are
> a teacher. How can you permit this to happen?" The next morning
> we buried our dead. They did the same. If it were not for the police,
> there would have been another battle. It was really the effects of war.
> To kill had become an easy thing to do. [51]

Violence was not confined to the camps. Nanzegue Tuo, whose liberation has been described above, told a dramatic story of how men in
his unit reacted to what they perceived as a racial insult:

> We were in Paris. One night the Parisians were going to show a film.
> They said that we, the soldiers, could not come to see that film. If
> we couldn't see the film, then we would make fools of them. We,
> the *Sénégalais*, were not pleased. We were angry. We took our weapons
> and encircled that cinema. We really bombarded that cinema. There
> were many, many dead Frenchmen. We, along with the Americans,
> had fought for them and now they didn't want us to come to their
> film. The Americans backed us up. No, no one did a thing to us.
> . . . Nothing happened to us because the Americans and the Rus-
> sians supported us. They could not react to what we had done. They
> could not. The Americans and the Russians said, "It was the French
> who sent you to war, and after the war, they had refused to let you
> go to their cinema. If that had happened in America, or even in
> Russia, they, the *tirailleurs*, would have been ranking officers.

Thus what you have done is not serious. Thus we support you." After
the bombardment they would not let us spend another night there.
They sent us away by train right away. We were all prisoners in that
train. We went the same day to Montauban. We spent only two days
at Montauban. [52]

Tuo Nanzegue perhaps used *"Paris"* and *"Parisian"* to mean "France"
and "the French," for the incident may be that refered to by Echenberg
as having occurred at St. Raphael near Cannes in August 1945, in which,
he writes, "two civilians were killed and several wounded before the
roughly 300 African soldiers were subdued." [53] The archives for this
period, while now open, remain uncatalogued, and it has been impossible
to determine if the events were one and the same.

Such incidents must have been grist for the mill of the analysts of
the army's political service. While admitting that little hard evidence
of nationalistic ideas among the released prisoners had been found,
nonetheless they warned de Gaulle's ministers that "it is possible that
many of them have always had these as a goal and are now highly susceptible to underground propaganda." [54] It is likely that the French
military was also troubled by the fact that *tirailleurs* in combat had,
in some cases, developed warm fraternal relationships with American
soldiers, both black and white — soldiers from a country thought of by
the French political establishment as traditionally hostile to colonialism.
There had already been ominous portents of the impact Americans might
have in the African colonies. American troops stationed in Dakar were
wildly popular with the people of Senegal. Spontaneous demonstrations of delighted welcome had turned to boos in the Cameroun when
a troop of infantrymen, outfitted in U.S. uniforms, were first thought
to be Americans and then found to be French. In the Côte d'Ivoire, in
Bouaké, following the visit of an American geographic survey mission,
African *évolués* began saying that France had promised to cede the colony
to the United States after the war. By report, there was widespread delight
at the prospect. [55]

Ivoirien veterans discussed their feelings. White GIs, many of whom
might have rioted had they been integrated with blacks of their own
nation, nevertheless ate, slept, and drank alongside African troops, and
by all accounts enjoyed these exotic encounters. Yet the *tirailleurs* did
take note of the segregation of black and white American troops and
appeared to regard it as yet another example of "European" peculiarity.
As Ditiemba Silué said,

The American *tirailleurs* — the blacks — were not mixed like we were.
They were a group apart. But the white Americans were with us.
When the battle was over, the American whites were very happy with

us, and said we were their real comrades. Let's go to town and drink! They took our hands. At first they didn't say why the black Americans didn't fight next to us. Afterward they told us someone had decided that we weren't strong enough alone, so they mixed us in with the white Americans. They told us that afterwards. . . . We were happy to fight alongside the Americans because the French behavior toward us was not good. We did not like them. We were glad to fight alongside the Americans because when we killed someone — a Frenchman would say he did it, but the Americans did not do things like that. They said — no — you killed him. I was the best. I killed the most. I was decorated after the war. I was decorated by Colonel Benoit. [58]

To most *tirailleurs*, unaware of the racial situation in the United States, seeing American blacks was an unforgettable experience, bringing with it a new realization that, with education and opportunity, ordinary Africans could become much more than laborers and soldiers for a colonial state. "We were at Marseilles with them," said Aoussi Eba, referring to the black Americans. "We were proud of them — pilots, officers!" [57] Siliouenissougui Silué, of the 13th RTS, remembered his sense of shock at first seeing black Americans:

I didn't know black Americans existed. I was surprised to see them. I had an American friend. We went out together. I saw one of them who looked like a Korhogolese. I spoke to him, but when he did not understand me, I knew he was not from Korhogo. We did not know where they came from. Slaves, eh! The elders used to speak of slaves and Samory, but not about things before that. [58]

Tuo Nahon was very impressed by Americans of any color.

If it were not for the Americans we would all be dead. It was the French who had sent for us. The Americans took all the power from the French when they arrived. They gave us aid, but they thought that the French and the Africans should stay together. The Americans loved us very much and they took care of us. [59]

It had not escaped the *tirailleurs*, of course, that in combat, white Frenchmen behaved very differently from the typical West African *colon*. "We were all together," remarked Sekongo Yenibiyofine, who had finished his regular military service in 1934 and was recalled in 1940.

The whites did no harm to anybody. We did all our work together, but we did not eat together. They brought us our food and they brought them their food. I felt equal to them. We did the same work, the same things. We talked together. There were no beatings — no

getting slapped. Here [in the Côte d'Ivoire] it was not the same. When
I came back the first time, there was no more equality. But for me,
when I came back, I was no longer afraid of whites. [60]

In the course of the various campaigns, moreover, the *tirailleurs* had
been able to contrast their conditions with those of soldiers in other
armies. Col. Henri Boileau reflected on this:

> These Africans saw the African soldiers from English colonies. These
> blacks also did not eat together [with the whites]. Even the French
> Canadians in the British Army could not adjust to English ways. They
> [the *tirailleurs*] saw the American Army—with black officers, black
> pilots. They understood what they were seeing. They understood
> it all. They talked about it. It was not a question of color. Yes, if
> there was a black and white together, the black usually did the work.
> But it was much more a question of literacy. [61]

The French authorities were undoubtedly correct in their view that
the war created a new type of West African. In almost total contrast
with those who had taken part in the Battle of France in 1940, the
Tirailleurs Sénégalais who fought in the liberation of Europe not only
had the great satisfaction of participating in one military victory after
another, but found themselves doing so alongside soldiers from all the
Allied nations. Yet if their horizons were greatly enlarged by the experience, many of them were astute enough to realize that the
brotherhood of the battlefield would not survive their repatriation to
the colonies of the AOF.

The paternalistic and largely successful system of overseeing the welfare
and the behavior of the *tirailleurs* which had evolved over a period of
eighty years developed serious problems in 1945. In a poverty-stricken
and disorganized France, there were shortages of provisions and clothing.
Discipline tended to be either overly strict or too lax. There was a dearth
of old Africa hands among those NCOs and officers now supervising
the *tirailleurs*, who awaited a repatriation seemingly delayed indefinitely.
A number of serious incidents occurred. Indeed, there were virtual
mutinies in some of the camps. The year of Allied victory, 1945, would
prove the most difficult of all in the history of the *Tirailleurs Sénégalais*.
Ouanlo Silué was one of those who arrived in France from the Côte
d'Ivoire in this difficult period. He completed his basic training in Bouaké.
"I was there four months," he remembered.

> The fifth month we took the ship for France. . . . I was happy to
> be going to France. I wanted to see it. I was not sure if there was
> a war or not. They sent us to Abidjan without saying why or where

we were going. . . . There was famine that year in France. Great
hunger. We stole raisins to eat. Yes, we were fed in camp but never
enough. Everyone [civilians] had tickets to get food with. They did
not want us to have any because we got food in camp. Things did
get better by the time I left. [62]

Repatriation

The French government attempted, on compassionate grounds, to
give former prisoners of war priority for repatriation. However, the limited
number of troopships available made the program a frustratingly slow
one for prisoners and combatants alike. So desperate did the military
authorities become in their quest for means of removing the African
troops from metropolitan soil, that some 400 were even shipped to Liver-
pool in October 1944, there to await British transport to West Africa.
A serious incident occurred when African NCOs invaded a British
sergeants' mess from which they had been barred. By the end of the
next month the British thankfully saw them off, determined never to
repeat the experiment. [63]

There were reports of near mutinies aboard ships taking groups of
prisoners home. As early as November 1944, Colonial Minister Pleven
ordered Governor-General Cournarie to move the returning *tirailleurs*
out of Dakar as rapidly as possible. "The prisoners of war," he warned,
"may be a factor in stirring up discontent among the people, especially
around Dakar where there are so many of them." [64] Thus, in the camps
in the AOF as in those in France, thousands of *Tirailleurs Sénégalais*,
with little to keep them interested or occupied, idle and bored, conscious that they had lost their value as combatants, became increasingly
resentful, restless, and prone to mutiny. That at Thiaroye near Dakar
was only the most serious of many incidents.

On 1 December 1944, almost 1,300 former prisoners of war refused
orders and took hostage the commander of the AOF forces. The
mutineers were met with a hail of gunfire. According to Echenberg's
account of the mutiny, 35 Africans were killed and about the same
number seriously wounded. Significantly enough, no lives were taken
by the mutineers. [65] A Senoufo of the class of 1941, Dossigutta Silué,
remembered the event:

I was stationed in Dakar, before de Gaulle was in charge. I was at
the camp in Balain, near Dakar. I worked in the infirmary. We were
orderlies—we worked with the sick. No, I never mixed with civilians.

There was an epidemic in town, so civilians came to spray the hospital. That is all. . . . Thiaroye? Yes, we knew about it. They had told the *tirailleurs* that they would get their money in Dakar. There they told them that the money had not arrived yet and they would get it in Abidjan. They were not pleased. The commandant arrived and told them to stay calm—they would get the money later, in Abidjan. They threw rocks at his car. He called the guards— *tirailleurs*—and told them to charge—that the men were mutineers. They fired on the mutineers. There were many dead that day. We were angry. We thought we might not get back to our villages. We might be killed too. The army fired upon the army—those were the orders. Our regiment was not far from them. They brought the bodies to us. [66]

Dossigutta was undoubtedly correct in identifying money as one of the major causes of unrest among the repatriates. All former POWs interviewed in this study insisted that, while still in France, they were promised compensation for their years of suffering. This also holds true for those who served in North Africa, the Levant, and Europe. Many maintain that they were given personal assurances by de Gaulle, though Ivoirien *tirailleurs* liked to believe that any high-ranking French officer was the great man himself. Panafolo Tuo recalled listening to "de Gaulle" on VE Day, 8 May 1945:

De Gaulle made us. He was truly a man. He told us to be calm—the ship will come one day and we will also pay you. All of you will get money and those who were in prison will have a great deal of money. He said they couldn't give it to us now, but that we would get it in Africa, but I got nothing. [67]

Several factors combined to heighten the soldiers' sense of outrage: nonpayment of back wages, promised bonuses which never materialized, and even where payments had been made, the worsening exchange rates between the French and West African francs. The repatriates seem to have arrived home with different understandings, having been given different information by their officers in Europe. Some expected to receive back pay from the years in prison, some expected bonuses, and others thought they had been promised both. In fact, France did pay bonuses to many of the repatriated men in the form of a demobilization allowance of between 500 and 1,000 francs. It was far less than anyone had anticipated. To defuse the situation, officers in the major camps of the AOF assured the men that additional sums would be paid them on arrival in their own districts. This information no doubt worried the local commandants, who had no money for the purpose and were left to deal with the escalating anger of the soldiers arriving at their last stop. Tuo Nanzegue, already inflamed by the cinema incident in France, was scarcely pacified by his reception in the Côte d'Ivoire:

> We came back and at Bouaké, everyone was given 1,000 francs. Then they said the rest of our money would be at Korhogo. They never said how much, just that we would get money. Up to now, there has been nothing, nothing. We were numerous, from the whole *département*. A truck was waiting at Mr. Escarré's place. We got on there. We ate nothing. They gave us nothing. They wanted us out as fast as possible. They were afraid of us. If we had slept there even one night, there would have been a palaver. They were in a rush to get us out. That same night we arrived in Korhogo, the truck took us to our villages. [68]

The exchange rate caused other problems. The French franc was devalued in 1945 to half that of the West African franc. Little attempt was made to explain international monetary matters to the returning men. Rumors of being cheated at home when changing money swept through the barracks and the ships. As a result, many *tirailleurs* had tried to change any money they had in French francs in Dakar but through civilians rather than the army authorities and often without success. Ditiemba Silué spoke of his experience in 1946:

> At Dakar the people were not honest. When you sent French money for exchange into our francs, they gave you only half. Not the same franc. At Abidjan we got off the boat ourselves to change our money. They hadn't heard about Dakar [that is, the mutiny at Thiaroye]. They tried to do the same thing to us. We said we would revolt. We said no! We said no! We found our old adjutant at Abidjan, at the depot, Sergeant Troulou, a Yacouba. He took our money and changed it at the normal rate—no cutting. Me, I had 25,000 francs. We did not get a demobilization bonus. It was just my savings—savings from my wages. [69]

Ditiemba Silué was, of course, not the only soldier to have returned with savings, whatever their source. There are references to men having as much as 80,000 francs, and administrators were warned to keep an eye on them. It was believed that their reluctance to change their money through the army was a result of their unwillingness to risk being questioned about its source. [70] Several former prisoners, when interviewed, insisted that they had been given money for working as houseboys for their German captors. [71] Nonetheless, French officials were convinced that much of the cash held by African soldiers, particularly those of de Gaulle's army, had to have come from illegal sources. [72] Their suspi-

cions were not totally without foundaton. Some *tirailleurs* had not scru-
pled to sell their American uniforms and equipment on the burgeoning
French black market, while others had traded in scarce luxury items.
Denis Yacé referred to this:

> I did not come back with the anything—just the 500 francs we had
> been given. Some did. They had made money on the black market
> in France. They would resell the cigarettes and chocolate the
> American Army gave us. American soldiers were a big part of the
> black market. They would sell us their uniforms and we'd resell them
> on the black market. The French were glad to buy them. Everyone
> was in it. [73]

Echenberg refers to one case in which French officers in charge of the
repatriation of POWs found a total of 18,000,000 francs in the possession of some 1,200 men. All insisted that their earnings were legitimate.
The French refused to believe them, although there is no evidence they
attempted to confiscate the funds. [74]

Colonial administrators feared that this new wealth, especially if earned
illegally, would impede the process of quick reintegration of the men
into traditional society, fostering defiance of chiefs, and thereby of French
rule. Messages were passed down from the commandants to the canton and village chiefs. The commandant of Korhogo, for example, was
warned about the dangerous state of mind of returning prisoners with
full pockets. [75]

If matters of money were of the most immediate concern to the politicians and functionaries of the colonial administration, the possibility
that the repatriates would be the spearhead of nationalistic activity, its
natural leaders, was always at the back of their minds. Throughout the
AOF, local commandants were instructed to keep a close watch on all
anciens combattants, particularly ex-POWs, and to report any possibly
subversive activities. In northern Côte d'Ivoire, the commandants had
a further specific concern. This centered around the return to their
districts of those who had fled into the Gold Coast and had "volunteered"
to serve in the British army, for the most part in the West African Frontier Force (WAFF). Their exact number is unknown, although Jean Rouch
estimated that 90 percent of the 27,000 men in the Gold Coast forces
were drawn from Francophone Africa. [76]

Those returning home from the Gold Coast had seen action not in
Europe but in the Far East. Regiments of the WAFF fought in Burma
with the Eighty-first Division from February 1944 to early 1945, when
they were withdrawn to India. Others were part of the Eighty-second
Division. The Third West African Brigade fought with Wingate's

renowned Chindits in 1944 before being withdrawn and attached to
General Stilwell's forces in May. Most did not return to Africa until
1946; 20,000 WAFF troops were shipped home between May and June
1946.[77] While still on board the troopships, British officers, armed with
specially issued pamphlets, carefully explained exactly the demobilization pay and bonuses to which they were entitled. All soldiers of French
origin could elect to collect all their money at once, including fifty-six
days back pay and allowances and a war gratuity, the latter two bonuses
amounting to approximately fifty pounds. This approach was in clear
contrast to the ignorance in which, as we have seen, the French army
kept its *tirailleurs*.[78]

Those of Ivoirien origin returning from the Far Eastern campaigns
were repatriated to the Gold Coast. There the British authorities continued to show a justifiable concern about the reception of the men upon
their return to French territory. They feared that French officialdom would
regard these men as deserters, since most of them had crossed into British
colonies "illegally"—in Vichy eyes, that is—during 1940–42. Despite
assurances from the governor of the Côte d'Ivoire that the veterans would
be allowed to return in uniform, exempted from all head taxes imposed
during their absence, and their savings, demobilization pay, and possessions protected from confiscation or taxation, the governor of the Gold
Coast remained skeptical. He doubted the good faith of those in a colony which was still significantly Vichy in spirit and was dominated by
colons who were certainly not yet fully reconciled to the Gaullist concept of a new empire.

In the light of these concerns, the British recommended that all Ivoirien
veterans of their forces be returned to the Côte d'Ivoire and other French
colonies in groups. Gold Coast Sessional Paper 5 of 1945 stated that
they should be accompanied by a "European officer or noncommissioned officer," noting that "if they do not, it is probable that they will
not receive these concessions."[79] In the event, these men appear generally
to have been allowed to cross the border unmolested. Of a group of
fifteen which passed through Upper Volta en route for Niger, a French
administrator commented on the sensation they caused. "Their appearance," he wrote, "contrasted strikingly with that of the demobilised French
tirailleurs."[80] Those poor *tirailleurs*! Transport had been found finally
for most of them by 1946. It is no wonder that the commandant in
Volta found a striking contrast between their appearance and that of
the African veterans of the British army. Not only did the Ivoirien
repatriates receive little or no money but their uniforms and equipment
were requisitioned by military authorities as soon as they docked in Abidjan. Since 1944, de Gaulle's desire to expand and equip his army had
been severely handicapped by shortages of matériel. One stopgap measure

had been to requisition that of discharged soldiers. Apparently, no exceptions were made for those who had been prisoners of war since 1940 or for those who had fought for the liberation of France. No one seemed concerned about the psychological effect of literally stripping these men of what few possessions they had. No attempt was made to explain why their clothes were being confiscated. This insensitive policy, particularly in the light of French fears about the state of mind of repatriated *tirailleurs*, is inexplicable. The effect was to anger even those men who had returned with little or no resentment, only happy to have survived the war.

We have met the ex-prisoner Ehouman Adou before. This is what happened to him:

> It was in Abidjan that they hurt us. They collected everything we had with us—all the gifts the whites had given us. They only left us one black uniform. At Port Bouët, they took all our suitcases. I had a big suitcase, a trunk; they took it away from me on the train. We spent two months there trying to get our things back. They gave us money for the train—that's all. [81]

Sekongo Yenibiyofine, another liberated prisoner, had a similar experience:

> No one came to welcome us when we got to Abidjan. They gave us new papers, because the Germans had taken ours. Then they took everything away from us except one shirt and one pair of shorts. We came back to our villages with nothing. They said nothing to us and they took everything. [82]

Some, like Gnoumagai Soro, were forewarned and managed to win a small victory:

> Those who had come back before us told us that they will take your uniforms at Abidjan. When we heard this, we got angry and we threw all our uniforms in the water. Better to do that than to see them in stores. When we arrived, they let us keep everything in our trunks—all the things we had bought in France. They opened them up and found no uniforms, so they let us take the trunks home. [83]

And so they came home, the prisoners, the infantrymen, the artillerymen. Some were survivors of a terrible defeat and long years of imprisonment; some were victors, liberators of France. All found they were expected to fade away, to be reabsorbed in their village societies, to cause no trouble, and to claim no compensation. Yet, unlike the past generations of *Tirailleurs Sénégalais*, these men found they had something new: an avenue of protest. In the Côte d'Ivoire, they found Félix Houphouët-Boigny and the *Rassemblement Démocratique Africain*. The colonial administration may have wanted no part of them, but the leaders of the new political movement in the Côte d'Ivoire, civilians all, recognized their potential as organizers, their standing as men of honor in their villages, and saw for them an important role. Many a *tirailleur* took the chance offered him of participating in a new struggle, this time for the liberation of his own homeland.

NOTES TO CHAPTER EIGHT

1. For the best guide to the deployment of the various African units which formed part of the Army of Africa in 1943–45, see Anthony Clayton, *France, Soldiers and Africa*, 137–52.

2. *Unités Combattantes des Campagnes 1939–1945*, 320; SHAT, *Les Grandes unités françaises, historique succinct: Campagnes de Tunisie et d'Italie* (Paris: Imprimerie Nationale, 1970), 463–67; *The United States Army in World War II*, vol. 3 (Washington, D.C.: U.S. Government Printing Office, 1951), 180.

3. Charles de Gaulle, *The Complete War Memoirs*, 612.

4. CMIDOM, *Journal de marche*, 13th RTS.

5. Interview 15.

6. Interview 46.

7. Interview 57.

8. *Les Grandes unités françaises*, 465.

9. Henri Michel, *The Second World War* (London: André Deutsch, 1975), 641.

10. The official designation of First French Army was not made until 19 September 1944 when various corps of the B Army and the old First DFL were regrouped. To avoid confusion, as regroupments were made continuously during this period, the writer has referred to the entire French Force as the 1st French Army. See Paul Gaujac, *L'Armée de la victoire: De la Provence à l'Alsace* (Paris: Charles Lavauzelle, 1985), 168. Also see Clayton, *France, Soldiers and Africa*, for more details of the regroupments.

11. Gaujac, *L'Armée de la victoire*, 120–21.

12. Henri Michel, *The Second World War*, 641–43.

13. Interview 90.

14. Interview 57.

15. De Gaulle, order no. 127, dd. 9 November 1944, Paris. See Gaujac, *L'Armée de la victoire*, 122.

16. De Gaulle order no. 124, dd. 7 November 1944, Paris: Ibid., 119.

17. Cesare Salmaggi and Alfredo Pallavisini, eds., *2194 Days of War* (New York: Gallery Books, 1979), 571.

18. Interview 57.

19. Interview 46.

20. Interview 66.

21. Gaujac, *L'Armée de la victoire*, 168.

22. Interview 108, *Tirailleur* song popular among troops fighting at Belfort, in Alsace.

23. Interview 73.

24. De Gaulle, *The Complete War Memoirs*, 704.

25. Interview 66.

26. Interview 15.

27. Interview 46.

28. Interview 53.

29. Interview 49.

30. For the "whitening" policy, see Myron Echenberg, "Morts pour la France," 373–74.

31. De Gaulle, *The Complete War Memoirs*, 671–72.

32. *Histoire et épopée des troupes coloniales*, 4th ed. (Paris: 1970), 402–3. Respectively, the regiments became the 21st, 6th, 23rd RIC.

33. De Gaulle, *The Complete War Memoirs*, 585.

34. Interview 108.

35. Ibid.

36. Interview 103. Adou remembered his release as taking place in June 1944. It must have occurred around 15 September when Nancy fell to Patton's Third Army.

37. Interview 71.

38. Interview 60.

39. Interview 69.

40. CMIDOM, Carton Guerre 39–45, Dossier TII IPCV II 3870.

41. Ibid., "La Résistance en Sologne," 126–27.

42. Interview 30.

43. Interview 15.

44. Interview 68.

45. Interview 46.

46. ANCI, René Pleven to Pierre Cournarie, dd. 31 October 1944. Carton 5355, Dossier XV–4/4.

47. Robert Bourgi, *Le Général de Gaulle et L'Afrique Noire*, 93.

48. Interview 103.

49. Interview 21. The occasion was probably the Bastille Day parade of 1945.

50. Interview 30.

51. Interview 102.

52. Interview 68.

53. Echenberg, "Morts pour la France," 378. Echenberg found the archives still closed for this event. There is a typographical error in the text which places the incident in 1944, but see his n. 73.

54. ANCI, Carton 5355, Dossier XV–4/4.

55. ANCI, Monthly *cercle* reports, Abidjan, Bouaké, February 1944. Carton 1555, Dossier X–55/14.

56. Interview 15.

57. Interview 102.

58. Interview 62. The session was interrupted for several minutes while the interviewer, at the request of those assembled, gave a brief history of the African slave trade.

59. Interview 46.

60. Interview 48.

61. Interview 40.

62. Interview 55.

63. Echenberg, "Morts pour la France," 375–76.

64. ANCI, René Pleven to Pierre Cournarie, op. cit.

65. Echenberg, "Tragedy at Thiaroye," 109–28, passim. See also Echenberg, "Morts pour la France," 337.

66. Interview 31.

67. Interview 30. In 1986, the writer was able to assist Panafolo Tuo in obtaining his pension at last, five years after his application was filed.

68. Interview 68.

69. Interview 21.

70. ANCI, Carton 1968, Dossier XXIII–15/11.

71. See interview 104.

72. ANCI, René Pleven to Pierre Cournarie, op. cit.

73. Interview 2.

74. Echenberg, "Tragedy at Thiaroye," 114.

75. ANCI, Carton 1555, Dossier X–55/14 (December 1944).

76. Jean Rouch, "Migrations en Ghana (Gold Coast)," *Journal de la Société des africanistes*, 26 (1956), 55.

77. Eugene P. A. Schleh, "Post-Service Careers of African World War Two Veterans: British East and West Africa with Particular Reference to Ghana and Uganda," Ph.D. diss. Yale University (1968), 34.

78. "Demobilisation and Resettlement of Gold Coast Africans in the Armed Forces," sessional paper 5, no. 5, of 1945, Gold Coast Colony, 2. For a broad picture of the repatriation of West African Troops, see Public Records Office, London, War Office Papers WO32/10822.

79. Gold Coast Sessional Paper 5, op. cit., 5.

80. ANCI, monthly report, December 1945. Carton 1555.

81. Interview 103.

82. Interview 48.

83. Interview 57.

9

Anciens Combattants and
the New Ivoirien Politics

The Making of a Militant

NAMONGO OUATTARA IS PRESIDENT OF the Korhogo section of the
national veterans organization, the *Association des Anciens Combattants et Victimes de la Guerre.* He was a strong partisan of Félix
Houphouët-Boigny's *Partie Démocratique de la Côte d'Ivoire* (PDCI)
and became in time secretary general of the local branch. He describes
himself as *"un militant de première heure."* Drafted from the class
of 1942, Namongo served first in Alexandria guarding German
prisoners of war and later saw action in Damascus during the bloody
1945 revolt in Syria and Lebanon against continued French domina-
tion. Repatriated to the Côte d'Ivoire and demobilized in January 1947,
Namongo became closely associated with Dramane, a son of the
venerable Province Chief Gbon Coulibaly. Dramane Coulibaly was
then the regional leader of the PDCI, which had become part of the
interterritorial movement, the *rassemblement Démocratique Africain*
(RDA). As a result of his political activities, Namongo was jailed for
six months in Odienné. In 1985, he spoke freely about the anger which
drove him to join the movement newly emerging in the Côte d'Ivoire:

> After the war, General de Gaulle had said that we, the Africans,
> had suffered greatly. Because of this he wished to raise our pay.
> General Catroux, who was in command of our regiment, the 14th
> RTS at Alexandria, said that if Africans had bread to eat that would
> suffice for them. Africans don't know, understand money. That is
> what made me angry. De Gaulle had said those words—we all knew

about it—but then they said that General Catroux had refused to increase our pay. That bread was enough for us. There was something else too. Before I had even left for the war, one thousand people from here had been sent to the *basse côte* for forced labor. Five hundred died—and five hundred returned home with huge sores on their feet.

When I returned to the Côte d'Ivoire in 1947, I found out that Houphouët had already started to end forced labor. And I thought again about the words of General Catroux and also of all those who had died over there, and I thought I will enlist in the cause of liberty for the Africans. I went to tell all the *anciens combattants* that they must help Houphouët-Boigny because of what he was doing about forced labor. [1]

The rise of the PDCI and the RDA have been treated in detail in a number of studies. [2] For the Côte d'Ivoire specifically, the works by Zolberg and Loucou are recommended. [3] To retell the general story of the growth of nationalist parties is not the intent of this chapter, which is concerned with the specific roles played by the ex-*tirailleurs* of World War II and, most of all, with their perceptions of the roles they were playing. The veterans of the Free French campaigns arrived home enthused by the rhetoric of Gaullist politicians and proud of the part they had taken in the liberation of France and the triumph of democracy over fascism in Europe. They also arrived angered by what they saw as the failure of the authorities, civil and military, to reward them for their efforts. They were not long in the Côte d'Ivoire before learning of the great hardships suffered on the home front during the Free French era. Many found that their families had gone hungry as their food had been requisitioned in unprecedented quantities and the demands for forced labor raised to levels hitherto unknown. [4] Their anger was compounded further as they talked with the old generation of veterans who had been repatriated after the fall of France, and learned that their military services had also gone largely unrecognized and unrewarded by the colonial authorities, whether in the Vichy or Free French era. These are the themes to be explored in this chapter.

Korhogo's War—The Home Front

For the *tirailleurs* in Europe the implications of the fall of France and the rise of Vichy were quite apparent. The Germans had, quite simply, won. In the Côte d'Ivoire, and even more so in the remoter parts of the colony such as Korhogo, it was not at all clear what was happening. There was, we have noted, scarcely a radio in Korhogo town. The level of information in the community was determined by what the commandant did or did not choose to tell people. Needless to say, he did not rush to inform them of the collapse of France. There was, however, one episode which certainly did not escape the attention of Gbon Coulibaly and his elders and probably caused comment in even the smallest villages: A crack appeared in the tiny French community itself.

Whatever regime was in power seemed irrelevant to the tiny enclave of French merchants and traders, concerned first and foremost with pursuing their own business interests. They depended, however, upon the colonial administration, one of the primary tasks of which was (as they saw it) to sustain a world in which commerce could flourish. The tranquility of that world was shattered by the fall of France. The British naval blockade virtually eliminated essential imports of spare parts, food, and most importantly, wine and gasoline. Rationing in the Côte d'Ivoire was introduced in late 1940. Allocation of the rare shipments which arrived in the colony's upcountry towns was the responsibility of district commandants. In such a situation of shortages, a potential for conflict between commercial and administrative interests was ever present.

In Korhogo, the merchants split into two factions, and the rivalry between them quickly took on political overtones. One side charged that the others were traitors, in open rebellion against Vichy authority, while the other side accused the commandant of favoring their rivals. For months, two of the five major French traders resident in Korhogo had been inundating Abidjan (including its chamber of commerce) with passionate protests by letters and telegrams. Their complaints ranged widely: gasoline, for example, was being unfairly allocated to others, and certain firms were being given all the contracts for the transport of forced laborers and soldiers to the railway at Ferkessedougou.[5] So bitter did the dispute become that the shipment of appropriated rice, essential to the plantations and timber concessions of the south, was threatened. One faction announced its intention of sending a complete report on the situation directly to Pétain. The other group, accused of Gaullist sympathies (for apparently one of them smoked English cigarettes), struck back by means of an anonymous and extremely scatological communication addressed to the Europeans of Korhogo. We spare the reader the more obscene parts of the letter, since a few passages will illustrate the level to which the disputants sank:

> Breathless, they have called me "Foetus, Anus, Shit" like a Roman emperor. Why not? Vespasian [slang for a *pissoir*] also left a great name behind him. . . . It is true, I am short—wasn't Napoleon too? And closer to us, Mussolini. But I have both great heart and intelligence. . . . They say I am illiterate, a rustic. Self-made man that I

am, I do not blush. I used to scratch the soles of my feet in public; to pee ostentatiously because I was proud of my virility; but a fat pig (if it is you, then I send you my greetings) can envy a donkey. I know that the truth is not always in good taste, and to enumerate my bouts with venereal disease in front of a group of prudish women. . . . So that these beasts cannot take any piece out of the pure diamond that is my being, using their false teeth on my dear friends. Have they not dared to compromise this high functionary of Koroko [i.e., commandant Darand] who addresses me familiarly (*tutoyer*) even though he hardly knows me. [6]

Reports of the affair reached Governor Deschamps in Abidjan. Korhogo was not the only place in the Côte d'Ivoire to experience such turmoil, but the situation there seemed to have assumed more serious dimensions than elsewhere. Deschamps ordered his chief inspector of administrative affairs, Pierre de Gentile, to proceed to Korhogo. He reported back to Deschamps in terms which reduced to absurdity the claims and counterclaims of the bickering participants. He did not refrain from using names.

What are the reasons for this animosity and of this attempt at removal [of Commandant Darand] leading up to this great fracas which seems a customary occurrence with M. Serville. If one believes M. Darand and the group of those faithful—who one could qualify as ardent—to Marshal Pétain, Messieurs Bernier, Ollivier, and Trabucato, they say that the animosity of the agitators Serville and Escarré originates from their "Gaullism" and that they desire to harm, at any price, M. Darand, who is not attached to their way of thinking on this subject.

The accused Serville and Escarré have put up photographs of Marshal Pétain everywhere, and they vehemently affirm their loyalty. As to the former, I am skeptical following the incident of his nonrepudiation [of de Gaulle] before me on January 15th, which was transformed the next morning into a written repudiation after stating that I had, basically, misunderstood. As for the latter, M. Escarré, at the request of the head of the colony, a file has been put together by the Administrator Darand, which has been sent to Abidjan. Five or six similar affidavits are included. [7]

Among these affidavits was one from the supposed smoker of English cigarettes, M. Serville.

I'm not a Gaullist, which is what you asked me. I never will be his agent. I disapprove of the actions in Gabon and at Dakar. I never have had any contact with them either directly or indirectly. It is true, like most others, I have followed somewhat, after the breakup of our country, perhaps longer than others did, the speeches of de Gaulle, but it is also true that with all the information that is now coming to us from France, my opinion is totally changed. I turn off my radio when the propaganda program comes from London and say, "Here is the little liar." I am French, completely, and I possess the necessary discipline to participate in the Renaissance of our country.[8]

It was all quite undignified and trivial. Governor Deschamps, however, saw a serious aspect to the matter. He was horrified at the prospect of having the chaotic situation revealed to the Vichy authorities, and he was furious with Commandant Darand for not having kept him informed from the beginning. Most of all, however, Deschamps was concerned about the effect of these displays upon the Senoufo and Dyula of Korhogo. "We are," he wrote, "completely astonished to learn that this great fracas in front of the natives is true."[9] But what was, truly, the effect upon Deschamps's "natives"? Colonial administrators had always been ultrasensitive to the image that the white man presented to the colonized. As far as we can tell, while the fracas could not have enhanced that image, it was not regarded by the people of Korhogo as having any great political significance.

The octogenarian Gbon Coulibaly had already been in power when Almamy Samory invaded the region in the 1890s. He had then welcomed the French as "liberators"; he had supported them throughout World War I; he had collaborated with them in the interwar period, providing forced labor and assisting in the collection of taxes and tributes; he had supported the recruiting drive for soldiers to defend France in 1939; and when France fell in 1940, he had found himself able to live comfortably with colonial officials who had switched their allegiance to Vichy. The French thought of him as a most trusted friend of France, and he became universally known as the Venerable Gbon. We do not know whether he found merely amusement in the "fracas" between the merchants, this local manifestation of the split between Vichy and de Gaulle, or whether it perhaps affected his attitude toward the French by diminishing his respect for them. Certainly Gbon's attitude was to change during the Free French era in the colony.

The transformation of the stagnant Vichy colonial economy in the Côte d'Ivoire into one requiring a massive *effort de guerre* under de Gaulle and the Free French brought much suffering to the Korhogo region. By 1944, military and forced labor recruitment quotas had been doubled. So, too, had production quotas for rice and other crops and such wild produce as latex. As the young men were sent to the south and food supplies were appropriated from their families, hunger became common and even localized famines occurred.[10] Ironically, the worst hardships of the war were encountered in 1944, the very year which opened with the Brazzaville Conference. [11]

The Brazzaville Conference was a gathering of French colonial administrators at which only a few Africans were present, and then strictly as observers. It recommended that major social, economic, and political reforms of the French colonial system should be instituted after the war. As news of this percolated to remote areas such as Korhogo, great interest and hope was aroused by the recommendation that forced labor should eventually be abolished. Like many of his counterparts elsewhere in the Colony, Gbon Coulibaly wondered why the measure could not be implemented immediately. Why wait?

Resentment and anger grew, particularly after local ceremonies were held to hail the liberation of Paris in August 1944. Surely, the Africans thought, the war must by now be over! Surely Gbon and his people deserved finally to be left to work for themselves and to consume and sell their own produce. When this did not happen, many Ivoiriens became determined to force reform upon the administration. The *tirailleurs* who returned home from their regiments or their prison camps found that while Gbon Coulibaly was still in power as province chief, he had finally reached the end of his toleration for French colonial policies and had openly joined the fight to end forced labor.

Korhogo Veterans and the PDCI-RDA

In 1943 Ivoiriens had been admitted to the hitherto all-white *Syndicat Agricole de la Côte d'Ivoire*. [12] However, after the Brazzaville Conference authorized the formation of nonpolitical African unions and associations, seven wealthy Ivoirien planters—Houphouët-Boigny, Lamine Touré, Kouame Adingra, Djibrille Diake, Kouame N'Guessan, Fulgence Brou, and Georges Kouassi—chose to form their own organization, the *Syndicat Agricole Africain* (SAA). They were actively supported by the new Governor, André Latrille. A reform-minded leftist who had served under Félix Eboué in the AEF, Latrille regarded the African planter-farmer, rather than the white *colon*, as the essential element in achieving the production goals of the *effort de guerre*. That he was correct can be seen from the actual production figures in Table 5 for the wartime era, which clearly indicate the weight of the African contribution to the Côte d'Ivoire's economy.

Launched on 3 September 1944, the immediate objective of the SAA was to bring about total dismantlement of the forced labor system, from which all African planters, regardless of the size of their operations,

Table Five
Cash Crop Production in the Côte d'Ivoire, 1938–1945   Metric tons grown by European and African Planters

Year	1938–39	1939–40	1940–41	1941–42	1943–44	1944–45
COFFEE:						
European	2,700	4,000	6,000	10,000	7,000	4,400
African	14,200 (84%)*	21,000 (84%)	22,000 (79%)	20,000 (67%)	28,000 (80%)	20,100 (82%)
COCOA						
European	4,500	5,000	5,000	4,000	2,000	1,500
African	49,900 (92%)	40,000 (89%)	40,000 (89%)	36,000 (90%)	16,000 (89%)	9,500 (86%)
PALM OIL						
European	0	0	0	0	0	0
African	3,871 (100%)	3,400 (100%)	5,000 (100%)	6,000 (100%)	4,000 (100%)	3,700 (100%)
PALM NUTS						
European	0	0	0	0	0	0
African	7,200 (100%)	5,000 (100%)	6,000 (100%)	7,000 (100%)	5,500 (100%)	6,600 (100%)
SHEA BUTTER						
European	0	0	0	0	0	0
African	263 (100%)	500 (100%)	1,000 (100%)	1,500 (100%)	1,400 (100%)	2,200 (100%)
COTTON						
European	0	0	0	0	0	0
African	1,587 (100%)	50 (100%)	1,000 (100%)	2,300 (100%)	1,250 (100%)	500 (100%)
RUBBER						
European	0	0	0	0	0	0
African	18 (100%)	64 (100%)	224 (100%)	370 (100%)	513 (100%)	1,275 (100%)
DRIED BANANAS						
European	0	0	0	150	445	1,380
African	0 (0%)	0 (0%)	0 (0%)	0 (0%)	0 (0%)	0 (0%)

SOURCE: ANCI, Carton 1555. Rapport Annuel du Gouverneur de la Côte d'Ivoire. Annex to André Latrille's 1944 report.
*Percentage of African production to total production.

had been unable to profit under Vichy decrees. It was the belief of the founders of the SAA that, with the abolition of forced labor, the free market in wage labor would rapidly expand and provide the Ivoirien planter with the workers he so desperately needed. In 1945 Gbon welcomed Houphouët-Boigny to Korhogo, as a representative of the SAA. Houphouët used the occasion to seek Gbon's collaboration in finding volunteer workers for the coming growing season. Gbon had his chiefs provide Houphouët with 1,500 men, convinced by the argument that Africans did not have to be coerced into supplying their labor but would respond to offers of fair wages and decent working conditions.

Throughout the Côte d'Ivoire, Africans rushed to join the SAA. By 1945, there were 20,000 members. The union, however, was rapidly transforming itself into a full-blown political organization. The PDCI was officially launched in April 1946. Six months later, under the leadership of Félix Houphouët-Boigny and Ouëzzin Coulibaly, it was instrumental in the founding of the overarching interterritorial movement, the RDA.

In Korhogo, Gbon strongly supported Houphouët and his slate of candidates for the Ivoirien Assembly in 1945, and in the following year likewise backed Houphouët's successful bid for election to the French National Assembly. Tuo Nahon came home from the army that year.

> When I got back the RDA hadn't got started. I came to Korhogo and went to say hello to Old Gbon. Gbon said that a young Baoulé is here who wants to get rid of forced labor. He gave us a paper about it. When we got home, we let all the villagers know about Houphouët and when the election came, Houphouët-Boigny won. All the *anciens combattants* voted for Houphouët—all of them—all of them. Our whole village too. Our canton chief was the first to support Houphouët, the first after Gbon. He was a great supporter of Houphouët. Thus no one could have not voted for Houphouët. No, it was not a question of force, it was because with Houphouët, forced labor was going to end. [13]

Why was Gbon Coulibaly's support so crucial for Houphouët and his colleagues? Strongly backed by his son Dramane, by virtue of the almost mystical respect he commanded, Gbon was the one figure who could directly appeal to, and win the support of, the embittered veteran *tirailleurs* not only of the Korhogo region but of much of the northern Côte d'Ivoire. By mobilizing the *anciens combattants*, he provided the PDCI-RDA with the nucleus of a political machine in the north. At this time the veterans were regarded as critical in spreading Houphouët's message, for regardless of their traditional status, the veterans were widely respected in their cantons and villages because of their military service. They were perceived by ordinary villagers as having an intimate under-

Namongo Ouattara, president of the Korhogo Veterans Association

standing of things alien and modern, and in particular of anything French. Military service had exempted them, *de facto*, from further administrative demands, and this added to their stature in a new post-war world which held promise of the abolition of that most detested of all colonial institutions, forced labor. They were men who appeared unafraid of either the commandant, his police, or even more importantly, the canton chiefs. What better bearers of Houphouët's tidings could the Venerable Gbon and his son find, than these men whose knowledge of the world had expanded so dramatically? Again, Namongo Ouattara speaks:

> There was a great change in us. Those who had been born in Korhogo, knew only the things of Korhogo, but those who had traveled everywhere did not have the same spirit. They had seen many things, done many things. They were more intelligent than those who had stayed. When they returned to work in their villages, they found Houphouët. Forced labor was impeding people's ability to work on their own account. We, the *anciens combattants,* were mighty in our efforts to explain things to the population. The system of forced labor fell. [14]

Gbon Coulibaly summoned all the *anciens combattants* to a meeting in Korhogo in 1946. Houphouët-Boigny addressed it. For both practical and ceremonial reasons, Dramane acted as interpreter. First, Houphouët needed to be certain that the veterans, whose French vocabulary tended to be limited to military and culinary matters, truly understood him. Second, customary Senoufo practice decrees that no important personage speak directly to his audience but must have his words "translated" by an intermediary, even when those words are spoken in the same language as that of his audience. That Houphouët's interpreter was the son of the only chief they had ever known was not lost upon the men. Yeo Nabetegue who, having barely escaped capture in 1940, was repatriated after the fall of France, recalls that first rally of the former Korhogolese *tirailleurs*:

> I joined very quickly because someone had taken over my lands. When I was in politics, I had the power to get it back. This village [Tagbanga] was with Houphouët—my little brother even worked in Houphouët's fields. I went to the big meeting in Korhogo. Houphouët said, "When you were soldiers, you worked for France. The men who left [as forced laborers] to pull the wood, worked for France. Now we all want to work for ourselves. After the first war, they promised to liberate us—to change the power. They did not do this. So you must help me to make this change so that all will work for themselves."
> I informed the village about who he was and what he said. . . .
> I said, "Here is one who can do it—make the change—take the power

from the hands of the whites." They accepted it. And it all came true. The village chief was an *ancien combattant* like me—no problem with him. The canton chief? No, all he was interested in was getting profits from sending men to pull wood. [15]

"Pulling wood" typified for these men perhaps the ultimate horror of the forced labor system. Namongo Ouattara graphically described what was involved.

Pulling—hauling tree trunks—huge logs that measured four meters by fifteen meters. You'd cut small logs then lay them down over two or three kilometers—a road of small wood. Then the trunks were chained. Two large, heavy chains were put around them—toward each end. Then, the wood was put on the small logs. One hundred people were on each side of the chains, while one man sat on the log, guiding the two chains. If the wood started to veer toward the left, he'd pull it straight. Those that were pulling the log could get run over if it fell off the rollers. If you didn't pull hard enough, the team leader would whip you, hard. If someone was killed, he was just thrown off to the side—like a dead chicken.

We chopped trees down too—with a hatchet, then we had to pull them all the way to the lagoon [at the coast]. If you started at seven in the morning, you had to pull until nightfall. Not even stopping to eat—you had to arrive first before they'd feed you. The white man was La Gosse—the head of the yard. If one day they decided you had to pull three logs and you didn't arrive by nightfall, you didn't eat. You just stayed with the wood until the next day. . . . How many you had to pull depended on their size. . . . The Mossi pulled wood as well as the Senoufo and worked on the plantations with us. Perhaps the men of the south are not strong enough. The Senoufo people rebelled. We did all the work in the Côte d'Ivoire—roads, even built the railway. All this without machines—nothing. It is we who did it all. [18]

There is little need to explain further why the Senoufo—remote as they might be from the centers of Ivoirien power and prosperity—were to become among the most ardent supporters of Félix Houphouët-Boigny and the PDCI-RDA.

And so the battle was joined. Most of the *anciens combattants* of Korhogo became engaged in a new struggle, that for the future of the Côte d'Ivoire. Lassina Coulibaly, chief of a Dyula section of Kapelé, commented on the esteem in which the veterans were held in this period:

The Dyula here respected the soldiers because they left for the army. Yes, it was forced upon them, but we made great sacrifices for them—

so that their sons would stay in good health during the war. Only one Senoufo [of Kapelé] died in the war. The rest came home. They had left group by group, and they came back the same way. The first to leave were the first to come back. They talked about all they had seen and done. Then, they commanded great respect here. They were like canton chiefs. When they spoke, no one else talked. They were greatly respected because they had seen the land of the whites. They fought the war. They were strong men. They were much honored. When there was a meeting of the *anciens combattants*, it was *chaud*! Because Houphouët told us he would end forced labor, and when he created the SAA and the men were well treated, all of us went his way. [17]

The Growth of the PDCI-RDA

Houphouët-Boigny took his message to *anciens combattants* throughout the Côte d'Ivoire. He told them they must now fight not for France but for their own country. They must join the RDA and use their special position to influence their people. And so they joined in droves. Already popular and well respected, they enhanced their standing by becoming enthusiastic defenders of the ordinary Ivoirien farmer and planter. [18] In the north, the administration tended to leave the *anciens combattants* to their own devices, seemingly in the hope that their enthusiasm for the new politics would wear itself out. In the south and west, considerable pressure was put on the veterans to conform to official policy, and the level of conflict rose as many of them refused to obey their chiefs or accept the *Indigénat*, the "native" law code which still, in 1946, remained in force. In the elections of that year, however, the franchise was extended to all veterans, who thus came to form a majority of the Ivoiriens eligible to vote. [19]

In 1945 and 1946 the colonial administration sought to destroy the burgeoning alliance between Houphouët and the *anicens combattants*. At the beginning of 1946, a new governor was appointed, M. Orselli. He was given a precise mission by Coste-Floret of the colonial ministry— namely to "suppress the RDA." [20] Although Orselli appeared to have little taste for the task, pointing out he had never dabbled in politics throughout his long career, he nevertheless obeyed orders. Attempts were made to convince or coerce former soldiers into supporting parties deemed no threat to French interests, parties dominated by traditional chiefs and financed by *colons* and even by colonial officials, such as the *Union Voltaïque* or the *Partie Progressiste de la Côte d'Ivoire*. Such attempts seem to have had mixed results. In the Mossi country of Upper Volta, many *anciens combattants* of the Ouagadougou area did indeed come out in support of the Moro Naba and his *Union Voltaïque*. They supported, apparently, his hopes of seeing the restoration of Upper Volta as a separate colony. In the Bobo-Dioulasso district of Upper Volta, by contrast, the veterans rallied behind the PDCI-RDA. As its commandant reported, "The *anciens combattants* are for the most part fervent partisans of Houphouët. They voted as one man for him."[21] And well they might, for Houphouët's closest comrade, Ouëzzin Coulibaly, was himself from the area and had become leader of the non-Mossi Voltaics.

Houphouët-Boigny's message was clear. He promised to work for freedom, higher prices for export crops, more schools and hospitals, and of course, an end to taxes and forced labor. If the French had created additional seats in the National Assembly for African deputies from both the AOF and the AEF, and had extended the franchise in limited ways, they received little credit for doing so. During the election campaign of 1945, Ivoirien militants working for Houphouët's election considered such measures no more than a prologue to the real reforms they had been awaiting ever since the Brazzaville Conference. The renowned Ivoirien writer, Bernard Dadié, voiced this view in Bouaké, speaking in the presence of the *cercle* commandant:

> France has not kept her promises. If France asks for black delegates, it is because she is afraid. Remember the proverb which says: When you have a pretty woman and you are afraid she might leave you for another and richer man, you must treat her well.[22]

Thompson and Adloff have advanced the view that "emotional ties between African and French veterans probably accounted for the unwavering loyalty shown by former African soldiers during the difficult post-war years."[23] This thesis is most definitely *not* borne out in the case in the Côte d'Ivoire. There were, of course, some veterans who held back from involvement in the new politics. The former prisoner of war, Ehouman Adou, was one who equivocated:

> The RDA invited me to take their card, and the *Progressivistes* invited me too. Each one offered me things. The *Progressivistes* offered me a rifle. I said no. I am French. I don't want either one of you. It was hot for a black then. One day the village called me—the whole village was RDA—and said, "You're not for us. You're not for the *Progressivistes*. Leave!" I told them, "No." I was born here, and I was staying. Of course, now I am a member of the RDA.[24]

More commonly, fear of the consequences of political involvement, rather than loyalty to France, was the paramount consideration. Tafolotien Soro of Napie, survivor of Elba and Belfort, spoke of this:

> The RDA was organized. You joined. You didn't join. Nowadays, everyone does and says what he wants. When the politics started, the canton chiefs were for the whites. They did not want the politics

of Houphouët. That is why many were afraid to join Houphouët. If you did—and were against your canton chief—he could cause trouble for you. Many were afraid. Those with hard heads were certain *anciens combattants* who joined Houphouët. But in 1946, here in Napie, only one person was RDA. We supported it, but secretly. No one here had the [membership] card—we were afraid of the canton chief. He was with the French, and they were in charge. No. We *anciens combattants* were not afraid, just tired from the war. What could the canton chief do? At a village near here, the villagers said that they would join the RDA. They [the police] came and took everyone, all the young boys, to Korhogo, to clean the streets. They beat them.[25]

The hesitation of some veterans notwithstanding, most gave their support to the rising nationalist movement. In the election of October 1945, Houphouët received the highest number of votes in the Ivoirien chamber reserved for *sujets* rather than *citoyens*. Against the 12,650 cast for him, 11,620 went to his opponent, the aged and illiterate Baloum Naba Tenga Ouedraogo, whose candidacy had been advanced by the Moro Naba.[26] In the election of 1946 the Moro Naba decided not to oppose Houphouët, presumably in the knowledge that Upper Volta was short-ly to regain its status as a separate territory. Houphouët received a stag-gering 21,099 votes of the 22,995 accepted as valid.[27] In both of these campaigns the veterans played a key role. Namongo Ouattara gives us a vivid picture of the times:

> We, the *anciens combattants*, had as our role the job of telling the people to follow Houphouët to end forced labor. Yes, the law was passed in 1946, but it did not end until 1950. . . . I was the one who led them—who sought them out. I went to every village to find the *anciens combattants*, and I told them to ask their villagers to follow Houphouët. I went from village to village. We had influence—power now. Before the war, one would have had to have gone first to the village chief, but not now. They listened and they talked. They were angrier than I was, but I was angrier than others. There were *anciens combattants* whose families had died because of forced labor—then they were sent to the army. They came back to find no one there—of course they were angry.[28]

By 1950 Houphouët-Boigny claimed, probably without too much exaggeration, that 99 percent of Ivoirien *anciens combattants* were members of the PDCI-RDA.[29] Aoussi Eba, the *tirailleur* who was to become a deputy in the Ivoirien parliament, spoke of the moral strength that his fellow ex-soldiers brought to the struggle:

> The *anciens militaires* were a force in the movement—an under-ground force. They told everyone what they had seen—done, in France. All the *anciens combattants* were with the RDA. We were

chosen to run for political office. But I spoke for all the *anciens combattants.* "I, I am not like you. I have fought the war." [30]

The readiness of the veterans to follow Houphouët undoubtedly
reflected the enthusiasm they felt for his programs of reform. They had,
however, their personal grievances. We have referred, and shall refer again,
to the matter of the payment of their pensions and bonuses. They also
frequently sought jobs in the administration, no matter how lowly, and
came to regard these as just rewards for having defended and taken part
in the liberation of France. That the Côte d'Ivoire was in financial straits,
and that most veterans were in fact illiterate and trained for little besides
combat, were unacceptable as explanations of why their applications
were rejected. They grew ever more disillusioned with the colony's administration. They began to create what the commandant in Man called
"problems" in their villages. [31] One of the main "problems" appears to
have been their total support for Houphouët. Several Man veterans
recalled those days:

> There were *anciens combattants* with Houphouët from the begin-
> ning. Sodie Gaston [dead], Sia Gaston [dead], and the president of
> the *anciens combattants,* Gondo François . . . Most of us returned
> to our villages after the politics had already started. We were very
> happy about it. First forced labor was suppressed, then there was
> the liberation of certain political prisoners. Yes, everyone knew about
> him [Houphouët]. . . . Those who had pulled the wood, when they
> said Houphouët was going to end it. [32]

In Gaoua, the commandant also complained that pensioned career
soldiers in his *cercle* were "showing independent tendencies for themselves
and their families—independent of authority, simply because they had
done their fifteen years of military service." [33] In Grand Lahou, the administrator refused to inform *anciens combattants* of the decree exempting
them from the *Indigénât,* and warned the then Governor Latrille that,
should they find out about it, veterans would then feel free to interfere
with the recruitment of forced laborers. "They will," he wrote, "believe
they have escaped all justice, all authority, even native." [34]

In Korhogo, as early as 1944, Senoufo ex-*tirailleurs* were involved in
several demonstrations, or what were referred to as "incidents." In one
of these, they had organized a protest against a canton chief. No less
than Governor André Latrille himself, happening to be on tour in the
north at the time, investigated the matter. Latrille, well known for his
"radical" view that Africans had legitimate grievances, evinced little sympathy for the commandant. In a report addressed to all his administrators,
he pointed out that "the attitude of the commandant of the *cercle* deter-
mines the spirit of the former *tirailleurs.*" The unfortunate comman-

dant in Korhogo probably received little comfort from Latrille's further comment that "the rest of the population disapproves of the aggressive attitude adopted by the *Tirailleurs Sénégalais* of Korhogo subdivision and makes that clear to them."[35]

Divided by a Common Uniform: Soldiers against Veterans

Appalled by the direction of French politics under the Fourth Republic which he had done so much to create, de Gaulle withdrew, temporarily, from public life in 1946. By then left-leaning reformists like Latrille had been eased out, or in some cases purged, from the colonial administration. The rebellion in Indochina, if it did not shake the foundations of the republic, persuaded it that colonial reform had gone too far. French policy took a dual path, economic advancement and political repression. The French government decided to draw upon its limited resources to finance rapid and real development in the colonies, so that these in turn could contribute to the reinvigoration of the shattered metropolitan economy. Economic development was funded on a scale hitherto unknown in France's colonial history. A series of ambitious agricultural, educational, industrial, and health projects was launched, designed to bring Francophone Africa into the European version of the twentieth century and into a new partnership, albeit a decidedly junior one, with the *métropole*. At the same time, however, investment in the colonies created the very real possibility of their moving slowly toward independence from the *métropole*. This prospect remained anathema to the politicians in Paris, especially the powerful and conservative *colon* lobby.

For the politicians the dilemma was how to reconcile economic liberalism with the perceived need to clamp down upon the "ominous" signs that new leaders in the colonies were becoming strongly influenced by anticolonial sentiments and even (heaven forbid!) left-wing ideologies. To those in the seat of power in the rue Oudinet, the growing influence of the RDA upon the peasants and planters of the AOF came to be seen as the most dangerous obstacle to the restructuring of the empire. Their worst fears seemed confirmed when RDA deputies in Paris accepted an alliance with the French Communist party in order to move their political agenda forward. Without this marriage of convenience, it seems clear that the small number of African deputies could have had little impact upon an Assembly which eventually grew, between 1947 and 1951, to 627 elected representatives of whom only fifteen were Africans.[36]

Conservatives dedicated to the preservation of the empire were horrified by these developments. Since the establishment of the communist-led *groupes des études* in the AOF under the momentarily liberalized regime of 1944, senior administrators in the colonies, as well as many within the resident white communities, had harbored deep suspicions about the true motivations of the Communist party vis-à-vis Africa. It should be remembered that much of the hostility toward de Gaulle among Europeans, in the Côte d'Ivoire as elsewhere, arose from his willingness to cooperate with Communist leaders of the Resistance. Two years after the war, however, de Gaulle and many others did indeed choose to forget the role these former allies had played in liberating France.

By the late 1940s, patriotic memories of the war had become of little import. In West Africa such considerations had no effect upon the decision to repress movements now viewed as dangerous, and first and foremost of them, the RDA. In the Côte d'Ivoire the campaign against the PDCI-RDA rapidly gained momentum. To hold a membership card was to be subjected to harassment and even imprisonment. *Ancien combattant*, wealthy planter or trader, canton chief and province chief—even those of Gbon Coulibaly's stature—found themselves facing the full might of colonial repression. Gbon himself was perhaps not taken entirely by surprise. Even in the first election of 1945, his house in Korhogo had been, on the orders of the governor, ringed with soldiers in an attempt to negate his influence on the voters.[37]

Repression, as always, fostered resistance. By January 1949, large-scale protests erupted. Violent confrontations between soldiers and crowds of demonstrators, with large contingents of *anciens combattants* in their ranks, took place throughout the colony. From Sinématiali in the north; Bongouanou and Bondoukou in the east; Bouaké, Dimbokro, Bouaflé, and Agboville in the center; and Daloa and Seguela in the west, RDA militants came out and demanded their rights. The RDA senator Biaka Boda (who was to disappear mysteriously one night in 1949, never to reappear) spoke for many Ivoiriens when he expressed the outrage felt at their treatment by an administration that appeared oblivious to the sacrifices made by their people during the war:

> The administration is afraid of the RDA. It is trying to suppress African liberty, like wounded panthers. These are the bad French; these are the bad administrators, who, during the war solicited our special affection, who today are reactionaries, and these are those who, during the war, ate our chickens, took our daughters. Some of us did not fire a gun but suffered terribly to furnish their products, rubber, in order that these administrators, the administrator of Daloa, who were part of that corrupt and decadent [Vichy] government which actually ruled France against the will of the French people.

France had been occupied by Germany. For its deliverance, the appeal was made to Africans who liberated France. The RDA has asked that the *anciens combattants*, the disabled, collect the same pension as the disabled veterans of the *métropole*. The corrupt government has to this day refused to grant us this equality, yet an African dies like a white and he has the same rights; he is a citizen exactly like the other. [38]

Boda's message was one that not only the Ivoirien leaders, but the *anciens combattants*, could enthusiastically endorse. Philippe Yacé, the *citoyen* who refused to be pulled back from the Belfort front in 1944, spoke of these years of political turbulence:

We, the *anciens militaires*, stayed in our villages when we came home. All stayed. We went without thinking of why or what we would see. But, the subjects, who were servants, had a crisis of conscience in France. We have liberated France. Why are we not free? We continue to be important in the politics of the nation. We had a special role to play—to accelerate the process. I made a speech, in Abidjan, in 1945, that was important to the SAA. We had a legitimate but different role in the movement. In 1950, they prevented meetings of the SAA. At one place where the SAA was trying to meet, French troops came armed to break it up. I stood up and said, "This is not a rendez-vous for arms, but for farmers. Do you see any guns among the people here?" And they backed down and left. It was the first day of May 1950. The best propagandists for Houphouët were the *anciens combattants*. [39]

A serious confrontation between RDA supporters and the administration occurred at Bouaflé in January 1950 after a meeting attended by Houphouët-Boigny and Ouëzzin Coulibaly. Ve Sabh from Man was serving part of his fifteen-year hitch there and was among those sent to break up the demonstration. "The RDA had really heated up then," he said.

There was a lot of palaver. They (our officers) sent us there to separate the people forcibly. Even the Lieutenant, Moussa Sano, was gravely hurt at Bouaflé. . . . By a machete cut. The RDA was meeting, and we went to separate them. There were so many at that meeting. We left. Moussa was with us. We had the machine gun and rifles which we were going to fire in the air. There were *anciens combattants* among the people. They could not understand why we fired on them. They were with the villagers. They kept coming. We fired above their heads. It was in front of the *gendarmes*'s camp—the camp that is there today. The lieutenant pulled out his pistol and fired in the air. The men fell upon him. They took away his pistol, then they cut him with the machete. He was gravely wounded. Two of us carried him to Faso hospital. When you see your officers being hurt, you cannot let them kill an officer even if they are your brothers. You cannot let them kill one of you. Moussa was not dead, but very badly hurt. We brought him to an African healer. We didn't tell anyone—if we had not done so, he would have died. The African doctor was a soldier, first class. We took Moussa out of the hospital.

Later Ouëzzin Coulibaly and Houphouët-Boigny passed in front of the African clinic, near the road. If I remember correctly, there was even a *sergent-chef*, a Corsican, who wanted to arrest Ouëzzin. It was a tense moment. The captain came and told us not to close the road. After Ouëzzin and Houphouët had gone by, the dead remained. After Moussa fell, they [the RDA supporters] believed that we would not shoot at them. They fell on us. We didn't want to hurt them, but they kept coming. They took the pom-pom gun [*canon-mitrailleuse*]. They started to fire on us. We had to fire back. It was lamentable. Because we had not fired first, they thought we would not. Then when we started shooting, the civilians ran away, into their houses. The soldiers fired into the houses—houses of mud brick. The bullets went right through them. There were too many meetings—too many people. The girls, the women, they encouraged the mob. We stopped them. We stood our ground. We arrested those who were trying to escape. [40]

The official count acknowledged only three civilian deaths at Bouaflé.

Ve Sabh was clearly disturbed by what had occurred, but nevertheless justified the response of the soldiers in the circumstances. *Tirailleurs* on active service, he said,

did not get into politics. It did not interest us. Then, when we left for Bouaflé, we knew then that we were [first and foremost] Ivoiriens. They—our people—did not understand that the Europeans had the power. They fell on us. They were our brothers, but they did not understand. They did not understand that we were their brothers. They had taken the pom-pom gun. They thought they had taken everything. We had to react. There were other incidents like that, but I was not involved in them. [41]

Alphonse Togba, a new recruit from Man who had signed up as a volunteer only a few months before, was also at Bouaflé. "My lieutenant, Moussa, was injured—by the natives," he said.

We fought the RDA for the sake of the whites. And Moussa was hurt. Then I went to Yamoussoukro. Everything was calm there. Moussa was replaced by a European captain, Laurent. Then we were sent to Toumodi, to the camp there. In January 1950 there was trouble at Dimbokro. [42]

The "trouble at Dimbokro" was of an even more serious nature. At least
fourteen Africans died there. [43] The district commandant, alarmed by
the size of a demonstration and not fully trusting the serving *tirailleurs*,
called in a unit of Syrian Alawites stationed in Bouaké to control the
situation. [44] Their presence had the opposite effect, inflaming the
demonstrators. In 1986 M. and Mme Delonges, French residents of Dimbokro since 1940, recalled the day:

> First they held a parade at the big market. The Africans here were
> asking for reforms. We lived here very comfortably with the Africans.
> I had, still have, a plantation with a house like this. I lived there and
> never had to lock a door. There was never a problem—and there
> were no problems during the war. Anyway I saw the parade, the
> marchers, and I asked my cook what was going on. They had called
> the military out. The commandant here was very indecisive. He did
> not want or did not know how to get respect from either the Africans
> or the whites. He called in the Alawites. . . . They're very tall—a
> race apart. They cause fear in others. Very handsome men. [45]

Why call in the Alawites? The answer is supplied by Alphonse Togba,
whose unit had been issued ammunition in order to keep the situation
in Dimbokro under control:

> We were camped where the *gardes du cercle* stayed. It was 25 January.
> A European corporal was hurt in town. Our commander found out
> about it and handed out ammunition. Usually we had our rifles but
> no ammunition, just blanks. We, the Ivoiriens, held a meeting. Our
> leaders—those who had been in the war—said, "Houphouët is in
> the city. They have given us ammunition to shoot our brothers. Thus,
> if they send us to town—do not shoot. That is what they want us
> to do." That is what they [our leaders] told us. But the commander's
> adjutant was at that meeting. He was from Burkina [i.e., Upper
> Volta]. He went to the captain to tell him we were protesting. That
> if we went to town, we had decided not to shoot. This was 27 January.
> When the captain heard that, he sent word to the *commandant de
> cercle*, who told him to take away our weapons and ammunition.
> Only from us, the Ivoiriens. There were others—Burkinabe and
> Malians—we, the Ivoiriens, were all locked in our huts. It was rotten.
> We could not go out.
> Two days later we saw soldiers arriving from Upper Volta, in battle
> dress, backpacks, all that. Then the *Garde Mobile*—the gendarmes—
> came from Dakar by plane, carrying machine guns. On 31 January
> they left camp with the Burkinabe. We could see the injured and the
> dead then—all civilians. We followed our leaders—that's why we were
> not in it, did not do it. They were twelve corpses that they made

us—the prisoners—put together in one grave. Five days later, Houphouët sent a telegram to the *commandant de cercle* telling him to disinter those bodies and put each one in an individual grave, with his name and his village marked. The commandant had to let us do it. Then the *Garde Mobile* left and the Burkinabe left. We stayed another three months in the region. January, February, March. Then they made us guardians for the *Progressivistes*, and we put the people of the RDA—the notables—in prison. We also confiscated all their rifles, spears. Only from the RDA, not from the *Progressivistes* who kept their rifles. [48]

Why did the *commandant de cercle* accede to Houphouët-Boigny's demand for the decent burial of the dead of Dimbokro? It must be remembered that Houphouët, whatever the local administration thought of him, was in his fifth year as deputy for the Côte d'Ivoire in the French National Assembly. Moreover, he was pressing for a commission to investigate inter alia the events in Bouaflé and Dimbokro. The report of this—the Damas—commission appeared in 1950. [47] Houphouët himself testified before it. He poured scorn on the official report that the Dimbokro deaths occurred after a crowd of 4,000 attacked the soldiers. No soldier received even a scratch, he observed.

Is it possible that those of you who knew our *tirailleurs* on the battlefield believe that when they were there, armed with rifles, being attacked by machetes held by 4,000 people—that not one soldier would get hurt—not one with the crowd only ten meters away? [48]

Nevertheless, this in a sense missed the point.

The real tragedy of Bouaflé and Dimbokro was that *anciens combattants* throughout the colony were enlisting in the RDA, while their countrymen, both new recruits and career soldiers, were still serving in the French army and were expected to repress the movement. Yet, perhaps for the first time in the Côte d'Ivoire, *Tirailleurs Sénégalais* on active duty recognized that there was a conflict between obedience to their commanders and loyalty to their own people. Those who agreed to hold their fire at Dimbokro were men who were now beginning to consider themselves first and foremost Ivoiriens. They were confronting Agni or Baoulé, with whom few of them were ethnically affiliated. Yet, they knew they should not fire upon them. The point, the paradoxical point, is that it was service in the army itself that had provided them with this growing sense of a national identity, transcending local particularisms. It was not that the army taught them anything of the new politics. Indeed, it discouraged any interest in politics among its ranks.

But the soldiers could not remain oblivious to the turmoil in their land. Sergeant Alphonse Dionkla, later to become canton chief of Blouno near Man, speaks of his experience:

> An African soldier could say nothing. At the bottom of our hearts, though, we were with them [the RDA]. I got fifteen days once at Bouaké because three of us went to a meeting of Houphouët at Sakasso. We did not know we had been seen. We got back to camp and they said, "Go to the office." There they said, "You were at the meeting held by the deputy Houphouët—fifteen days!" [We had gone] to hear—to listen to what he, the deputy, had to say. It was good for us. [49]

The Korhogo region did not escape the effects of repression. Lassina Coulibaly of Kapelé, no relation to Gbon, recalls that period and the role played by Gbon's son, Dramane:

> Those of this village wanted peace. If someone is seeking peace, we will follow him. We followed Dramane. Yes, the whole village, we wanted peace, not trouble. In 1952, four people from this village were taken to prison. They were accused of being spies for Dramane. They spent four months in jail. I was one of those four. We were imprisoned in Korhogo—four months in prison. Then they made us pay a fine of 200 francs each. We could not support people like that—never! Those people, they danced—they had a party. "The men of the RDA are in prison!" No one dared say a word—only Dramane spoke up for us. Only one person supported us. And when Houphouët won, then *we* danced. It was us, those in the villages— we were the delegates. If we found a Dyula or a Senoufo, it was our job to tell him to follow Dramane and Houphouët. The whole region—we covered it. We went everywhere to explain things. Some listened, others understood nothing, but we campaigned for Houphouët-Boigny. He who had ended forced labor—this man won. He never even gave us five francs, but we were very interested because we could now work for ourselves—be left alone—not work for others in forced labor—but be free. It was not a question of money, but of liberty. [50]

Ladji Kanigui Coulibaly was another who worked closely with Dramane. He remembered:

> Houphouët had to come to see old Gbon to get him to help suppress forced labor. Before he came he was told about Dramane, the son of old Gbon who worked for the railway. If Dramane was not with him, he would not be received. So Houphouët had to find

Dramane to ask him to come with him to see his father, old Gbon. They came and it was there that Houphouët told Dramane to tell his father that he wanted to end forced labor. And that Gbon must help him. When the whites came to him again to ask for men to do forced labor—don't send them! Old Gbon must say no! There are no more men who will do that.[51]

Dramane and Gbon Coulibaly were both to suffer for their support of Houphouët and the RDA. In 1950, Dramane was arrested by the commandant of Odienné, 60 miles west of Korhogo, ostensibly for not carrying his identity card. Three days later, on 27 April, M. Buggia, chief aide to Governor Péchoux, arrived to confront him. According to Dramane, Buggia told him,

> You have annoyed me since 1946. Today you are under arrest and you will remain in prison as long as possible. I am going to Korhogo to tell your father to quit the RDA. If he refuses, I will kick him out. You will see, you will receive a severe sentence. If the charges against you are insufficient, I will look for others. You can be sure that I will find them. In one month, you'll see, for you, for all the men of the RDA, there will be nothing but prison.[52]

RDA supporters in Korhogo, then, felt the heavy hand of government repression as did those throughout the Côte d'Ivoire. But few were to remain as bitter as those loyal to Dramane. Ladji Kanigui speaks again:

> I was at all the meetings. I never missed one. Before Dramane came here with Houphouët, he told Houphouët that if I come with you to do these political things, my job will be finished. Houphouët replied, "If your job is taken away from you, you will be my prime minister." I was the right arm of Dramane—only sleep separated us. He told me everything—it was because I had suffered too much from forced labor. . . . He did everything for Houphouët—he was arrested in Odienné and spent six months in prison in Bassam. When the work was finished, Houphouët did not make Dramane prime minister. He did not even put him in the political bureau; he was just a plain deputy until his death. He had promised everything, but he gave nothing.[53]

Gbon Coulibaly, the man who had preferred to welcome the French rather than to continue to accede to the demands of Samory, was forced publicly to renounce the RDA, and to say that he wished to belong to no party.[54] It did not save his position. On 18 March 1950, his salary as province chief was suspended.[55] Gbon's power, if not his inviolate authority, was transferred to another of his sons, Bema. A bitter enemy of Dramane, Bema remained the spokesman for the proadministration faction of canton chiefs until the RDA struggle ended in victory. The wounds of that fratricidal conflict remain unhealed to this day.

In 1950, Houphouët-Boigny, testifying before the Damas Commission, pointed out that his party was not led by foreigners, whether Communists (which had been the accusation) or by capitalists (which had occurred to no one) but reminded them that "the French Communists proved their loyalty by their defense of the nation invaded by the Teutonic hordes, something known and appreciated by all."[56] As the 1950s rolled on, however, the RDA broke its connections with the Communist party. Houphouët-Boigny joined the socialist government of Premier Guy Mollet in 1956 as minister of state. In that year, the *Loi-Cadre* granted universal suffrage to all French Africans over the age of twenty-one.[57]

Charles de Gaulle returned to power in February 1958. Houphouët was included in his first cabinet. De Gaulle toured AOF during that summer and campaigned vigorously for approval of the referendum to establish the Fifth Republic and a French Union, within which the territories of the former AOF and AEF would be granted autonomy while continuing to enjoy a close association with France. The great majority of West African *anciens combattants* had, of course, never actually served under de Gaulle. Most of them, however, as we have seen, had by 1958 come to regard him as "their" general, the man who spoke for veterans everywhere, the legendary figure who now represented a reborn France and not the repressive colonial power that had tried to smash the RDA. In the referendum campaign, the Gaullists made a special effort to capitalize upon this widespread devotion. From Paris, they produced a lavish brochure, complete with photographs of the *Tirailleurs Sénégalais* in action, calling on them to demonstrate their solidarity not only with de Gaulle but with their fellow veterans in France itself.

> On 28 September the *anciens combattants* of the overseas territories will say YES to the REFERENDUM. They will say YES because they were bound together with their comrades of the metropole at Verdun, at Koufra, in Morocco, in Provence in 1944, in Indochina, in Algeria. . . . on all these battlefields, the basis was formed for a GREAT COMMUNITY which the future CONSTITUTION can only make more solid and more vibrant. They will say YES because this Community which is already their achievement will bring them: the certainty that their sacrifices, their courage, their devotion, will have given birth to a humane endeavor in which will be blended the destiny of men in love with liberty, justice and progress . . . that these feelings which link them to their brothers-in-arms of the metropole, which were forged on the battlefields will be present in Peace and in the Union,

Yeo Mohoouo (left) and friend

a matter to develop and to perpetuate . . . a guaranty of the prestige and of the position which is owed to them. BY SAYING YES, they will know that they have remained faithful to the LEADER who, once before, led them down the avenue of GLORY and of HONOR.[58]

The authors of the brochure gauged the situation accurately. On 28 September the vast majority of voters, including the ex-*tirailleurs* of the Côte d'Ivoire, approved the referendum. That this was so was guaranteed by the fact that Houphouët and virtually all Ivoirien politicians had urged the YES vote. The Côte d'Ivoire became independent two years later.

Everyone regarded Houphouët as the architect of nationhood. Among those who had fought in the liberation of France, however, de Gaulle is given his due place. The Senoufo veteran, Yeo Mohoouo, spoke to a widespread belief that the general had actually "promised" independence in France's desperate hours. We never thought about actual independence, he reflected, "but before starting the war, General de Gaulle promised us that if we fought the war—fought hard after this war—he would liberate all the states—we would be free citizens. De Gaulle kept his promise. We are free." [59]

Those who had fought for the liberation of France—the motherland—had been constantly assured that they were thereby fighting for the Côte d'Ivoire—for their homeland if not for its freedom. It is true that many of them would continue to serve in the French Army, and see action in Indochina and Algeria, and it is also true that, almost to a man, they look back on their service with pride. Leaders of the new states of Francophone Africa do not hesitate to remind France of the sacrifices made by its former African subjects. "There is not a Burkinabe," the late President Thomas Sankara of Burkina-Faso pointed out, "who does not remember an uncle or a father who died so that France could be free." [60] Yet such lofty sentiments were directed from West Africa to France. In 1958, de Gaulle had appealed from France to West Africa. His appeal to the *anciens combattants* was, in a real sense, their last moment in the political spotlight, their last moment of collective importance to France. They had another battle to fight, but it was not as soldiers but former soldiers, and it was not to be on behalf of France.

NOTES TO CHAPTER NINE

1. Interview 27.

2. Ruth Schachter Morgenthau, *Political Parties in French-Speaking West Africa* (Oxford: Clarendon Press, 1964). Thomas Hodgkin, *Nationalism in Colonial Africa* (London: Frederick Muller, 1956) and *African Political Parties* (Harmondsworth: Penguin, 1961); John D. Hargreaves, *West Africa: The Former French States* (Englewood Cliffs, N.J.: Prentice-Hall, 1967); and *Decolonization in Africa* (New York: Longman, 1979); *Le Rassemblement démocratique africain dans la lutte anti-impérialiste* (Abidjan: Centre D'Edition et de Diffusion Africaines, 1986). An excellent source which includes considerable testimony of participants can be found in the two volumes published on the occasion of the fortieth anniversary of the RDA, *Actes du Colloque International de Yamoussoukro, 18–25 octobre 1986*.

3. Aristide R. Zolberg, *One-Party Government in the Ivory Coast* (Princeton, N.J.: Princeton University Press, 1964), Jean-Noël Loucou, "Les Premières Elections de 1945 en Côte d'Ivoire," *Annales d'histoire de l'université d'Abidjan* 4, ser. 1 (1976): 5–33, and "Aux origines du parti démocratique de la Côte d'Ivoire," *Annales d'histoire de l'université d'Abidjan* 5, ser. 1 (1977): 81–105.

4. Lawler, "Reform and Repression under the Free French," 94–99 passim.

5. ANCI, Pierre de Gentile, "Rapport d'un mission dans le cercle de Korhogo (Relations entre la commerce et l'administration, et répartition de l'essence)," 5 February 1941. Carton 3039.

6. Ibid.

7. Ibid., 12.

8. ANCI, letter to de Gentile, 16 January 1941. Carton 3039, Dossier V45–36/510.

9. Ibid.

10. Catherine Aubertin, *Histoire et création d'une région sous-developée* (Abidjan: OSTROM, May 1980), 14.

11. For a detailed account of the proceedings of the Brazzaville Conference, see *La Conférence Africaine Française, 1944 Brazzaville, Congo* (Algiers: Commissariat aux Colonies).

12. Morgenthau, *Political Parties in French-Speaking West Africa*, 177.

13. Interview 46.

14. Interview 45.

15. Interview 76.

16. Interview 45.

17. Interview 41.

18. Joachim Bony, "La Côte d'Ivoire sous la colonisation française," 1110.

19. While precise statistics for the Côte d'Ivoire are not available, according to Thompson and Adloff, serving soldiers and veterans composed 58 percent of the electorate in Dahomey. (*French West Africa* [Palo Alto, Calif.: Stanford University Press, 1957], 58).

20. M. Damas, *Rapport no. 11348 sur les incidents survenus en Côte d'Ivoire*, 3 vols. in 1 (1950 reprint, Abidjan: Imprimerie Nationale, 1965), 97–98.

21. ANCI, Carton 1555, monthly report, October 1945.

22. Ibid., commandant's report, Bouaké, October 1945.

23. Thompson and Adloff, *French West Africa*, 228.

24. Interview 103.

25. Interview 75.

26. F. J. Amon d'Aby, *La Côte d'Ivoire dans la cité africaine*, 55–57. Morgenthau, *Political Parties in French-Speaking West Africa*, 178–81.

27. Morgenthau, 181–82.

28. Interview 27.

29. Damas, *Rapport*, 72, testimony of Félix Houphouët-Boigny.

30. Interview 102.

31. ANCI, Carton 1555, monthly political report, Man, October 1945.

32. Interview 80.

33. ANCI, Carton 1555, monthly political report, Gaoua, 26 October 1944.

34. Ibid., monthly political report, Grand Lahou, July 1944.

230 *Soldiers of Misfortune*

35. Ibid., governor's monthly political report, March 1944.
36. Morgenthau, *Political Parties in French-Speaking West Africa,* 79.
37. Damas, *Rapport,* testimony of André Latrille, 1067.
38. Ibid., report by André Buttavand, commandant of Daloa, of Boda's speech on 18 November 1949 to 500 people, 851.
39. Interview 49.
40. Interview 82.
41. Ibid.
42. Interview 86.
43. Damas, *Rapport,* testimony of Félix Houphouët-Boigny, 26 June 1950, 68.
44. Ibid., testimony of Robert Leon, 4 July 1950, 77.
45. Interview 101.
46. Interview 86.
47. For the events in Bouaflé and Dimbokro, see Damas, *Rapport,* especially evidence of Félix Houphouët-Boigny, 68–69; evidence of André Buttavand, 905; and "Procès-Verbal des opérations de maintien de l'ordre les 21 et 22 janvier 1950 à Bouaflé," 914.
48. Ibid., testimony of Félix Houphouët-Boigny, 68.
49. Interview 81.
50. Interview 41.
51. Interview 99.
52. Damas, *Rapport,* testimony of Dramane Coulibaly, 623; testimony of Bamara Coulibaly, Dramane's brother, 788–90.
53. Interview 99.
54. Damas, *Rapport,* testimony of Gbon Coulibaly, 785–86.
55. Ibid., testimony of Bamara Coulibaly, 788–90.
56. Ibid., testimony of Félix Houphouët-Boigny, 72.
57. Law of 23 June 1956, Article 10.
58. Original pamphlet in possession of the author. A copy can be found in Northwestern University Library, Africana.
59. Interview 17.
60. *New York Times* (23 August 1987).

10

Epilogue

Sekongo Yessongui

> Ils étaient de Ouaga, Conakry et Dakar
> Du Niger, du Mali, de la Côte d'Ivoire.
> Ils étaient des soldats de la France d'antan.
> Qui peut fermer sa porte à l'un de leurs enfants?[1]

THIS SONG, IN HONOR OF THE *Tirailleurs Sénégalais*, is from an album cut by Nanou Guily in Abidjan in 1987. These former soldiers of France, Guily is asking, how can France have closed her door on any one of them? Sekongo Yessongui might well have raised the same question. After having been taken from his village of Kakologo, near Napiedougou in the prefecture of Korhogo, for forced labor in the forests of the south, he was then recruited into the *Tirailleurs Sénégalais* from the class of 1933. He served for three years, two of them in France. In 1936, he returned to his village, only to be recalled, as a reservist, to the colors in 1939. His regiment was one of the many to fight the desperate battle against the German Pantzer divisions which swept across the Meuse in May 1940. On three occasions he narrowly escaped capture. "Thank God I had a strong fetish," he remarked. "It made me invisible."[2] Eventually, long after the Armistice, he was repatriated. He returned to his village, only to find his wife had gone off with another man. He took up farming again, remarried, had five more children, and for more than forty years had been trying to claim the pension, *la retraite de combattant*, to which he was entitled. The first step in the process was to secure a *carte de combattant*.

I first met him in his village on 3 February 1986. Hospitable, gracious, humorous, and seemingly still vigorous, Yessongui had a superb memory.

231

Sekongo Yessongui and family

He showed me, among his other papers, all as carefully protected from the elements as was possible in a mud house, the letter he had received from France in 1984. It informed him that his application for the combatant's card had been approved and that all that was needed to complete the process was an additional passport-sized photograph. He had immediately complied. He received no further communication on the matter. At his request, I took the relevant correspondence back to Korhogo and, on his behalf drafted a letter of inquiry to the *Hautes Pyrénées Services des Anciens Combattants* in Pau (France). Shortly thereafter, I returned to Kakologo to obtain his signature and to collect another photograph for enclosure with the letter. The photograph was waiting for me, but it was too late. I learned that he had died on 2 March, suddenly. Neither he nor his family would ever receive what was owed him by a country which had first sent him to pull wood in the forests and then twice called him to serve in its army.

Although these circumstances were especially poignant, I had by then interviewed dozens of *anciens combattants* with similar stories to tell. Tuo Nahon, we have seen, went willingly to war eager to rescue his elder brother, a prisoner of the Germans since 1940. Years later, when both were back in Napié, Tuo's brother finally received notification that his pension had been granted. "They sent a paper, that my older brother must go to Abidjan within two weeks," Tuo remembered. "He died the next week. After all he had suffered!"[3] I became well acquainted with many such tales of the bureaucratic delays and inefficiencies encountered by Africans seeking military pensions. Indeed, along with my tape recorder, cameras, cooler, and assorted writing materials, I now traveled from village to village with a complete set of official regulations and application forms given me, along with their blessing, by Korhogo's honorary French consul, Maurice Menjuc, and his assistant, Mme Michèle Turcan.

I came to know every *sous-préfet* in the region, for it was often necessary to bring the *anciens combattants* in person to their offices to acquire copies of birth certificates, identity cards, declarations that the men in question were indeed alive, and the myriad of other documents and fiscal stamps required by the process. These *sous-préfets,* many of them serving officers in the Ivoirien Army, proved to be both sympathetic and cooperative. I had also become an infrequent and somewhat unwelcome visitor at the French consulate and *Office des Anciens Combattants et Victimes de la Guerre* in Abidjan, taking packets of applications to the capital. On rare but extremely happy occasions, I was delegated by the Korhogo consulate actually to deliver papers (and the inevitable accompanying forms) to *anciens combattants* in remote villages, finally granting them their pensions.

I came to understand what Namongo Ouattara, president of the Korhogo section of the Ivoirien *anciens combattants*, had meant early in October 1985, when I had first asked his assistance in locating veterans of World War II. He consulted his council and then invited me to his compound to announce the decision. They agreed to give me the list of their members in the prefecture, and they did so in the hope that my work would in some way resolve the many problems facing Senoufo and Dyula veterans most of whom were illiterate in French. "We will help you and we hope that you will help us," Namongo said. I am pleased that I was able to provide them with some small measure of assistance, for each of the more than a hundred *anciens combattants* I interviewed in the Côte d'Ivoire certainly did everything they could for me.

Consigned to Oblivion

Yeo Porio, it will be remembered, was one of the very few Senoufo ever to volunteer for the army. Nearly fifty years later, he had acquired almost legendary status on this account, the subject of a mixture of both admiration for his boldness and scorn for his folly. Looking back over the years since his enlistment in 1939, he reflected on the sad state to which former *tirailleurs* had been reduced by 1986. "After the war," he said,

> those from Mali, Upper Volta, and Guinea got their money. Only the Ivoirien *tirailleurs* never received theirs. They [the French] were wicked, because we had saved them from the Germans. Today, we, the *anciens combattants*, are the lowliest. They give us nothing—do nothing for us—nothing at all. They even beat the *anciens combattants*. Yes! Here! In the other countries, they pay their veterans—here not a cent. Look if you don't eat, you cry. It is the same as being beaten. Even with my pension, I have to go collect it four times a year. I was wounded four times. I only got the combatant's pension, I did not get the bonus paid to the wounded. [4]

On 7 August 1960, the Côte d'Ivoire became independent. None of the fathers of the new nation had ever served in the army. The ranks of the new Assembly did contain some *anciens combattants*, several of whom like Philippe Yacé, Guy Nairay, and Aoussi Eba, would fill important positions in the government over the years. The ordinary *ancien combattant*, however, the private of the *tirailleur* regiments, was back in his village, apparently in the process of being reabsorbed in his traditional milieu. There he still commanded respect, still continued to challenge any perceived assaults on his honor, and still saluted his dead comrades. Nanlougo Soro, who had gone to fight the battle for France well prepared with his amulets, spoke of these matters:

> We are taken notice of more than the rest. When an *ancien combattant* dies in the village, we wear our uniforms. We shoot in the air for him. We have a parade in our village for him. We go to the house of the dead man and shoot our rifles in the air—in front of the house. After that, we stand guard over his body and carry it back to his tomb. When he is put in his grave, we fire again as it is being lowered. [5]

But even proud men like Nanlougo Soro knew they had little place in the new Côte d'Ivoire.

The mass of World War II veterans found their accomplishments—their travel abroad, their combat experience, their French (albeit often marginal)—becoming progressively less important. They grew older, watching a new generation arise. Its members were taught French in primary schools. They were learning a new history, an African history which no longer began with *nos ancêtres les Gaulois*. There was, moreover, by then a new Ivoirien army. Its soldiers had little interest in listening to the stories of an older generation about a war that was over, or to their complaints about their difficulty in claiming the pensions to which they were entitled. Kouhona Yeo returned from the war in 1947. "When we got back to the village, we were looked up to. Then. Now they have an African army, and we are not given any consideration at all." [6] Even those recruited from post-war classes felt a sense of disillusionment. Zie Coulibaly fought in Indochina for two years and was demobilized in 1962. "I did not want to leave the army," he said.

> I wanted my fifteen years. But now the Côte d'Ivoire was independent—and there was not room for all of us. They only took those with skills, drivers, mechanics. I had asked to become a driver, but I didn't get it. I served eleven years and have a half-pension. [7]

Ve Sabh of Man, class of 1948, saw action in Indochina and Algeria. He was one of those to be accepted into the Ivoirien army. Nevertheless, he too had a sense of being overtaken by the changing times. In 1960, he observed,

> many wanted to go into the Ivoirien army. We were transferred, chosen, to build the new army—to train the young. . . . At first we said we must make the Ivoirien army stronger than the French army. We trained them. Today they are the generals, the colonels. In the French army, we had done everything. These men knew nothing prac-

Zie Coulibaly wears his medals from Indochina and Algeria

tical. We knew how the French trained the young soldier. We tried to force them the same way. But, by the end, the army had entered politics. We were afraid to let them go. We wanted to do for them what had been done for us, but they could not continue to the finish. They went into politics. They did not want us to apply the things that we had learned. [8]

Virtually all *anciens combattants* interviewed were sensitive to, and bitterly resented, the changes in attitude which left them with a sense of alienation from the new nation. The comment of Yetidaanna Yeo, who had served in North Africa and the Levant, was typical:

They are not admired — respected. The others who stayed here and worked for themselves cannot understand that I was working for them, too, when I was in the military. I did it for the country. If I had been killed, I would have been *mort pour la patrie.*[9]

The sharpshooter and famed hunter, Ditiembe Silué, spoke in the same vein. "They don't care about us," he claimed. "They only care about the *anciens combattants* of the Ivoirien army now. We fought for France and we have nothing. They give us nothing."[10]

The sentiments expressed by these Senoufo were echoed by veterans in other parts of the country. Even in Man, with its ancient warrior tradition which supposedly conferred upon the veteran a most honored place in society, Salifou Bogbe ("97828, class of 1942!") and Bientot Gbeyone voiced much the same complaints:

I recognize that we are respected by the president and by ministers. They know that we fought for the liberty of Africa. But, below that level — *préfets,* everyone else — even when we wear our decorations — they have no respect for us. None from the civilians, none from our families. Even if an *ancien combattant* is in uniform on his moped, even in a car, they [police, customs, etc.] stop us. We shed our blood for them, but they do not give us any consideration at all. The veterans do not have the political power to get things. We receive no respect. Already by the time we got our liberty, the RDA, the civilians, were in place. We did not have enough money, enough power. We had no resources, even to hold meetings. We are not respected by the civilian population — whether they are in politics or not. They do not understand us. They said to us at a meeting these words which cut us: "You have suffered for France, but not for us."[11]

There were veterans who took a rather more positive view of the part they had played in building the new nation. Namongo Ouattara, whom we have met so often before, was among these. Once the struggle for independence had been fought and won, due in no small degree to the efforts of *anciens combattants* like himself, some turned to affairs at the village level, particularly primary schools. While serving in the army, the importance of education had come as a revelation to many of the illiterate Senoufo conscripts. The change came about as the Senoufo *tirailleur* saw educated recruits promoted, put in offices, and generally given an easier time during military training. From their military service, they learned the importance of "paper."

This was a radical change in the attitudes of men raised in a society which had resisted the impressment of boys into schools far more than of soldiers into the army. The Senoufo had always preferred to keep their sons on the land. Several veterans spoke of how the Korhogo Catholic Mission had "recruited" pupils in much the same way as the army had recruited soldiers, by *la force*! *Gardes* arrived in the villages and took "volunteers." [12] By contrast, many veterans talked of their role in bringing education to their villages after the war. They not only sent their own children, male and female, to school but were leaders in the movement to build new primary schools. Namongo Ouattara explained:

> In my village (Pokaha), I now understood the need for development. I built a school with housing for the teachers. I have built many schools. I planted a great field of yams and rice and used that money to build these schools. Yes, many had the thought that they needed to build schools, but they did not have the means to do it by themselves. They explained things to the people—we must contribute money to build schools. Some villagers understood and gave money; others did not. Certain *anciens combattants* understood very well what was needed, and they worked hard—others did not. At Pangarikaha, it was the *anciens combattants*, Pelibé, Silué, and the others—who called the villagers together and explained that they needed to have a school. [13]

Nevertheless, by 1986, even Namongo Ouattara had come to feel that his contribution to the new nation, as to the previous colonial regime, was all but forgotten. He had become, as he said, simply a bothersome old man. With what energy he had left, he concentrated on securing those few benefits to which he believed service to France had entitled him and his fellow veterans.

Slowly but surely, the outcome of the battle for pensions became the measure by which veterans were judged within the community. Sadly, an *ancien combattant* struggling to claim the monies due him for years spent in the French army became an object first of pity, finally of disdain. Respect was reserved for the veteran who had either come back from the war with cash or who, exceptionally, had been able subsequently to establish his right to a pension. Poverty, a universal feature of Senoufo society, became a stigma when it was an *ancien combattant* who was poor. Listen to M'ba Coulibaly, a quarter chief in the prosperous Dyula village of Wareniéne:

> We do not respect the *anciens combattants* at all. We even are better than them. They returned with much force—they came back with the strength to work. Those men who left for the war. We who stayed—we worked for the old, made our little economies. Those who were in the war worked for the whites. They were not paid. Thus when they came back without money—their fathers—who had had other people working for them—had money and they got it. Those who just went to the war and came back have nothing, but those who did fifteen years and who returned after the fifteen years are better than them because they made a great deal of money. [14]

This, then, was the last battle that *anciens combattants* would fight—and, most of them, lose.

Pensions: The Last and Lost Battle

Africans who had served fifteen years in the French army were entitled to the *pension de retraite*, with rights of survivorship to legal wives, that is, to those married under civil law. [15] Such pensions were supposed to start upon discharge. Their applications were facilitated by the fact that they were all, to some degree or other, literate in French, and that most were given the correct paperwork by the army before being released. Nevertheless, there were some bureaucratic delays, particularly arising from the confusion of the Vichy period. In 1947, Governor Durand estimated that 10 percent of the career men in the Côte d'Ivoire, discharged between 1942 and 1946, had still to establish their claims. [16] This situation was, however, a temporary one. Most if not all of these veterans were able in time to draw their money.

A considerable proportion of the Ivoirien career men are to be found, for reasons we have touched on earlier, in the Man region in the west. There, in the late 1980s, the local *association des anciens combattants* was relatively well-organized and active and, most importantly, was led by a man well connected in the PDCI-RDA. In addition to a large veterans hall in town, the association owns a 450-acre coffee and cocoa plantation. Formerly the property of a French settler, President Houphouët-Boigny purchased it in 1963 and gave it to the *anciens combattants* of Man. The officials of the organization maintain fairly close relations with the staff of Abidjan's *Bureau des Anciens Combattants* and with the French embassy. This enables them to operate effectively within the shifting bureaucratic system whenever pension problems arise. That the veterans' organization in Korhogo is, relative to that in Man, ineffective reflects more than anything the fact that there are so few ex-career soldiers in that region. When the officers of the association there petitioned the Ivoirien government in 1985 for a grant of 500 acres of farmland in order to generate income for their section, they received no reply. [17]

If the career soldier was well treated in comparison with men enlisted only for the duration, it does seem that the French government also made special efforts to meet the claims of those eligible for the *pensions d'invalide*, awarded to men disabled by wounds or disease during their service, and the supplementary *pensions des grands mutilés*, reserved to amputees. Gabriel Moyehi of Man, who lost his foot not in World War II but in Indochina, was impressed by the care he received when evacuated to French hospitals:

> I wrote to my father. . . . I didn't say I had been wounded. He would have died. After Mont Olivier, I went to Fréjus. There they did all the paper. I came back to Marseille, and they fitted the first appliance. I began to walk. I did not want to leave France. I was not happy to have to come home. Here, if you walk with a cane, they laugh at you. I was ashamed. I left on my legs—now to come home? The colonel, the doctor, said, "You have your mother, your father there. You must go to them." I said I had shame. The colonel said, "All the papers are finished. Go to Man and wait for your pension." I got home on 17 August 1953. There was no one waiting for me. I went home. My father saw me with the cane. He started to cry. I said do not cry. It was the war. A man is a man. [18]

Nevertheless, all was not what it seemed. In 1946, Governor Latrille had had to complain continually to the Military Bureau that many disabled veterans were experiencing long delays in receiving their pension cards. [19] Eventually, however, most disabled Ivoirien veterans, like the fifteen-year men, did collect their pensions.

Far less fortunate were those veterans, whether conscripts or volunteers, who were eligible only for the *retraite de combattant*. This pension is paid to any veteran on reaching age 60 (and since 1984, 65) who had served a minimum of 90 days in a combat zone. [20] The pension has no rights of survivorship to widows. Such was the magnitude of the problems in handling these pensions, not only in the Côte d'Ivoire but throughout the AOF, that in 1949 the French government appointed a special commission to investigate the matter on the spot. Headed by

Gabriel Moyehi

Henri Liger, the delegation interviewed some 25,000 *anciens combattants*. Formal pension claims were made by over 9,000 of them, of which almost 5,000 were granted immediately and the rest deferred for further consideration. [21]

The good intentions of France may or may not be at issue. The problem facing the *ancien combattant* was the sheer complexity of the process by which he had to establish his rights to the *retraite de combattant*. Before applying, he had to possess a combatant's card, *la carte de combattant*, to prove he had completed 90 days in combat. To obtain this, however, he had first to produce written evidence of the units in which he had served, the dates of that service, and in the case of a prisoner of war, the camps in which he was incarcerated. There was an extraordinary amount of luck in it. In the most difficult position were those *tirailleurs* who had been repatriated after the fall of France. They arrived home, for the most part, with no papers. Equally difficult was the situation of many prisoners of war, particularly those released early for medical reasons to the care of Vichy, whose papers had been confiscated by the German camp authorities. Still others had had their papers destroyed in battle, whether in the Levant, North Africa, or Europe. Those who had served in the Free French period were the exception, for they were often issued with cards before discharge, or could otherwise put together the necessary documentation.

A typical experience was that of the former prisoner of war, Tuo Donatoho. "The Germans took my *livret militaire* and never gave it back," he said. On his repatriation, he reached Abidjan to find that his tribulations were far from ended:

> There was a very bad colonel. He took all our clothes away and only gave us two pairs of shorts, one shirt, and the old red cap of the *tirailleur*. Then we were sent home. I now had lost everything. . . . No one tried to help me. I never got a new *livret militaire*. I wrote to Libourne [in France] five times. I never got a reply. I have no pension. I came back to my village—I have never moved since.[22]

Those who did return to the Côte d'Ivoire with papers preserved them with loving care, often enclosing them in specially purchased plastic envelopes. Nonetheless the ravages of insects, damp, and fire have wreaked their inevitable havoc. Worse, many of the military papers turned out to be nearly unreadable and often incomplete, lacking those crucial entries which would document the magic number of 90 days. Worse still, even those whose documents appeared to be complete continued to encounter rejection. Aoussi Eba, who served as chief of the *Ivoirien Bureau des Anciens Combattants* in Abidjan during the 1970s, commented:

> Is it difficult, for there are many who did fight in the war, but not for ninety days. But he cannot understand that—he tells you that he was at the front. And he was! In principle, you look at their papers to see what dates the book places them with what units—campaigns. You have to count the days—ninety days in combat. There is a document which lists all the units in combat during 1939–45. You look to see if there is a date first. If he believes the file is truthful—that the soldier did fight in the war—he will send the file to France.[23]

It may be thought that the lot of the Ivoirien *ancien combattant* would have improved with independence. It is sad to have to say that this was not the case. Despite the fact that pensions paid by the French government to ex-soldiers represent a much-needed source of hard currency in the Côte d'Ivoire, Ivoirien administrations have shown little interest in assisting *anciens combattants* in collecting their dues. An *Office des Anciens Combattants et Victimes de la Guerre* (OACVG) was established immediately after the war to help them. Since independence, however, its main concern has been with veterans of the Ivoirien army and, even so, the OACVG was left without a director from 1985 to early 1987. During this hiatus, it was run by a single Ivoirien sergeant, who appeared to have the power to decide whether claims by veterans of World War II would or would not be forwarded to France. Even when they were, and after the forms were correctly filled in and the dossier complete, it might take two years for the material to pass through the seemingly endless labyrinth of the French military bureaucracy before appearing finally in the applicant's village in the form of the highly prized *carte de combattant*. It is at this point that the other set of forms, including one to certify that the man was born and another to certify that he had not died, have to be forwarded to the French embassy in Abidjan, which, having satisfied itself at its leisure that the forms truly are complete, returns them once more to the OACVG for that organization to post them to France. All of this routinely takes another two years. If the *ancien combattant* is, by good fortune, still alive at the end of these proceedings, he can finally start to collect his pension. In 1984, only 1,250 Ivoiriens were doing so.[24]

Those fortunate enough to stay the course did not, need it be said, find themselves among the wealthy of the Côte d'Ivoire. Independence was to have a profound, if unforeseen, effect upon pensions. In the negotiations between France and her colonies which took place in preparation for the severing of ties, all financial arrangements had to be reviewed, including pensions paid to former functionaries, police, *tirailleurs*, and the like. By Article 71 of the Law of 26 December 1959, France first reduced the pensions of the African veterans to one-seventh that of their counterparts who were French citizens, and then froze them with no provision for any indexing to a rising cost-of-living. Some Ivoiriens tried, and in a few cases succeeded, in gaining French nationality, but this was not an option for the vast majority. Aoussi Eba attempted to rectify the situation during his tenure as head of the OACVG but, as he explains, to little avail:

> The African pension is practically nothing, but the European pension is indexed—it's increased by 30, 50, 60, 80, 100 percent because their pensions are indexed to the inflation rate. . . . Complete inequality between the French and the Africans. Around 1975, I left to go to Paris to speak to the minister for *anciens combattants*—I think his

name was Tripolet. We talked about pensions at this time. I told him about the great difference between the two pensions. M. Tripolet responded, "What you eat in Africa—rice, millet, things like that cost practically nothing. Here we eat beefsteak and bread." "All right," I said, "I'll move to France and eat beefsteak and bread. Is it possible for me to do so?" No! We stayed together for some hours, but we could not find a compromise—a solution. [25]

There was widespread bitterness in the Korhogo area in the late 1980s. Insofar as the volume of complaint is diminishing it is because the old soldiers are dying off, not because their demands are being met. Korhogo has, of course, felt the problem most acutely, so few of its veterans being entitled to the *pension de retraite*, so many only to the *retraite de combattant*, if even that. Retired career soldiers from the area are few, so uncommon a phenomenon among the Senoufo and Dyula that virtually all *anciens combattants* can name every one of them. They lack influence. Most of them, after completing their fifteen years service in the army, appear to have chosen not to resettle in their villages but to live on their pensions in the towns of the region. On the face of it, this seems natural enough. They would be likely to seek the better amenities offered by larger centers. While this may have been so, three of those career men interviewed offered different explanations. These had to do with the demands made upon them in their villages, the envy they encountered, and although they were reluctant to allude to this, their fear of becoming the victims of witchcraft. One Senoufo, Fonon Gano of Boundiali, taken from the class of 1929, spoke of his experience:

> When I came home the village people were afraid to approach me. Even the *cercle* guards were afraid of a soldier, so naturally the peasants were even more afraid. I was the only one who came back— the only *ancien militaire*. That is still true. I moved though, after a few years, because everyone in the village wanted money from me. In Korhogo, the people have a better character. There [in the village], everyone kept saying, "Give me money—Give me!" [26]

Madio Yeo was from the class of 1944 and retired with his pension in 1959, having seen service in Europe and combat in Algeria and Indochina. He soon left his village, however, and settled in the town of Sinématiali. His pension brought him, he thought, nothing but trouble. He was envied by the villagers, and he believed they had tried to bewitch or poison him so that he went mad for three years. [27] A third career man, Ouanlo Silué, an official in the Veterans' Association, maintained that Madio's experience was not unusual: "Anyone with money in a village is envied to death by the others." That, said Ouanlo, is why he himself also lives in Sinématiali. [28]

Madio Yeo displays his strength

Korhogo has its section of the *Association des Anciens Combattants*, and in 1949 had its own *maison des combattants*, built with money provided by the Liger Mission.[29] It is symptomatic of the situation of the Korhogo veterans that the government chose to tear the office down in the late 1960s to make way for a bank. The head of the section, Namongo Ouattara, does go to extraordinary lengths to locate and assist the hundreds of those entitled to combatant pensions, but they are scattered in remote villages throughout the region. Over seventy years old, without an office, without funds for transport, without photocopying facilities, he can only do so much. He has, however, received some help from French residents in Korhogo who have shown concern for the plight of the veterans. Out of his own pocket, the honorary French consul Maurice Menjuc maintains an office, and he and his assistant, Michèle Turcan, have devoted an inordinate amount of their time to assisting *anciens combattants*. On one of his periodic tours in the mid-1980s, the French ambassador—a not insignificant personage even in an independent Côte d'Ivoire—assured the Korhogo veterans still striving to establish their pensions that he would intercede on their behalf. It was, however, all too late. Most Korhogolese *anciens combattants* had, in fact, given up the struggle. So, it seems, had most of the World War II veterans throughout the Côte d'Ivoire. War memorials everywhere crumble through neglect. The men who served in the *Tirailleurs Sénégalais* have slipped into a kind of half-world. Largely ignored in their own country, their sacrifices on behalf of France are now little known to a new generation of French.

Twenty years ago Anita Glaze attended the funeral of an "unknown Senoufo soldier," one who was killed in a war of long ago. "The proper rituals," she learned,

> had never been observed, and as a result he was causing some of the troubles currently plaguing the village. He was said to have spoken in a dream to one villager, who then sought counsel with the elders. The villager and the elders consulted with many *Sando* diviners, who transmitted the message from the ancestors (*kuubele*) that the village must call out the Poro society for a ritual funeral. [30]

Who, we may wonder, will put to rest the Senoufo soldiers who laid down their lives on the battlefields of World War II, or who perished in the German prisoner of war camps? It is somehow ironic that the last time the men of the *tirailleur* regiments made the headlines was during the emotional Klaus Barbie trial held in Lyon in the summer of 1987. Jacques Vergès, chief counsel for the defense, posed a question in his opening statement.

> Why, among all the memorials held in Lyon for the different ethnic groups murdered by the Nazis, was none held for the very first Nazi victims in Lyon, the 200 *Sénégalais* massacred by the Germans, the *Tirailleurs Sénégalais*, massacred because of their race? Do crimes against humanity not bring forth emotion, not merit commemoration unless [they] hit . . . Europeans? [31]

Surely they, the men who have spoken of their own experiences for this book, deserve a finer epitaph than that—merit more than a brief mention in the trial of a notorious Nazi war criminal.

Notes to Chapter Ten

1. Nanou Giuly, *Les Tirailleurs*, Abidjan, 1987 (author's translation).
2. Interview 59.
3. Interview 46.
4. Interview 18.
5. Interview 35.
6. Interview 66.
7. Interview 4.
8. Interview 82.
9. Interview 10.
10. Interview 15.
11. Interview 80.
12. Interview 5.
13. Interview 45.
14. Interview 19.
15. Conversation with M. Jacquemin, French consular official in charge of veterans affairs, 10 October 1985. In 1984, 398 Ivoirien widows were collecting survivors' pensions.
16. ANCI, Carton 3276, Dossier V–23–34, "Mémento pour survie à la régularisation des droits acquis par anciens militaires," Abidjan, May 1947.
17. Letter, Namongo Ouattara and Soma Koné to minister of agriculture, Abidjan, dd. 7 October 1985, copy in personal files of author.
18. Interview 78.
19. ANCI, Carton 1311, Dossier XXI–41/10, 1946.
20. Due to the higher mortality rate in the Côte d'Ivoire, raising the age of eligibility for pensions from 60 to 65 effectively deprived many of their entitlement, since no survivors' benefits are included.
21. Damas, *Rapport*, 593.
22. Interview 5.
23. Interview 102. The list of combat units referred to by M. Eba is *Unités Combattantes des campaignes 1939–1945; Période du 3 septembre 1939 au 8 mai, 1945.*
24. Conversation with M. Jacquemin, 10 October 1985.
25. Interview 102.
26. Interview 39.
27. Interview 58.
28. Interview 55.
29. Damas, *Rapport,* 593.
30. Anita Glaze, *Art and Death in a Senufo Village*, 155.
31. *Le Monde* (3 July 1987).

Appendix
Interviews

No.	Name	Date	Location	Language Used	Years Served	Combat Unit	Volunteer?	Pension?	POW?
1	Guy Ahizi-Eliam	23 Oct 85	Abidjan	French	4	6 RTS	Y		
2	Denis Yace	24 Oct 85	Abidjan	French	4	1 DFL			
3	Edmond N'Guetta	24 Oct 85	Grand Bassam	French	7	24 RTS	Y	Y	Y
4	Zie Coulibaly	4 Nov 85	Korhogo	French	11		Y	Y	
5	Daouda Tuo Donatoho	5 Nov 85	Pokaha	Nafara	6	1 RAC			Y
6	Jean Nandin	5 Nov 85	Pokaha	French	4		Y	Y	
7	Mipiema Soro	5 Nov 85	Pokaha	Nafara	5			Y	
8	Tonienigue Soro	5 Nov 85	Pokaha	Nafara	5		Y		
9	Soma Kone	6 Nov 85	Korhogo	Djeli	5	15 RTS	Y		
10	Yetidaanna Yeo	7 Nov 85	Nidienkaha	Tyebari	8				
11	Ouattara	7 Nov 85	Nidienkaha	Tyebari					
12	Navaga Ouattara	7 Nov 85	Siliekaha	Fr/Tyebari	3				
13	Drissa Ouattara	11 Nov 85	Korhogo	Fr/Tyebari					
14	Daouda Tuo-Donatoho	13 Nov 85	Pokaha	Nafara	6	1 RAC			
15	Ditiemba Silue	14 Nov 85	Moroviné	Fodonon	5	13 RTS			
16	Elders	15 Nov 85	Pokaha	Nafara					
17	Yeo Mohoouo	15 Nov 85	Pangarikaha	Fr/Nafara	7	1 DFL	Y	Y	
18	Yeo Porio	15 Nov 85	Pangarikaha	Nafara	3	6 RTS	Y	Y	
19	M'Ba Coulibaly	16 Nov 85	Waraniené	Dyula					Y
20	Bey Coulibaly	18 Nov 85	Korhogo	French	7		Y		

No.	Name	Date	Location	Language Used	Years Served	Combat Unit	Volunteer?	Pension?	POW?
21	Ditiemba Silue	19 Nov 85	Moroviné	Fodonon	5	13 RTS			
22	Zondoho	21 Nov 85	Lataha	Fodonon					
23	Zana Tuo	21 Nov 85	Lataha	Fr/Fodonon	11	14 RICM			Y
24	Tuo Ouna	22 Nov 85	Kolokaha	Tyebari	3	4 RTS		Y	
25	Farnan Kone	22 Nov 85	Noufoun	Fr/Tyebari	7	24 RTS	Y	Y	Y
26	Zie Soro	25 Nov 85	Kolokpo	Kassabeli	4				
27	Namongo Ouattara	27 Nov 85	Korhogo	Fr/Nafara	6			Y	
28	Soro Nougbo	28 Nov 85	Noubougnonka	Fr/Nafara	5	44 RICMS		Y	
29	Pelibe Tuo	28 Nov 85	Pangarikaha	Fr/Nafara	8	24 RTS		Y	Y
30	Panafolo Tuo	29 Nov 85	Sirasso	Tyebari	8	16 RTS		Y	Y
31	Dossigutta Silue	29 Nov 85	Sirasso	Tyebari	3				
32	Laqui Konde	29 Nov 85	M'Bala	Fr/Dyula	5	8 RTS			
33	Garkite Kambo	7 Dec 85	Dida	Fr/Lobi	15		Y	Y	
34	Djirigue Soro	10 Dec 85	M'Bala	Fr/Tyebari	6	6 RTS			
35	Namlougo Soro	10 Dec 85	M'Bala	Tyebari		15 RTS			
36	Yéo Tibeya	11 Dec 85	Napiédougou	Fr/Nafara	5	10 RTS	Y		
37	Tuo Lielourou	11 Dec 85	Napiédougou	Fr/Nafara	8	5 RTS			Y
38	Tiozon Soro	24 Dec 85	Natiokobadara	Nafara	4				
38	Somogo Yeo	24 Dec 85	Natiokobadara	Fr/Nafara	5				
39	Fonon Gano	24 Dec 85	Korhogo	French	17	13 RTS	Y	Y	

#	Name	Date	Place	Language	No.	Archive	Y	Y	Y
40	Henri Boileau	7 Jan 86	Abidjan	French			Y		
41	Lassina Coulibaly	9 Jan 86	Kapelé	Dyula	5				
42a	Dianguina Coulibaly	9 Jan 86	Kapelé	Fr/Dyula	5	12 RTS			
42b	Dianguina Coulibaly	14 Jan 86	Kapelé	Dyula	7	7 RTS			
43	Tuo Mahan	15 Jan 86	Guiembé	Fodonon	7	1 RTS			
44	Tiorna Yeo	15 Jan 86	Guiembé	Fodonon	3	10 RTS			
45	Namongo Ouattara	16 Jan 86	Korhogo	Fr/Nafara				Y	
46	Tuo Nahon	17 Jan 86	Guiembé	Fr/Fodonon	6	13 RTS		Y	
47	Djomopine Yeo	17 Jan 86	Guiembé	Koufoulo	4				
48	Sekongo Yenibiyofine	17 Jan 86	Nourfré	Koufoulo	5				Y
49	Phillipe Yace	17 Jan 86	Korhogo	French	7	1 DFL			
50	Fonfola Silue	21 Jan 86	Guiembé	Fr/Fodonon	4	1 RIC			
51	Torna Sokongo	21 Jan 86	Guiembé	Fodonon	5	1 RAC			Y
52	Veterans of Guiembé	21 Jan 86	Guiembé	Fr/Fodonon	4				
53	Nahoua Silue	25 Jan 86	Guiembé	Fr/Tyebari	3	8 RTS			
54	Yeo Yehoua	25 Jan 86	Guiembé	Fr/Fodonon	3	5 RTS			
55	Ouanlo Silue	28 Jan 86	Sinématiali	French	15		Y	Y	
56	Peleguitamnadio Yeo	28 Jan 86	Sinématiali	Fr/Nafara	8	6 RAC		Y	Y
57	Gnoumagai Soro	29 Jan 86	Sinématiali	Nafara	6	4 RTS			
58	Madio Yeo	29 Jan 86	Sinématiali	French	15		Y	Y	
59	Sekongo Yessongui	3 Feb 86	Kakologo	Tyebari	5	1 RTS			
60	Tionnina Soro	3 Feb 86	Kakologo	Fr/Tyebari	8				
61	Mme Porotio Tuo	3 Feb 86	Kakologo	Tyebari					
62	Siliouenissougui Silue	4 Feb 86	Guiembé	Fodonon	5	13 RTS			
63	Duondiana Yeo	4 Feb 86	Guiembé	Fr/Fodonon	5	24 RTS			
63	Founwo Yeo	4 Feb 86	Guiembé	Fr/Fodonon	5	24 RTS			Y

No.	Name	Date	Location	Language Used	Years Served	Combat Unit	Volunteer?	Pension?	POW?
64	Namble SILUE	4 Feb 86	Guiembé	Fr/Fodonon	6	2 BM	Y		
64	Namongo SILUE	4 Feb 86	Guiembé	Fr/Fodonon	6	2 BM	Y		
65	Lapon SILUE	15 Feb 86	Topinakaha	Nafara	5				
66	Yeo KOUHONA	18 Feb 86	Blagbokaha	Nafara	3				
67	Donipoho SEKONGO	18 Feb 86	Blagbokaha	Fr/Nafara	5	17 BM			
68	Tuo NANZEGUE	18 Feb 86	Takplakaha	Fr/Nafara	9				Y
69	Somongo SORO	19 Feb 86	Kogotonkaha	Fr/Nafara	7	12 RTS		Y	Y
70	Yeo MOHOOUO	23 Feb 86	Pangarikaha	Fr/Nafara	7	1 DFL	Y	Y	
71	Gmbale SORO	24 Feb 86	Dossemekaha	Fr/Tyebari	8	12 RTS		Y	Y
72	Tienfolo SILUE	25 Feb 86	Dikodougou	Fr/Fodonon	8			Y	Y
73	Sadjiri MAIDANA	25 Feb 86	Tiere	Fr/Dyula	5	13 RTS		Y	
74	Nanga SORO	26 Feb 86	Tenecokaha	Fr/Nafara	6	4 RTS		Y	
75	Tafolotien SORO	26 Feb 86	Tenecokaha	Fr/Nafara	5	4 RTS			
76	Yeo NABETEGUE	27 Feb 86	Tagbanga	Tyebari	3			Y	
77	Soro KOLO	28 Feb 86	Lataha	Fr/Tyebari	3	6 RTS		Y	
78	Gabriel MOYEHI	12 Mar 86	Man	French	3	6 RTS	Y	Y	
79	Fe LIA	12 Mar 86	Sisea	French	8	14 RTS	Y	Y	Y
80	Vets of Man Plantation	12 Mar 86	Sisea	French				Y	
81	Alphonse DIONKLA	13 Mar 86	Podiagouine	French	15	17 RTS	Y	Y	
82	Ve SABH	17 Mar 86	Man	French	15	5 BM	Y	Y	

No.	Name	Place	Date	Language	No.	Unit				
83	Albert BROUSSE	Man	18 Mar 86	French	5	1 DIC	Y			
84	BIE-DOUMA	Man	18 Mar 86	French	15			Y	Y	
85	André FEBAOUI	Man	18 Mar 86	Fr/Yacouba	15	14 RTS	Y	Y	Y	
86	Alphonse TOGBA	Man	18 Mar 86	French	15				Y	
87	Corporal GUEPLEU	Koulinlé	19 Mar 86	Fr/Yacouba	8	4 RTS	Y		Y	
88	Pierre VA MESSIE	Banlé	19 Mar 86	French	10	12 RTS		Y	Y	
89	Jacquet FLORENT	Man	20 Mar 86	French	15					
90	Kiwalte KAMBOU	Bouna	25 Mar 86	French	15	15 BM		Y		
91	Tilire KAMBIRE	Bouna	25 Mar 86	Fr/Lobi	15	17 RTS		Y	Y	
92	Kangouté KATAKIE	Bouna	25 Mar 86	French						
93	Baba CAMARA	Bouna	25 Mar 86	French						
94	Nambilogo SILUE	Nakaha	8 Apr 86	Fr/Nafara	8	2 RAC	Y	Y		
95	Ouattama SORO	Kalaha	10 Apr 86	Fr/Fodonon	8	9 DIC	Y	Y		
96	Sandona SORO	Kalaha	10 Apr 86	Fr/Fodonon	3	25 RTS				
97	Diofounon YEO	Kalaha	10 Apr 86	Fr/Fodonon	4	6 RAC				
98	Nimougolo COULIBALY	Korhogo	11 Apr 86	Tyebari						
99	Ladji Kanigui COULIBALY	Korhogo	14 Apr 86	Tyebari						
100	Benoit Kouassi EHOU	Grand Bassam	23 Apr 86	French	8					
101	M and Mme DELONGES	Dimbokro	29 Apr 86	French						
102	Aoussi EBA	Grand Bassam	5 May 86	French	5					
103	Ehouman ADOU	Vitre II	7 May 86	French	7	1 DIC		Y	Y	Y
104	Emile DAGBA	Lebleko	10 May 86	French	4	12 RTS	Y	Y	Y	
105	Pierre BEUGLOT	Kotobi	26 May 86	French			Y			
106	Seidou Bily CAMARA	Bouna	14 Jun 86	Dyula						
107	Mamourou CAMARA	Bouna	14 Jun 86	Dyula						
108	Gérard FAIVRE	Paris	23 Jul 86	French	3	8 RTS			Y	
109	Henri WINCKLER	Toulon	26 Aug 86	French	18			Y	Y	

Bibliography

Abadie, Maurice, *La Défense des colonies*, Paris: Charles Lavauzelle, 1937.

Adloff, Richard and Virginia Thompson, *French West Africa*, Palo Alto, Calif.: Stanford University Press, 1957.

Aghlon, Raoul, *L'Epopée de la France combattante*, New York: Editions de la Maison, 1943.

Amon d'Aby F. J. *La Côte d'Ivoire dans la cité africaine*, Paris: Editions Larose, 1951.

Angoulvant, G. *La Pacification de la Côte d'Ivoire, 1908–1915*, Paris: Editions Larose, 1916.

Aubertin, Catherine, *Histoire et création d'une région sous-developée*, Abidjan: Centre OSTROM de Petit Bassam (May, 1980).

Austin, Dennis, *Politics in Ghana 1916–60*, Oxford: Oxford University Press, 1970.

Bâ, Hampaté, *L'Etrange Destin de Wangrin*, Paris: Union Générale d'Editions, 1973.

Balesi, Charles John, *From Adversaries to Comrades-In-Arms: West Africans and the French Military, 1885–1918*, Waltham, Mass.: Crossroads Press 1979.

Balima, Albert Salfo, *Genèse de la Haute-Volta*, Ouagadougou: Presses Africaines, 1969.

Barlone, D. *A French Officer's Diary (22 August 1939–1 October 1940)*, Cambridge: Cambridge University Press, 1942.

Bassett, Thomas J. "Food, Peasantry and the State in the Northern Ivory Coast: 1898–1982," Ph.D. diss. University of California, Berkeley, 1984.

Berteil, Louis, *L'Armée de Weygand*, Paris: Editions Albatros, 1975.

Bonnet, G. *Mémorial de l'empire: à la gloire des troupes coloniales*, Toulouse: Sequana, 1941.

Bony, Joachim, "La Côte d'Ivoire sous la colonisation française et le prélude à l'émancipation 1920–1947: Genèse d'une nation," Ph.D. diss. Université de Paris I, Sorbonne, 1980.

Bouche, Denise, "Le Retour de l'Afrique Occidentale Française dans la lutte contre l'ennemi aux côtes des alliés." *Revue d'histoire de la deuxième guerre mondiale* 29, no. 114, (April 1979): 41–68.

Bourgi, Robert, *Le Général de Gaulle et l'Afrique Noire; 1940–1969*, Abidjan: Nouvelles Editions Africaines, 1980.

Breuer, William B. *Operation Torch: The Allied Gamble to Invade North Africa*, New York: St. Martin's Press, 1986.

Buell, Raymond, *The Native Problem in Africa*, 2 vols., London: Macmillan, 1965.

Burman, Ben Lucien, *Miracle on the Congo; Report from the Free French Front*, New York: John Day Company, 1941.

Carver, Michael, *Dilemmas of the Desert War*, Bloomington: Indiana University Press, 1986.

Chaffard, Georges, *Les Carnets secrets de la décolonisation*, vol. 1, Paris: Calmann-Levy, 1965.

Chailley, Marcel, *Histoire de l'Afrique Occidentale Française, 1638–1959*, Paris: Berger-Levrault, 1968.

Chénet, Daniel, *Qui a sauvé l'Afrique?*, Paris: L'Elan, 1949.

Clayton, Anthony, *France, Soldiers and Africa*, London: Brassey's, 1988.

Cohen, William B. "The Colonial Policy of the Popular Front," *French Historical Studies* 7, no. 3 (1972): 368–93.

―――, *Rulers of Empire: The French Colonial Service in Africa*, Stanford: Hoover Institution Press, 1971.

La Conférence Africaine Française, 1944: Brazzaville, Congo, Algiers: Commissariat aux Colonies, 1944.

Coquery-Vidrovitch, C. "Vichy et l'industrialisation aux colonies," *Revue d'histoire de la deuxième guerre mondiale* 29 (April 1979): 69–94.

Cornevin, Marianne, *Histoire de l'Afrique contemporaine*, Paris: Petite Bibliothèque Payot, 1978.

Coulibaly, Sinali, *Le Paysan Senoufo*, Abidjan: Nouvelles Editions Africaines, 1978.

Cousturier, Lucie, *Des Inconnus chez moi*, Paris: Editions de la Sirène, 1920.

Crocker, W. R. *On Governing Colonies*, London: Allen & Irwin, 1947.

Crowder, Michael, *Colonial West Africa*, London: Frank Cass and Company, 1978.

―――, *West Africa under Colonial Rule*, Evanston, Il.: Northwestern University Press, 1960.

―――, "West Africa and the 14–18 War," *Bulletin de l'IFAN* 30, no. 1, series B, (January 1968) 227–45.

Damas, M., *Rapport no. 11348 sur les incidents survenus en Côte d'Ivoire*, 3 vols. in 1, 1950. Reprint, Abidjan: Imprimerie Nationale, 1965.

Darcourt, Pierre, *Armée d'Afrique; La revanche des drapeaux*, Paris: La Table Ronde, 1972.

Dartigues, Louis, *Des Coloniaux au Combat; La 1ére D.I.C. en 1939–1940*, Bordeaux: Amicales des Anciens de la 1ére D.I.C., 1971.

Davis, Shelby Cullom, *Reservoirs of Men: A History of the Black Troops of French West Africa*, Geneva: Kundig, 1934.

de Gaulle, Charles, *The Complete War Memoirs of Charles de Gaulle*, translated by Richard Howard, New York: Simon and Schuster, 1968.

de Gobineau, Hélène, *Noblesse d'Afrique*, Paris: Fasquelle, 1946.

de la Gorce, Paul-Marie, *The French Army*, New York: G. Braziller, 1963.

de Martonne, E. "La vérité sur les Tirailleurs Sénégalais," *Outre-Mer* 7, no. 1 (March 1935) 27–45.

Deschamps, Hubert, *Roi de la brousse; Mémoires d'autres mondes*, Paris: Berger-Levrault, 1975.

Devéze, Michel, *La France d'outre-mer; De l'empire colonial à l'union française, 1938–1947*, Paris: Librairie Hachette, 1948.

d'Houp, Jean-Marie, "Prisonniers de la guerre française témoins du défaute allemande," *Guerres mondiales et conflits contemporains*, no. 150 (1988) 77–98.

Diawara, Bakary, "L'école William Ponty de 1930 à 1950; la Formation d'une élite nouvelle ivoirienne," *Annales Université d'Abidjan*, series 1–10, Abidjan (1982), 171–82.

Doumbi-Fakoly, *Morts pour la France*, Paris: Karthala, 1983.

Duboc, A. *Les Sénégalais au service de la France*, Paris: E. Malfère, 1939.

du Gard, Maurice Martin, *La Carte impériale*, Paris: Editions André Bonne, 1949.

_____, *La Drame de l'Afrique Française; Choses vues 1940*, Paris: Sequana, 1941.

Durand, André, *History of the International Committee of the Red Cross from Sarajevo to Hiroshima*, Geneva: Henry Dunant Institute, 1984.

Echenberg, Myron, *Colonial Conscripts: The Tirailleurs Sénégalais in French West Africa, 1857–1960*, Portsmouth, N.H.: Heinemann, 1991.

_____. " 'Faire du nègre': Military Aspects of Population Planning in French West Africa, 1920–1940" in *African Population and Capitalism: Historical Perspectives* edited by D. D. Cordell and J. Gregory, Boulder, Colo. and London: Westview Press, 1987.

_____. "Slaves into Soldiers: The Social Origins of the *Tirailleurs Sénégalais*" in *Africans in Bondage*, edited by Paul E. Lovejoy. African Studies Program, Madison: University of Wisconsin, 1986, 311–33.

_____. "Morts pour la France; the African Soldier in France during the Second World War," *Journal of African History* 26, no. 4 (1985) 373–80.

_____. "Les Migrations militaires en Afrique Occidentale Française, 1900–1945," *Canadian Journal of African Studies* 14, no. 3 (1980) 429–50.

_____. "Tragedy at Thiaroye: The Senegalese Soldiers' Uprising of 1944" in *African Labor History*, edited by R. Cohen, J. Copans, and P. Gutkind. Beverly Hills, Calif.: Sage Publications, 1978, 109–28.

_____. "Paying the Blood Tax: Military Conscription in French West Africa, 1914–1929," *Canadian Journal of African Studies* 9, no. 2 (1975), 171–92.

France d'outremer. La Vie de l'empire français: Guide colonial à l'usage des parents et de leurs enfants, Paris: Sarazin, 1939.

Gallienne, Marcel, *De Psichari à De Gaulle*, Paris: La Pensée Universelle, 1978.

Gaujac, Paul, *L'Armée de la victoire: de la Provence à l'Alsace 1944*, Paris: Charles-Lavauzelle, 1985.

_____, *La Bataille et la libéération de Toulon; 18 au 28 août 1944*, Paris: Fayard, 1984.

Gbagbo, Laurent, *La Côte d'Ivoire: Economie et société à la veille de l'indépendance, (1940–1960)*, Paris: Editions l'Harmattan, 1982.

General X [Bührer], *Aux Heures Tragiques de l'Empire (1938–1941)*, Paris: Office Colonial d'Edition, 1947.

Gentil, Pierre, *Les Troupes du Sénégal de 1816 à 1890*, vol. 1, *Soldats du Sénégal du Colonel Schmaltz au Général Faidherbe*, Dakar: Nouvelles Editions Africaines, 1978.

_____, ed., *Derniers chefs d'un Empire*, Paris: Académie des Sciences d'Outre-Mer, 1972.

Glaze, Anita, *Art and Death in a Senufo Village*, Bloomington: Indiana University Press, 1981.

Gold Coast Colony, "Demobilisation and Resettlement of Gold Coast Africans in the Armed Forces," Sessional Paper 5, no. 5 of 1945, Accra, 1945.

Guerlain, Robert, *A Prisoner in Germany*, London: Macmillan, 1944.

Gunderson, W. C. "Village Elders and Regional Intermediaries: Differing Responses to Change in the Korhogo Region of the Ivory Coast," Ph.D. diss. Indiana University, 1975.

Hargreaves, John D. *Decolonization in Africa*, New York: Longman, 1988.

_____. *West Africa: The Former French States*, Englewood Cliffs, N.J.: Prentice-Hall, 1967.

Headrick, Rita, "African Soldiers in World War II," University of Chicago, October 1976. Typescript.

Histoire et épopée des troupes coloniales, 4th ed. Paris, 1970.

Hodgkin, Thomas, *African Political Parties*, Harmondsworth: Penguin, 1961.

_____. *Nationalism in Colonial Africa*, London: Frederick Muller, 1956.

Holas, Bohumil, *Les Toura: Esquisse d'une civilisation montagnarde de Côte d'Ivoire*, Paris: Presses Universitaires de France, 1962.

_____. *Les Senoufo (y compris les Minianka)*, Paris: Presses Universitaires de France, 1957.

Hyman, Jacques Louis, *Léopold Sédar Senghor*, Edinburgh: University of Edinburgh Press, 1971.

Irving, David, *The Trail of the Fox*, New York: Dutton, 1977.

Israel, Adrienne, "Measuring the War Experience: Ghanian Soldiers in World War II," *Journal of Modern African Studies* 25, no. 1 (1987): 159–68.

Joseph, Gaston, *Côte d'Ivoire*, Paris: Librairie Arthème Fayard, 1944.

Killingray, David, "Military and Labour Recruitment in the Gold Coast During the Second World War," *Journal of African Studies* 23, (1982): 83–95.

Langer, William, *Our Vichy Gamble*, New York: Knopf, 1947.

Launay, Robert, *Traders without Trade: Responses to Change in Two Dyula Communities*, Cambridge: Cambridge University Press, 1982.

Lawler, Nancy, "Reform and Repression under the Free French: Economic and Political Transformation in the Côte d'Ivoire, 1942-45, *Africa* 60, no. 1 (1990): 88–110.

Liddell-Hart, B. H. *History of the Second World War*, New York: Putnam, 1971.

Loucou, Jean-Noël, *Histoire de la Côte d'Ivoire* : Vol. 1, *La Formation des Peuples*, Abidjan: Centre d'Edition et de Diffusion Africaines, 1984.

_____. "La Deuxième guerre mondiale et ses effets en Côte d'Ivoire," *Annales d'histoire de l'université d'Abidjan* 8, series 1, (1980): 181–207.

_____. "Aux origines du parti démocratique de la Côte d'Ivoire," *Annales d'histoire de l'université d'Abidjan* 5, series 1, (1977): 81–105.

_____. "Les Premières élections de 1945 en la Côte d'Ivoire," *Annales d'histoire de l'université d'Abidjan* 4, series 1, (1976): 5–33.

_____. "La Vie politique en Côte d'Ivoire de 1932 à 1952," Ph.D. diss. University of Aix-en-Provence, 1976.

Louveau, Edmond, *"Au Bagne": Entre les griffes de Vichy et de la milice*, Bamako: Soudan Imprimerie, 1947.

Ly, Abdoulaye, *Mercenaires noires; notes sur une forme de l'exploitation des africains*, Paris: Présence Africaine, 1957.

Manns, Adrienne, "The Role of Ex-Servicemen in Ghana's Independence," Ph.D. diss. John Hopkins University, 1984.

Marshall, D. Bruce, *The French Colonial Myth and Constitution-Making in the Fourth Republic*, New Haven, Conn.: Yale University Press, 1973.

Messenger, Charles, *The Tunisian Campaign*, Shepperton, Surrey: Ian Allen, 1982.

Michel, Henri, *The Second World War*, London: André Deutsch, 1975.

Michel, Marc, *L'Appel à l'Afrique: Contributions et réactions à l'effort de guerre en A.O.F. (1914–1919)*, Paris: Publications de la Sorbonne, 1982.

———. "La Genèse du recrutement de 1918 en Afrique noire française," *Revue française d'histoire d'outre-mer* 58, no. 213 (1971): 433–50.

Mille, Pierre, "L'Empire colonial et la guerre," *Notre Combat* 1 (10 November 1939).

Mommsen, W. J. *Max Weber zur Politik im Weltkrieg. Schriften und Reden 1914–1918*, Tübingen, Germany: J. C. B. Mohr, 1988.

Morgenthau, Ruth Schachter, *Political Parties in French-Speaking West Africa*, Oxford: Clarendon Press, 1964.

Mortimer, Edward, *France and the Africans, 1944–1960, A Political History*, London: Faber and Faber, 1969.

Murphy, Robert, *Diplomat among Warriors*, New York: Doubleday, 1964.

N'Dumbe III, Kumia, "Black Africa and Germany During the Second World War" in *Africa and the Second World War*, Paris: UNESCO, 1985, 51–75.

———, *Hitler voulait l'Afrique*, Paris: Editions d'Harmattan, 1980.

Nyo, Général, "Le problème de nos cadres africains," *Tropiques* 54, no. 385 (June 1956): 33–40.

Ollandet, Jerome, *Brazzaville, capitale de la France libre, Histoire de la résistance française en Afrique (1940–1944)*, Paris: Editions de la Savane, 1980.

Ouattara, Tiona Fernand, "Les Tiembara de Korhogo; des Origines à Péléforo Gbon Coulibaly (1962): Evolution historique, politique, sociale et économique d'un tar Senoufo," Ph.D. diss, Université de Paris I, June 1977.

Paxton, Robert O. *Vichy France: Old Guard and New Order, 1940–1944*, New York: Knopf, 1972.

———. *Parades and Politics at Vichy*, Princeton, N.J.: Princeton University Press, 1966.

La Première Division Française Libre. Epopée d'une reconquête, 1946.

Le Rassemblement démocratique africain dans la lutte anti-impérialiste, Abidjan: Centre d'Edition et de Diffusion Africaines, 1986.

RDA: Actes du Colloque International de Yamoussoukro, 18–25 Octobre 1986, Abidjan: Centre d'Edition et de Diffusion Africaines, 1986.

République de la Côte d'Ivoire. Carte des religions de l'Afrique Noire, Abidjan: Centre des Hautes Etudes Administratives sur l'Afrique et l'Asie Modernes, 1957.

Richard-Molard, Jacques, *Afrique Occidentale Française*, Paris: Editions Berger-Levrault, 1952.

Rouch, Jean, "Migrations en Ghana (Gold Coast)," *Journal de la Société des Africanistes* 26 (1956): 33–196.

———. "Contribution à l'histoire des Songhay," *Mémoires de l'institut français d'Afrique noire* 29 (1953): 141–259.

Roux, Genevieve, "La Presse ivoirienne: Miroir d'une société," Ph.D. diss. Université René Descartes, Paris, 1975.

Sabben-Clare, E. E. "African Troops in Asia," *African Affairs* 44 (October 1945): 151–57.

Salmaggi, Cesare and Alfredo Pallavisini, eds. *2194 Days of War*, New York: Gallery Books, 1979.

Saurat, Denis, "Attention au Tchad," *La France Libre* 2, no. 8 (20 June 1941): 142–46.

Schleh, Eugene P. A. "Post-Service Careers of African World War Two Veterans: British East and West Africa With Particular Reference to Ghana and Uganda," Ph.D. diss. Yale University, 1968.

Schwartz, A. *La vie quotidienne dans un village Guéré*, Abidjan: Institut Africain pour le Développement Economique et Social, 1975.

Service historique de l'armée de la terre, *Les Grandes unités françaises, historique succinct, Campagnes de Tunisie et d'Italie*, Paris: Imprimerie Nationale, 1970.

Shirer, William, *The Rise and Fall of the Third Reich*, New York: Simon and Schuster, 1960.

Siordet, Frederic, *L'Oeuvre du Comité International de la Croix-Rouge pendant la seconde guerre mondiale*, Geneva, International Committee of the Red Cross, 1947.

Siriex, Paul-Henri, *Félix Houphouët-Boigny*, Paris: Nouvelles Editions Africaines, 1975.

Société d'études pour le développement économique et social, *Région de Korhogo*, Abidjan, 1965.

Spears, Edward, *Fulfilment of a Mission: Syria and Lebanon 1941–1944*, London: Archon Books, 1977.

Summerscales, John, "The War Effort of the French Colonies," *African Affairs*, 39 (April 1940): 123–28.

Suret-Canale, Jean, *French Colonialism in Tropical Africa: 1900–1945*, translated by Till Gottheimer, London: C. Hurst, 1971.

Tate, H. R. "The French Colonial Empire," *African Affairs* 39, (October 1940): 322–30.

Tevoedjre, Albert, *L'Afrique révoltée*, Paris: Présence Africaine, 1958.

Thompson, Paul, *The Voice of the Past. Oral History*, Oxford: Oxford University Press, 1978.

The United States Army in World War II, Vol. 3, Washington, D.C.: U.S. Government Printing Office, 1951.

Unités Combattantes des campagnes 1939–1945; Période du 3 septembre 1939 au 8 mai 1945, Bulletin officiel du Ministère de la Guerre, Paris: Charles Lavauzelle.

Vincent, Jean-Noel, *Les Forces français libres en Afrique: 1940–1943*, Paris: Ministère de l'Armée de Terre: Service Historique, 1983.

Wallerstein, Immanuel, *The Road to Independence, Ghana and the Ivory Coast*, Paris: Mouton & Co., 1964.

Watson, John, *Echec à Dakar, septembre 1940*, translated by Daniel Martin, Paris: Laffont, 1968.

Weiskel, T. C. *French Colonial Rule and the Baule People: Resistance and Collaboration, 1889–1911*, Oxford: Clarendon Press, 1980.

Wilks, Ivor, *Wa and the Wala*, Cambridge: Cambridge University Press, 1989.

Wilson, H. Maitland, *Report by the Supreme Allied Commander Mediterranean to the Combined Chiefs of Staff on the Operations in Southern France, August 1944*, London: H. M. Stationery Office, 1946.

Zolberg, Aristide R. *One-Party Government in the Ivory Coast*, Princeton, N.J.: Princeton University Press, 1969.

Index

Abidjan, 42, 52, 123, 129, 136, and Chamber of Commerce, 27, 205
Abron, support for de Gaulle, 165–66; *see also* Kouadio Adjoumani; Kouamé Adingra
Adingra, *see under* Kouamé Adingra
Afrika Korps, 155
Agboville, 219
Agni, 223
Alawites, 222–23
Alexandria, 141–42, 203
Algeria, 55, 156–57, 163, 167, 228; *see also* Operation Torch
American soldiers, relations with West Africans, 184–85, 190–93
Angoulvant, Gabriel, 12
Armistice (1940) 93, 126, terms of, 117, 123, and Armistice Army, 93, 108–109, 117–18, 133–34, 150, 157, 180
army, conditions of service
    bonuses, 127–38, 195–96, 198
    food, 56, 72–73
    housing, 57
    marriage allowances, 50, 73–74
    pensions, 80, 239–46
    punishments, 58
Army of the Levant, 141, 147
assimilation policy, 15, 130
Association des anciens combattants, 203
Atlantic Charter, 14
atrocities, 102, 109; *see also* Erquinvillers

Baloum Naba Tenga, 25, 216
Bambara, as lingua franca, 48, 62
Baoulé, 57–58, 223
Barbie, Klaus, 246
Barraud, General, 26, 28
Bataillon d'Afrique, 19
Bataillon de Gorée, 19
Bataillon du Sénégal, 19
Bathurst, 134
Batié, 123–24
battle honors, Elba, 172, Toulon, 176
Belfort, liberation of, 178–80
Belgium, 75, 78, 79, 141
Bema Coulibaly, 226
Berlin, 103

Besson, General, 85
Biaka Boda, 219
Bir Hakeim, battle of, 154–55
black market, 196–97
Blum, Leon, 129, 132
Bobo-Dioulasso, 48, 56, 123, 215
Boisson, Pierre, 122–23, 125–26, 130, 132, 134, 163–64, 166–67
Bondoukou, 25, 219
Bongouanou, 219
Bonnard, Lieutenant, 123–24
Bordeaux. 75, 77, 123, 189
Boromo, 130
Bouaflé, 219–21, 223
Bouaké, 48, 52, 56–58, 61, 129, 136, 191, 219
Bouillon, Captain, 123
Bouna, 42, 48, 56, 123–24
Brazzaville Conference, 208, 215
Brou, Fulgence, 208
Buggia, M., 225
Burkina Faso, *see under* Upper Volta
Burma campaign, 197–98

Cameroun, 122, 125, 167
Cannes, landings, 174
Casablanca, landings, 156–58
Catholic Church, 68, 69, 71–72, 122, 132, 138, 164
Catroux, Georges, 143, 145, 152, 203–204
Cazaud, General, 155
censuses
    local, 42; 1954, 12–13; 1963, 8, 12
Chad, 134, 154
Chartres, 94, 103
Chevillot, Lieutenant, 123
chiefs, 72, 129–30
    and military recruitment, 25–26, 42–45, 52
    relations with veterans, 197, 212–14
    and party politics, 214–16
Chindits, 197–98
Churchill, Winston, 142, 143, 156
Clemenceau, Georges, 24
Comité pour le ravitaillement des prisonniers de guerre, 107

A NOTE ABOUT THE AUTHOR

A graduate of Trinity College Dublin, Nancy Lawler obtained her Ph.D. from Northwestern University. She is Professor of Economics and History at Oakton College, Des Plaines, Illinois. She is currently working on a study of Free French espionage and propaganda efforts directed at Vichy-controlled West Africa during the Second World War.